The Ligh

A Tale of the North C

Irving Bacheller

Alpha Editions

This edition published in 2022

ISBN : 9789356892187

Design and Setting By
Alpha Editions
www.alphaedis.com
Email - info@alphaedis.com

Contents

PREFACE

The Light in the Clearing shone upon many things and mostly upon those which, above all others, have impassioned and perpetuated the Spirit of America and which, just now, seem to me to be worthy of attention. I believe that spirit to be the very candle of the Lord which, in this dark and windy night of time, has flickered so that the souls of the faithful have been afraid. But let us be of good cheer. It is shining brighter as I write and, under God, I believe it shall, by and by, be seen and loved of all men.

One self-contained, Homeric figure, of the remote countryside in which I was born, had the true Spirit of Democracy and shed its light abroad in the Senate of the United States and the Capitol at Albany. He carried the candle of the Lord. It led him to a height of self-forgetfulness achieved by only two others—Washington and Lincoln. Yet I have been surprised by the profound and general ignorance of this generation regarding the career of Silas Wright, of whom Whittier wrote these lines:

"Man of the millions thou art lost too soon!
Portents at which the bravest stand aghast
The birth throes of a future strange and vast
Alarm the land. Yet thou so wise and strong
Suddenly summoned to the burial bed,
Lapped in its slumbers deep and ever long,
Hear'st not the tumult surging over head.
Who now shall rally Freedom's scattering host?
Who wear the mantle of the leader lost?"

The distinguished Senator who served at his side for many years, Thomas H. Benton of Missouri, has this to say of Silas Wright in his *Thirty Years' View*:

"He refused cabinet appointments under his fast friend Van Buren and under Polk, whom he may be said to have elected. He refused a seat on the bench of the Supreme Court of the United States; he rejected instantly the nomination of 1844 for Vice-President; he refused to be put in nomination for the Presidency. He spent that time in declining office which others did in winning it. The offices he did accept, it might well be said, were thrust upon him. He was born great and above office and unwillingly descended to it."

So much by way of preparing the reader to meet the great commoner in these pages. One thing more is necessary to a proper understanding of the final scenes in the book—a part of his letter written to Judge Fine just before the Baltimore convention of 1844, to wit:

"I do not feel at liberty to omit any act which may protect me from being made the instrument, however honestly and innocently, of further distractions.

"Within a few days several too partial friends have suggested to me the idea that by possibility, in case the opposition to the nomination of Mr. Van Buren should be found irreconcilable, a compromise might be made by dropping him and using my name. I need not say to you that a consent on my part to any such proceeding would justly forfeit my standing with the democracy of our state and cause my faith and fidelity to my party to be suspected everywhere.... To consent to the use of my name as a candidate under any circumstances, would be in my view to invite you to compromise the expressed wishes and instructions of your constituents for my personal advancement. I can never consent to place myself in a position where the suspicion of acting from such a motive can justly attach to me....

"If it were proper I could tell you with the most perfect truth that I have never been vain enough to dream of the office of President in connection with my own name, and were not Mr. Van Buren the candidate of our State, I should find just as little difficulty as I now do, in telling you that I am not and can not under any circumstances be a candidate before your convention for that office."

According to his best biographer, Jabez Hammond, Mr. Wright still adhered to this high ground in spite of the fact that Mr. Van Buren withdrew and requested his faithful hand to vote for the Senator.

There were those who accused Mr. Wright of being a spoilsman, the only warrant for which claim would seem to be his remark in a letter: "When our enemies accuse us of feeding our friends instead of them never let them lie in telling the story."

He was, in fact, a human being, through and through, but so upright that they used to say of him that he was "as honest as any man under heaven or in it"

For my knowledge of the color and spirit of the time I am indebted to a long course of reading in its books, newspapers and periodicals, notably *The North American Review, The United States Magazine and Democratic Review, The New York Mirror, The Knickerbocker, The St. Lawrence Republican*, Benton's *Thirty Years' View*, Bancroft's *Life of Martin Van Buren*, histories of Wright and his time by Hammond and Jenkins, and to many manuscript letters of the distinguished commoner in the New York Public Library and in the possession of Mr. Samuel Wright of Weybridge, Vermont.

To any who may think that they discover portraits in these pages I desire to say that all the characters—save only Silas Wright and President Van Buren and Barton Baynes—are purely imaginary. However, there were Grimshaws and Purvises and Binkses and Aunt Deels and Uncle Peabodys in almost every rustic neighborhood those days, and I regret to add that Roving Kate was on many roads. The case of Amos Grimshaw bears a striking resemblance to that of young Bickford, executed long ago in Malone, for the particulars of which case I am indebted to my friend, Mr. H.L. Ives of Potsdam.

THE AUTHOR.

BOOK ONE

Which is the Story of the Candle and the Compass

CHAPTER I

THE MELON HARVEST

Once upon a time I owned a watermelon. I say once because I never did it again. When I got through owning that melon I never wanted another. The time was 1831; I was a boy of seven and the melon was the first of all my harvests. Every night and morning I watered and felt and surveyed my watermelon. My pride grew with the melon and, by and by, my uncle tried to express the extent and nature of my riches by calling me a mellionaire.

I didn't know much about myself those days except the fact that my name was Bart Baynes and, further, that I was an orphan who owned a watermelon and a little spotted hen and lived on Rattle road in a neighborhood called Lickitysplit. I lived with my Aunt Deel and my Uncle Peabody Baynes on a farm. They were brother and sister—he about thirty-eight and she a little beyond the far-distant goal of forty.

My father and mother died in a scourge of diphtheria that swept the neighborhood when I was a boy of five. For a time my Aunt Deel seemed to blame me for my loss.

"No wonder they're dead," she used to say, when out of patience with me and—well I suppose that I must have had an unusual talent for all the noisy arts of childhood when I broke the silence of that little home.

The word "dead" set the first mile-stone in the long stretch of my memory. That was because I tried so hard to comprehend it and further because it kept repeating its challenge to my imagination. I often wondered just what had become of my father and mother and I remember that the day after I went to my aunt's home a great idea came to me. It came out of the old dinner-horn hanging in the shed. I knew the power of its summons and I slyly captured the horn and marched around the house blowing it and hoping that it would bring my father up from the fields. I blew and blew and listened for that familiar halloo of his. When I paused for a drink of water at the well my aunt came and seized the horn and said it was no wonder they were dead. She knew nothing of the sublime bit of necromancy she had interrupted—poor soul!

I knew that she had spoken of my parents for I supposed that they were the only people in the world who were dead, but I did not know what it meant to be dead. I often called to them, as I had been wont to do, especially in the night, and shed many tears because they came no more to answer me. Aunt Deel did not often refer directly to my talents, but I saw, many times, that no-wonder-they-died look in her face.

Children are great rememberers. They are the recording angels—the keepers of the book of life. Man forgets—how easily!—and easiest of all, the solemn truth that children do *not* forget.

A few days after I arrived in the home of my aunt and uncle I slyly entered the parlor and climbed the what-not to examine some white flowers on its top shelf and tipped the whole thing over, scattering its burden of albums, wax flowers and sea shells on the floor. My aunt came running on her tiptoes and exclaimed: "Mercy! Come right out o' here this minute—you pest!"

I took some rather long steps going out which were due to the fact that Aunt Deel had hold of my hand. While I sat weeping she went back into the parlor and began to pick up things.

"My wreath! my wreath!" I heard her moaning.

How well I remember that little assemblage of flower ghosts in wax! They had no more right to associate with human beings than the ghosts of fable. Uncle Peabody used to call them the "Minervy flowers" because they were a present from his Aunt Minerva. When Aunt Deel returned to the kitchen where I sat—a sorrowing little refugee hunched up in a corner—she said: "I'll have to tell your Uncle Peabody—ayes!"

"Oh please don't tell my Uncle Peabody," I wailed.

"Ayes! I'll have to tell him," she answered firmly.

For the first time I looked for him with dread at the window and when he came I hid in a closet and heard that solemn and penetrating note in her voice as she said:

"I guess you'll have to take that boy away—ayes!"

"What now?" he asked.

"My stars! he sneaked into the parlor and tipped over the what-not and smashed that beautiful wax wreath!"

Her voice trembled.

"Not them Minervy flowers?" he asked in a tone of doleful incredulity.

"Ayes he did!"

"And tipped over the hull what-not?"

"Ayes!"

"Jerusalem four-corners!" he exclaimed. "I'll have to—"

He stopped as he was wont to do on the threshold of strong opinions and momentous resolutions.

The rest of the conversation was drowned in my own cries and Uncle Peabody came and lifted me tenderly and carried me up-stairs.

He sat down with me on his lap and hushed my cries. Then he said very gently:

"Now, Bub, you and me have got to be careful. What-nots and albums and wax flowers and hair-cloth sofys are the most dang'rous critters in St. Lawrence County. They're purty savage. Keep your eye peeled. You can't tell what minute they'll jump on ye. More boys have been dragged away and tore to pieces by `em than by all the bears and panthers in the woods. When I was a boy I got a cut acrost my legs that made a scar ye can see now, and it was a hair-cloth sofy that done it. Keep out o' that old parlor. Ye might as well go into a cage o' wolves. How be I goin' to make ye remember it?"

"I don't know," I whimpered and began to cry out in fearful anticipation.

He set me in a chair, picked up one of his old carpet-slippers and began to thump the bed with it. He belabored the bed with tremendous vigor. Meanwhile he looked at me and exclaimed: "You dreadful child!"

I knew that my sins were responsible for this violence. It frightened me and my cries increased.

The door at the bottom of the stairs opened suddenly.

Aunt Deel called:

"Don't lose your temper, Peabody. I think you've gone fur 'nough—ayes!"

Uncle Peabody stopped and blew as if he were very tired and then I caught a look in his face that reassured me.

He called back to her: "I wouldn't 'a' cared so much if it hadn't 'a' been the what-not and them Minervy flowers. When a boy tips over a what-not he's goin' it purty strong."

"Well don't be too severe. You'd better come now and git me a pail o' water—ayes, I think ye had."

Uncle Peabody did a lot of sneezing and coughing with his big, red handkerchief over his face and I was not old enough then to understand it. He kissed me and took my little hand in his big hard one and led me down the stairs.

After that in private talks uncle and I always referred to our parlor as the wolf den and that night, after I had gone to bed, he lay down beside me and told the story of a boy who, having been left alone in his father's house one day, was suddenly set upon and roughly handled by a what-not, a shaggy old hair-cloth sofy and an album. The sofy had begun it by scratchin' his face and he had scratched back with a shingle nail. The album had watched its chance and, when he stood beneath it, had jumped off a shelf on to his head. Suddenly he heard a voice calling him:

"Little boy, come here," it said, and it was the voice of the what-not.

"Just step up on this lower shelf," says the old what-not. "I want to show ye somethin'."

The what-not was all covered with shiny things and looked as innocent as a lamb.

He went over and stepped on the lower shelf and then the savage thing jumped right on top of him, very supple, and threw him on to the floor and held him there until his mother came.

I dreamed that night that a long-legged what-not, with a wax wreath in its hands, chased me around the house and caught and bit me on the neck. I called for help and uncle came and found me on the floor and put me back in bed again.

For a long time I thought that the way a man punished a boy was by thumping his bed. I knew that women had a different and less satisfactory method, for I remembered that my mother had spanked me and Aunt Deel had a way of giving my hands and head a kind of watermelon thump with the middle finger of her right hand and with a curious look in her eyes. Uncle Peabody used to call it a "snaptious look." Almost always he whacked the bed with his slipper. There were exceptions, however, and, by and by, I came to know in each case the destination of the slipper for if I had done anything which really afflicted my conscience that strip of leather seemed to know the truth, and found its way to my person.

My Uncle Peabody was a man of a thousand. I often saw him laughing and talking to himself and strange fancies came into my head about it.

"Who be you talkin' to?" I asked.

"Who be I talkin' to, Bub? Why I'm talkin' to my friends."

"Friends?" I said.

"The friends I orto have had but ain't got. When I git lonesome I just make up a lot o' folks and some of 'em is good comp'ny."

He loved to have me with him, as he worked, and told me odd tales and seemed to enjoy my prattle. I often saw him stand with rough fingers stirring his beard, just beginning to show a sprinkle of white, while he looked down at me as if struck with wonder at something I had said.

"Come and give me a kiss, Bub," he would say. As he knelt down, I would run to his arms and I wondered why he always blinked his gray eyes after he had kissed me.

He was a bachelor and for a singular reason. I have always laid it to the butternut trousers—the most sacred bit of apparel of which I have any knowledge.

"What have you got on them butternut trousers for?" I used to hear Aunt Deel say when he came down-stairs in his first best clothes to go to meeting or "attend" a sociable—those days people just went to meeting but they always "attended" sociables—"You're a wearin' `em threadbare, ayes! I suppose you've sot yer eyes on some one o' the girls. I can always tell—ayes I can! When you git your long legs in them butternut trousers I know you're warmin' up—ayes!"

I had begun to regard those light brown trousers with a feeling of awe, and used to put my hand upon them very softly when uncle had them on. They seemed to rank with "sofys," albums and what-nots in their capacity for making trouble.

Uncle Peabody rarely made any answer, and for a time thereafter Aunt Deel acted as if she were about done with him. She would go around with a stern face as if unaware of his presence, and I had to keep out of her way. In fact I dreaded the butternut trousers almost as much as she did.

Once Uncle Peabody had put on the butternut trousers, against the usual protest, to go to meeting.

"Ayes! you've got 'em on ag'in," said Aunt Deel. "I suppose your black trousers ain't good 'nough. That's 'cause you know Edna Perry is goin' to be there—ayes!"

Edna Perry was a widow of about his age who was visiting her sister in the neighborhood.

Aunt Deel wouldn't go to church with us, so we went off together and walked home with Mrs. Perry. As we passed our house I saw Aunt Deel looking out of the window and waved my hand to her.

When we got home at last we found my aunt sitting in her armchair by the stove.

"You did it—didn't ye?—ayes," she demanded rather angrily as we came in.

"Done what?" asked Uncle Peabody.

"Shinin' up to that Perry woman—ain't ye?—ayes! I see you're bound to git married—ayes!"

I had no idea what it meant to get married but I made up my mind that it was something pretty low and bad. For the moment I blamed Uncle Peabody.

Aunt Deel's voice and manner seemed to indicate that she had borne with him to the limit of her patience.

"Delia," said my uncle, "I wouldn't be so—"

Again he checked himself for fear of going too far, I suppose.

"My heart! my heart!" Aunt Deel exclaimed and struggled to her feet sobbing, and Uncle Peabody helped her to the lounge. She was so ill the rest of the day that my uncle had to go for the doctor while I bathed her forehead with cold water.

Poor Uncle Peabody! Every step toward matrimony required such an outlay of emotion and such a sacrifice of comfort that I presume it seemed to be hardly worth while.

Yet I must be careful not to give the reader a false impression of my Aunt Deel. She was a thin, pale woman, rather tall, with brown hair and blue eyes and a tongue—well, her tongue has spoken for itself. I suppose that she will seem inhumanly selfish with this jealousy of her brother.

"I promised ma that I would look after you and I'm a-goin' to do it—ayes!" I used to hear her say to my uncle.

There were not many married men who were so thoroughly looked after. This was due in part to her high opinion of the Baynes family, and to a general distrust of women. In her view they were a designing lot. It was probably true that Mrs. Perry was fond of show and would have been glad to join the Baynes family, but those items should not have been set down against her. There was Aunt Deel's mistake. She couldn't allow any humanity in other women.

She toiled incessantly. She washed and scrubbed and polished and dusted and sewed and knit from morning until night. She lived in mortal fear that company would come and find her unprepared—Alma Jones or Jabez Lincoln and his wife, or Ben and Mary Humphries, or "Mr. and Mrs. Horace Dunkelberg." These were the people of whom she talked when the neighbors came in and when she was not talking of the Bayneses. I observed that she always said "Mr. and Mrs. Horace Dunkelberg." They were the conversational ornaments of our home. "As Mrs. Horace

Dunkelberg says," or, "as I said to Mr. Horace Dunkelberg," were phrases calculated to establish our social standing. I supposed that the world was peopled by Joneses, Lincolns, Humphries and Dunkelbergs, but mostly by Dunkelbergs. These latter were very rich people who lived in Canton village.

I know, now, how dearly Aunt Deel loved her brother and me. I must have been a great trial to that woman of forty unused to the pranks of children and the tender offices of a mother. Naturally I turned from her to my Uncle Peabody as a refuge and a help in time of trouble with increasing fondness. He had no knitting or sewing to do and when Uncle Peabody sat in the house he gave all his time to me and we weathered many a storm together as we sat silently in his favorite corner, of an evening, where I always went to sleep in his arms.

He and I slept in the little room up-stairs, "under the shingles"—as uncle used to say. I in a small bed, and he in the big one which had been the receiver of so much violence. So I gave her only a qualified affection until I could see beneath the words and the face and the correcting hand of my Aunt Deel.

Uncle made up the beds in our room. Often his own bed would go unmade. My aunt would upbraid him for laziness, whereupon he would say that when he got up he liked the feel of that bed so much that he wanted to begin next night right where he had left off.

I was seven years old when Uncle Peabody gave me the watermelon seeds. I put one of them in my mouth and bit it.

"It appears to me there's an awful draft blowin' down your throat," said Uncle Peabody. "You ain't no business eatin' a melon seed."

"Why?" was my query.

"'Cause it was made to put in the ground. Didn't you know it was alive?"

"Alive!" I exclaimed.

"Alive," said he, "I'll show ye."

He put a number of the seeds in the ground and covered them, and said that that part of the garden should be mine. I watched it every day and by and by two vines came up. One sickened and died in dry weather. Uncle Peabody said that I must water the other every day. I did it faithfully and the vine throve.

"What makes it grow?" I asked.

"The same thing that makes you grow," said Uncle Peabody. "You can do lots of things but there's only one thing that a watermelon can do. It can just grow. See how it reaches out toward the sunlight! If we was to pull them vines around and try to make 'em grow toward the north they wouldn't mind us. They'd creep back and go reachin' toward the sunlight ag'in just as if they had a compass to show 'em the way."

It was hard work, I thought, to go down into the garden, night and morning, with my little pail full of water, but uncle said that I should get my pay when the melon was ripe. I had also to keep the wood-box full and feed the chickens. They were odious tasks. When I asked Aunt Deel what I should get for doing them she answered quickly:

"Nospanks and bread and butter—ayes!"

When I asked what were "nospanks" she told me that they were part of the wages of a good child. I was better paid for my care of the watermelon vine, for its growth was measured with a string every day and kept me interested. One morning I found five blossoms on it. I picked one and carried it to Aunt Deel. Another I destroyed in the tragedy of catching a bumblebee which had crawled into its cup. In due time three small melons appeared. When they were as big as a baseball I picked two of them. One I tasted and threw away as I ran to the pump for relief. The other I hurled at a dog on my way to school.

So that last melon on the vine had my undivided affection. It grew in size and reputation, and soon I learned that a reputation is about the worst thing that a watermelon can acquire while it is on the vine. I invited everybody that came to the house to go and see my watermelon. They looked it over and said pleasant things about it. When I was a boy people used to treat children and watermelons with a like solicitude. Both were a subject for jests and both produced similar reactions in the human countenance.

Aunt Deel often applied the watermelon test to my forehead and discovered in me a capacity for noise which no melon could rival. That act became very familiar to me, for when my melon was nearing the summit of its fame and influence, all beholders thumped its rounded side with the middle finger of the right hand, and said that they guessed they'd steal it. I knew that this was some kind of a joke and a very idle one for they had also threatened to steal me and nothing had come of it.

At last Uncle Peabody agreed with me that it was about time to pick the melon. I decided to pick it immediately after meeting on Sunday, so that I could give it to my aunt and uncle at dinner-time. When we got home I ran for the garden. My feet and those of our friends and neighbors had literally worn a path to the melon. In eager haste I got my little wheelbarrow and ran with it to the end of that path. There I found nothing but broken vines! The melon had vanished. I ran back to the house almost overcome by a feeling of alarm, for I had thought long of that hour of pride when I should bring the melon and present it to my aunt and uncle.

"Uncle Peabody," I shouted, "my melon is gone."

"Well I van!" said he, "somebody must 'a' stole it."

"Stole it?" I repeated the words without fully comprehending what they meant.

"But it was my melon," I said with a trembling voice.

"Yes and I vum it's too bad! But, Bart, you ain't learned yit that there are wicked people in the world who come and take what don't belong to 'em."

There were tears in my eyes when I asked:

"They'll bring it back, won't they?"

"Never!" said Uncle Peabody, "I'm afraid they've et it up."

He had no sooner said it than a cry broke from my lips, and I sank down upon the grass moaning and sobbing. I lay amidst the ruins of the simple faith of childhood. It was as if the world and all its joys had come to an end.

"You can't blame the boy," I heard Uncle Peabody saying. "He's fussed with that melon all summer. He wanted to give it to you for a present."

"Ayes so he did! Well I declare! I never thought o' that—ayes!"

Aunt Deel spoke in a low, kindly tone and came and lifted me to my feet very tenderly.

"Come, Bart, don't feel so about that old melon," said she, "it ain't worth it. Come with me. I'm goin' to give you a present—ayes I be!"

I was still crying when she took me to her trunk, and offered the grateful assuagement of candy and a belt, all embroidered with blue and white beads.

"Now you see, Bart, how low and mean anybody is that takes what don't belong to 'em—ayes! They're snakes! Everybody hates 'em an' stamps on 'em when they come in sight—ayes!"

The abomination of the Lord was in her look and manner. How it shook my soul! He who had taken the watermelon had also taken from me something I was never to have again, and a very wonderful thing it was—

faith in the goodness of men. My eyes had seen evil. The world had committed its first offense against me and my spirit was no longer the white and beautiful thing it had been. Still, therein is the beginning of wisdom and, looking down the long vista of the years, I thank God for the great harvest of the lost watermelon. Better things had come in its place—understanding and what more, often I have vainly tried to estimate. For one thing that sudden revelation of the heart of childhood had lifted my aunt's out of the cold storage of a puritanic spirit, and warmed it into new life and opened its door for me.

In the afternoon she sent me over to Wills' to borrow a little tea. I stopped for a few minutes to play with Henry Wills—a boy not quite a year older than I. While playing there I discovered a piece of the rind of my melon in the dooryard. On that piece of rind I saw the cross which I had made one day with my thumb-nail. It was intended to indicate that the melon was solely and wholly mine. I felt a flush of anger.

"I hate you," I said as I approached him.

"I hate you," he answered.

"You're a snake!" I said.

We now stood, face to face and breast to breast, like a pair of young roosters. He gave me a shove and told me to go home. I gave him a shove and told him I wouldn't. I pushed up close to him again and we glared into each other's eyes.

Suddenly he spat in my face. I gave him a scratch on the forehead with my finger-nails. Then we fell upon each other and rolled on the ground and hit and scratched with feline ferocity.

Mrs. Wills ran out of the house and parted us. Our blood was hot, and leaking through the skin of our faces a little.

"He pitched on me," Henry explained.

I couldn't speak.

"Go right home—this minute—you brat!" said Mrs. Wills in anger. "Here's your tea. Don't you ever come here again."

I took the tea and started down the road weeping. What a bitter day that was for me! I dreaded to face my aunt and uncle. Coming through the grove down by our gate I met Uncle Peabody. With the keen eyesight of the father of the prodigal son he had seen me coming "a long way off" and shouted:

"Well here ye be—I was kind o' worried, Bub."

Then his eye caught the look of dejection in my gait and figure. He hurried toward me. He stopped as I came sobbing to his feet.

"Why, what's the matter?" he asked gently, as he took the tea cup from my hand, and sat down upon his heels.

I could only fall into his arms and express myself in the grief of childhood. He hugged me close and begged me to tell him what was the matter.

"That Wills boy stole my melon," I said, and the words came slow with sobs.

"Oh, no he didn't," said Uncle Peabody.

"Yes he did. I saw a piece o' the rin'."

"Well by—" said Uncle Peabody, stopping, as usual, at the edge of the precipice.

"He's a snake," I added.

"And you fit and he scratched you up that way?"

"I scratched him, too."

"Don't you say a word about it to Aunt Deel. Don't ever speak o' that miserable melon ag'in to anybody. You scoot around to the barn, an' I'll be there in a minute and fix ye up."

He went by the road with the tea and I ran around to the lane and up to the stable. Uncle Peabody met me there in a moment and brought a pail of water and washed my face so that I felt and looked more respectable.

"If Aunt Deel asks ye about them scratches you just tell her that you and Hen had a little disagreement," said my uncle.

She didn't ask me, probably because Uncle Peabody had explained in his own way, and requested her to say nothing.

The worst was over for that day but the Baynes-Wills feud had begun. It led to many a fight in the school yard and on the way home. We were so evenly matched that our quarrel went on for a long time and gathered intensity as it continued.

One day Uncle Peabody had given me an egg and, said that there was a chicken in it.

"All ye have to do is to keep it warm an' the chicken will come to life, and when the hen is off the nest some day it will see light through the shell and peck its way out," he explained.

He marked my initials on the egg and put it under a hen and by and by a little chicken came out of the shell. I held it in my palm—a quivering, warm handful of yellow down. Its helplessness appealed to me and I fed and watched it every day. Later my uncle told me that it was a hen chick and would be laying eggs in four months. He added:

"It's the only thing it can do, an' if it's let alone it'll be sure to do it. Follows a kind of a compass that leads to the nest every time."

This chicken grew into a little spotted hen. She became my sole companion in many a lonely hour when Uncle Peabody had gone to the village, or was working in wet ground, or on the hay rack, or the mowing machine where I couldn't be with him. She was an amiable, confiding little hen who put her trust in me and kept it unto the day of her death, which came not until she had reached the full dignity of mature henhood.

She was like many things on the farm—of great but unconsidered beauty. No far-fetched pheasant was half so beautiful as she. I had always treated her with respect, and she would let me come and sit beside her while she rolled in the dust and permit me to stroke her head and examine her wonderful dress of glossy mottled satin. She would spread her glowing sleeves in the sunlight, and let me feel their downy lining with my fingers and see how their taut snug-fitting plumes were set.

I remember a day when she was sitting on her nest with that curious expression in her eyes which seemed to say, "Please don't bother me now for this is my busy time," I brought three little kittens from their basket in the wood-shed and put them under her. The kittens felt the warmth of her body and began to mew and stir about. I shall never forget the look of astonishment in the little hen as she slowly rose in her nest and peered beneath her body at the kittens. She looked at me as if to say that she really couldn't be bothered with those furry things any longer—they made her so nervous. She calmly took hold of one of them with her bill and lifted it out of the nest. She continued this process of eviction until they were all removed, when she quietly sat down again.

Slowly her right hand rose above her

I mention this only to show that the hen and I had come to terms of intimacy and mutual understanding. So when I saw Wills' dog catch and kill her in the field one day, where she was hunting for grasshoppers, I naturally entertained a feeling of resentment. I heard the cries of the hen and ran through the orchard and witnessed the end of the tragedy and more. Away down in the meadow I saw the dog and farther away "the Wills boy," as we then called him, running toward his home. The dog had run away as I approached and when I picked up the lifeless body of my little friend the hills seemed to lift up their heads and fall upon me. Of course that Wills boy had set the dog on her. I shall write no more of that hour of trial. Such little things make history, and it is necessary that the reader should understand me.

One June day of the next summer Uncle Peabody and I, from down in the fields, saw a fine carriage drive in at our gate. He stopped and looked intently.

"Jerusalem four-corners!" he exclaimed. "It's Mr. and Mrs. Horace Dunkelberg."

My heart beat fast at thought of the legendary Dunkelbergs. Uncle looked me over from top to toe. "Heavens!" he exclaimed. "Go down to the brook and wash the mud off yer feet an' legs."

I ran for the brook and before I had returned to my uncle I heard the horn blow.

"The Dunkelbergs!—the Dunkelbergs! Come quick!" it seemed to say.

Uncle had tied a red handkerchief around his neck and was readjusting his galluses when I returned. In silence we hurried to the house. As we drew near I heard the voice of Mrs. Horace Dunkelberg and that of another woman quite as strange to my ear—a high-pitched voice of melting amiability. It was the company voice of my Aunt Deel. I had observed just a faint suggestion of it when the neighbors came, or when meeting was over, but I had never before heard the full-fledged angelicity of her company voice. It astonished me and I began to regard her as a very promising old lady. Uncle Peabody, himself, had undergone a change in the presence of the Dunkelbergs. He held his neck straighter and smiled more and spoke with greater deliberation.

Mr. Dunkelberg was a big, broad-shouldered, solemn-looking man. Somehow his face reminded me of a lion's which I had seen in one of my picture-books. He had a thick, long, outstanding mustache and side whiskers, and deep-set eyes and heavy eyebrows. He stood for half a moment looking down at me from a great height with his right hand in his pocket. I heard a little jingle of coins down where his hand was. It excited my curiosity. He took a step toward me and I retreated. I feared, a little, this big, lion-like man. My fears left me suddenly when he spoke in a small squeaky voice that reminded me of the chirping of a bird.

"Little boy, come here and I will make you a present," said he.

It reminded me of my disappointment when uncle tried to shoot his gun at a squirrel and only the cap cracked.

I went to him and he laid a silver piece in the palm of my hand. Aunt Deel began to hurry about getting dinner ready while Uncle Peabody and I sat down on the porch with our guests, among whom was a pretty blue-eyed girl of about my own age, with long, golden-brown hair that hung in curls.

"Sally, this is Barton Baynes—can't you shake hands with him?" said Mrs. Dunkelberg.

With a smile the girl came and offered me her hand and made a funny bow and said that she was glad to see me. I took her hand awkwardly and made no reply. I had never seen many girls and had no very high opinion of them.

My attentive ears and eyes began to gather facts in the history of the Dunkelbergs. Mr. Dunkelberg had throat trouble, and bought butter and cheese and sent it to Boston, and had busted his voice singing tenor, and was very rich. I knew that he was rich because he had a gold watch and chain, and clothes as soft and clean as the butternut trousers, and a silver ring on his finger, and such a big round stomach. That stomach was the most convincing feature of all and, indeed, I have since learned that the rounded type of human architecture is apt to be more expensive than the angular.

As we sat there I heard the men talking about the great Silas Wright, who had just returned to his home in Canton. He had not entered my consciousness until then.

While I sat listening I felt a tweak of my hair, and looking around I saw the Dunkelberg girl standing behind me with a saucy smile on her face.

"Won't you come and play with me?" she asked.

I took her out in the garden to show her where my watermelon had lain. At the moment I couldn't think of anything else to show her. As we walked along I observed that her feet were in dainty shiny button-shoes. Suddenly I began to be ashamed of my feet that were browned by the sunlight and scratched by the briers. The absent watermelon didn't seem to interest her.

"Let's play house in the grove," said she, and showed me how to build a house by laying rows of stones with an opening for a door.

"Now you be my husband," said she.

Oddly enough I had heard of husbands but had only a shadowy notion of what they were. I knew that there was none in our house.

"What's that?" I asked.

She laughed and answered: "Somebody that a girl is married to."

"You mean a father?"

"Yes."

"Once I had a father," I boasted.

"Well, we'll play we're married and that you have just got home from a journey. You go out in the woods and then you come home and I'll meet you at the door."

I did as she bade me but I was not glad enough to see her.

"You must kiss me," she prompted in a whisper.

I kissed her very swiftly and gingerly—like one picking up a hot coal—and she caught me in her arms and kissed me three times while her soft hair threw its golden veil over our faces.

"Oh I'm so glad to see you," she said as she drew away from me and shook back her hair.

"Golly! this is fun!" I said.

"Ask: 'How are the babies?'" she whispered.

"How are the babies?" I asked, feeling rather silly.

"They're fine. I'm just putting them to bed."

We sat on the grass and she had a stick which she pretended to be dressing and often, after she had spanked the stick a little, she made a noise through closed lips like that of a child crying.

"Now go to sleep and I'll tell you a story," said she.

Then she told pretty tales of fairies and of grand ladies and noble gentlemen who wore gold coats and swords and diamonds and silks, and said wonderful words in such a wonderful way. I dare say it prospered all the better in my ears because of the mystery by which its meanings were partly hidden. I had many questions to ask and she told me what were fairies and silks and diamonds and grand ladies and noble gentlemen.

We sat down to one of our familiar dinners of salt pork and milk gravy and apple pie now enriched by sweet pickles and preserves and frosted cake.

A query had entered my mind and soon after we began eating I asked:

"Aunt Deel, what is the difference between a boy and a girl?"

There was a little silence in which my aunt drew in her breath and exclaimed, "W'y!" and turned very red and covered her face with her napkin. Uncle Peabody laughed so loudly that the chickens began to cackle. Mr. and Mrs. Dunkelberg also covered their faces. Aunt Deel rose and went to the stove and shoved the teapot along, exclaiming:

"Goodness, gracious sakes alive!"

The tea slopped over on the stove. Uncle Peabody laughed louder and Mr. Dunkelberg's face was purple. Shep came running into the house just as I ran out of it. I had made up my mind that I had done something worse than tipping over a what-not. Thoroughly frightened I fled and took refuge behind the ash-house, where Sally found me. I knew of one thing I would never do again. She coaxed me into the grove where we had another play spell.

I needed just that kind of thing, and what a time it was for me! A pleasant sadness comes when I think of that day—it was so long ago. As the Dunkelbergs left us I stood looking down the road on which they were disappearing and saw in the sky and the distant, purple hills and sloping meadows the beauty of the world. The roaring aeroplane of a humming bird whirled about me and sped through the hollyhock towers. I followed and watched the tiny air-ship sticking its prow in their tops, as if it would have me see how wonderful they were, before it sped away. Breast deep in the flowers I forgot my loneliness for a few minutes. But that evening my ears caught a note of sadness in the voice of the katydids, and memory began to play its part with me. Best of all I remembered the kisses and the bright blue eyes and the soft curly hair with the smell of roses in it.

CHAPTER II

I MEET THE SILENT WOMAN AND SILAS WRIGHT, JR.

Amos Grimshaw was there in our dooryard the day that the old ragged woman came along and told our fortunes—she that was called Rovin' Kate, and was said to have the gift of "second sight," whatever that may be. It was a bright autumn day and the leaves lay deep in the edge of the woodlands. She spoke never a word but stood pointing at her palm and then at Amos and at me.

I was afraid of the old woman—she looked so wild and ragged. I have never seen a human being whose look and manner suggested a greater capacity for doing harm. Yet there was a kindly smile on her tanned face when she looked at me. Young as I was, the truth came home to me, somehow, that she was a dead but undeparted spirit and belonged to another world. I remember the tufts of gray hair above her blue eyes; the mole on the side of her aquiline nose; her pointed chin and small mouth. She carried a cane in her bony right hand and the notion came to me that she was looking for bad boys who deserved a cudgeling.

Aunt Deel nodded and said:

"Ayes, Kate—tell their fortunes if ye've anything to say—ayes!"

She brought two sheets of paper and the old woman sat down upon the grass and began to write with a little stub of a pencil. I have now those fateful sheets of paper covered by the scrawls of old Kate. I remember how she shook her head and sighed and sat beating her forehead with the knuckles of her bony hands after she had looked at the palm of Amos. Swiftly the point of her pencil ran over and up and down the sheet like the movements of a frightened serpent. In the silence how loudly the pencil seemed to hiss in its swift lines and loops.

My aunt exclaimed "Mercy!" as she looked at the sheet; for while I knew not, then, the strange device upon the paper, I knew, by and by, that it was a gibbet. Beneath it were the words: "Money thirst shall burn like a fire in him."

She rose and smiled as she looked into my face. I saw a kind, gentle glow in her eyes that reassured me. She clapped her hands with joy. She examined my palm and grew serious and stood looking thoughtfully at the setting sun.

I see, now, her dark figure standing against the sunlight as it stood that day with Amos in its shadow. What a singular eloquence in her pose and gestures and in her silence! I remember how it bound our tongues—that silence of hers! She covered her eyes with her left hand as she turned away from us. Slowly her right hand rose above her head with its index finger extended and slowly came down to her side. It rose again with two fingers showing and descended as before. She repeated this gesture until her four bony fingers had been spread in the air above her. How it thrilled me! Something jumped to life in my soul at the call of her moving hand. I passed a new gate of my imagination, I fancy, and if I have a way of my own in telling things it began that moment.

The woman turned with a kindly smile and sat down in the grass again and took the sheet of paper and resting it on a yellow-covered book began to write these words:

"I see the longing of the helper. One, two, three, four great perils shall strike at him. He shall not be afraid. God shall fill his heart with laughter. I hear guns, I hear many voices. His name is in them. He shall be strong. The powers of darkness shall fear him, he shall be a lawmaker and the friend of God and of many people, and great men shall bow to his judgment and he shall—"

She began shaking her head thoughtfully and did not finish the sentence, and by and by the notion came to me that some unpleasant vision must have halted her pencil.

Aunt Deel brought some luncheon wrapped in paper and the old woman took it and went away. My aunt folded the sheets and put them in her trunk and we thought no more of them until—but we shall know soon what reminded us of the prophet woman.

The autumn passed swiftly. I went to the village one Saturday with Uncle Peabody in high hope of seeing the Dunkelbergs, but at their door we learned that they had gone up the river on a picnic. What a blow it was to me! Tears flowed down my cheeks as I clung to my uncle's hand and walked back to the main street of the village. A squad of small boys jeered and stuck out their tongues at me. It was pity for my sorrows, no doubt, that led Uncle Peabody to take me to the tavern for dinner, where they were assuaged by cakes and jellies and chicken pie.

When we came out of the tavern we saw Benjamin Grimshaw and his son Amos sitting on the well curb. Each had a half-eaten doughnut in one hand and an apple in the other. I remember that Mr. Grimshaw said in a scolding manner which made me dislike him:

"Baynes, I'm glad to see you're so prosperous. Only the rich can afford to eat in taverns. Our dinner has cost us just three cents, an' I wouldn't wonder if I was worth about as much as you are."

My uncle made no reply and we passed on to a store nearly opposite the well, where I became deeply interested in a man who had tapped me in the stomach with his forefinger while he made a sound like the squealing of a rat. Then he said to Uncle Peabody:

"Look at that man out there by the well! He's the richest man in this section o' country. He owns half o' this village. I wouldn't wonder if he was worth fifty thousand dollars at least. What do ye suppose he spent for his dinner?"

"Three cents," said my uncle.

"Guess again—it was a cent and a half. He came in here and asked how much were the doughnuts. I told him they were a cent a piece. He offered me three cents for four of them—said it was all the change he had. He and his boy are eating them with some apples that they had in their pockets."

I remember how my uncle and the man laughed as the latter said: "His wealth costs too much altogether. 'Tain't worth it"—a saying which my uncle often quoted.

Thus early I got a notion of the curious extravagance of the money worshiper. How different was my uncle, who cared too little for money!

At Christmas I got a picture-book and forty raisins and three sticks of candy with red stripes on them and a jew's-harp. That was the Christmas we went down to Aunt Liza's to spend the day and I helped myself to two pieces of cake when the plate was passed and cried because they all laughed at my greediness. It was the day when Aunt Liza's boy, Truman, got a silver watch and chain and her daughter Mary a gold ring, and when all the relatives were invited to come and be convinced, once and for all, of Uncle Roswell's prosperity and be filled with envy and reconciled with jelly and preserves and roast turkey with sage dressing and mince and chicken pie. What an amount of preparation we had made for the journey, and how long we had talked about it! When we had shut the door and were ready to get into the sleigh our dog Shep came whining around us. I shall never forget how Uncle Peabody talked to him.

"Go back, Shep—go back to the house an' stay on the piaz," he began. "Go back I tell ye. It's Christmas day an' we're goin' down to ol' Aunt Liza's. Ye can't go way down there. No, sir, ye can't. Go back an' lay down on the piaz."

Shep was fawning at my uncle's foot and rubbing his neck on his boot and looking up at him.

"What's that ye say?" Uncle Peabody went on, looking down and turning his ear as if he had heard the dog speak and were in some doubt of his meaning. "Eh? What's that? An empty house makes ye terrible sad on a Chris'mas day? What's that? Ye love us an' ye'd like to go along down to Aunt Liza's an' play with the children?"

It was a clever ruse of Uncle Peabody, for Aunt Deel was softened by his interpretation of the dog's heart and she proposed:

"Le's take him along with us—poor dog! ayes!"

Then Uncle Peabody shouted:

"Jump right into the sleigh—you ol' skeezucks!—an' I'll cover ye up with a hoss blanket. Git in here. We ain't goin' to leave nobody alone on Chris'mas day that loves us—not by a jug full—no, sir! I wouldn't wonder if Jesus died for dogs an' hosses as well as for men."

Shep had jumped in the back of the sleigh at the first invitation and lay quietly under his blanket as we hurried along in the well-trod snow and the bells jingled. It was a joyful day and old Shep was as merry and well fed as the rest of us.

How cold and sad and still the house seemed when we got back to it in the evening! We had to drive to a neighbor's and borrow fire and bring it home with us in a pail of ashes as we were out of tinder. I held the lantern for my uncle while he did the chores and when we had gone to bed I fell asleep hearing him tell of Joseph and Mary going to pay their taxes.

In the spring my uncle hired a man to work for us—a noisy, brawny, sharp-featured fellow with keen gray eyes, of the name of Dug Draper. Aunt Deel hated him. I feared him but regarded him with great hope because he had a funny way of winking at me with one eye across the table and, further, because he could sing and did sing while he worked—songs that rattled from his lips in a way that amused me greatly. Then, too, he could rip out words that had a new and wonderful sound in them. I made up my mind that he was likely to become a valuable asset when I heard Aunt Deel say to my Uncle Peabody:

"You'll have to send that loafer away, right now, ayes I guess you will."

"Why?"

"Because this boy has learnt to swear like a pirate—ayes—he has!"

Uncle Peabody didn't know it but I myself had begun to suspect it, and that hour the man was sent away, and I remember that he left in anger with a number of those new words flying from his lips. A forced march to the upper room followed that event. Uncle Peabody explained that it was wicked to swear—that boys who did it had very bad luck, and mine came in a moment. I never had more of it come along in the same length of time.

One day in the spring when the frogs were chanting in the swamp land, they seemed to be saying, "Dunkelberg, Dunkelberg, Dunkelberg, Dunkelberg," from morning to bedtime. I was helping Uncle Peabody to fix the fence when he said:

"Hand me that stake, Bub. Don't be so much of a gentleman."

I handed the stake to him and then I said:

"Uncle Peabody, I want to be a gentleman."

"A gentleman!" he exclaimed as he looked down at me thoughtfully.

"A grand, noble gentleman with a sword and a gold watch and chain and diamonds on," I exclaimed.

He leaned against the top rail of the fence and looked down at me and laughed.

"Whatever put that in yer head?" he asked.

"Oh, I don't know—how do ye be it?" I demanded.

"They's two ways," said he. "One is to begin 'fore you're born and pick out the right father. T'other is to begin after you're born and pick out the right son. You can make yerself whatever you want to be. It's all inside of a boy and it comes out by and by—swords and gold and diamonds, or rags an' dirt an' shovels an' crowbars."

I wondered what I had inside of me.

"I guess I ain't got any sword in me," I said.

"When you've been eating green apples and I wouldn't wonder," he answered as he went on with his work.

"Once I thought I heard a watch tickin' in my throat," I said hopefully.

"I don't mean them things is really in ye, but the power to git 'em is in ye," said Uncle Peabody. "That's what I mean—power. Be a good boy and study yer lessons and never lie, and the power'll come into ye jest as sure as you're alive."

I began to watch myself for symptoms of power.

After I ceased to play with the Wills boy Uncle Peabody used to say, often, it was a pity that I hadn't somebody of my own age for company. Every day I felt sorry that the Wills boy had turned out so badly, and I doubt not the cat and the shepherd dog and the chickens and Uncle Peabody also regretted his failures, especially the dog and Uncle Peabody, who bore all sorts of indignities for my sake.

In the circumstances I had to give a good deal of time to the proper education of my uncle. Naturally he preferred to waste his time with shovels and rakes. But he soon learned how to roll a hoop and play tag and ball and yard off and how to run like a horse when I sat on his shoulders. It was rather hard on him, after his work in the fields, but he felt his responsibility and applied himself with due diligence and became a very promising child. I also gave strict attention to his talent for story-telling. It improved rapidly. Being frank in my criticism he was able to profit by all his failures in taste and method, so that each story had a fierce bear in it and a fair amount of growling by and by. But I could not teach him to sing, and it was a great sorrow to me. I often tried and he tried, but I saw that it wasn't going to pay. He couldn't make the right kind of a noise. Through all this I did not neglect his morals. If he said an improper word—and I regret to say that he did now and then—I promptly corrected him and reported his conduct to Aunt Deel, and if she was inclined to be too severe I took his part and, now and then, got snapped on the forehead for the vigor of my defense. On the whole it is no wonder that Uncle Peabody wearied of his schooling.

One day when Uncle Peabody went for the mail he brought Amos Grimshaw to visit me. I had not seen him since the day he was eating doughnuts in the village with his father. He was four years older than I—a freckled, red-haired boy with a large mouth and thin lips. He wore a silver watch and chain, which strongly recommended him in my view and enabled me to endure his air of condescension.

He let me feel it and look it all over and I slyly touched the chain with my tongue just to see if it had any taste to it, and Amos told me that his grandfather had given it to him and that it always kept him "kind o' scairt."

"Why?"

"For fear I'll break er lose it an' git licked," he answered.

We went and sat down on the hay together, and I showed him the pennies I had saved and he showed me where his father had cut his leg that morning with a blue beech rod.

"Don't you ever git licked?" he asked.

"No," I answered.

"I guess that's because you ain't got any father," he answered. "I wish I hadn't. There's nobody so mean as a father. Mine makes me work every day an' never gives me a penny an' licks me whenever I do anything that I want to. I've made up my mind to run away from home."

After a moment of silence he exclaimed:

"Gosh! It's awful lonesome here! Gee whittaker! this is the worst place I ever saw!"

I tried to think of something that I could say for it.

"We have got a new corn sheller," I said, rather timidly.

"I don't care about your corn shellers," he answered with a look of scorn.

He took a little yellow paper-covered book from his pocket and began to read to himself.

I felt thoroughly ashamed of the place and sat near him and, for a time, said nothing as he read.

"What's that?" I ventured to ask by and by.

"A story," he answered. "I met that ragged ol' woman in the road t'other day an' she give me a lot of 'em an' showed me the pictures an' I got to readin' 'em. Don't you tell anybody 'cause my ol' dad hates stories an' he'd lick me 'til I couldn't stan' if he knew I was readin' 'em."

I begged him to read out loud and he read from a tale of two robbers named Thunderbolt and Lightfoot who lived in a cave in the mountains. They were bold, free, swearing men who rode beautiful horses at a wild gallop and carried guns and used them freely and with unerring skill, and helped themselves to what they wanted.

He stopped, by and by, and confided to me the fact that he thought he would run away and join a band of robbers.

"How do you run away?" I asked.

"Just take the turnpike and keep goin' toward the mountains. When ye meet a band o' robbers give 'em the sign an' tell 'em you want to join."

He went on with the book and read how the robbers had hung a captive who had persecuted them and interfered with their sport. The story explained how they put the rope around the neck of the captive and threw the other end of it over the limb of a tree and pulled the man into the air.

He stopped suddenly and demanded: "Is there a long rope here?"

I pointed to Uncle Peabody's hay rope hanging on a peg.

"Le's hang a captive," he proposed.

At first I did not comprehend his meaning. He got the rope and threw its end over the big beam. Our old shepherd dog had been nosing the mow near us for rats. Amos caught the dog who, suspecting no harm, came passively to the rope's end. He tied the rope around the dog's neck.

"We'll draw him up once—it won't hurt him any," he proposed.

I looked at him in silence. My heart smote me, but I hadn't the courage to take issue with the owner of a silver watch. When the dog began to struggle I threw my arms about him and cried. Aunt Deel happened to be near. She came and saw Amos pulling at the rope and me trying to save the dog.

"Come right down off'm that mow—this minute," said she.

When we had come down and the dog had followed pulling the rope after him, Aunt Deel was pale with anger.

"Go right home—right home," said she to Amos.

"Mr. Baynes said that he would take me up with the horses," said Amos.

"Ye can use shank's horses—ayes!—they're good enough for you," Aunt Deel insisted, and so the boy went away in disgrace.

I blushed to think of the poor opinion he would have of the place now. It seemed to me a pity that it should be made any worse, but I couldn't help it.

"Where are your pennies?" Aunt Deel said to me.

I felt in my pockets but couldn't find them.

"Where did ye have `em last?" my aunt demanded.

"On the haymow."

"Come an' show me."

We went to the mow and search for the pennies, but not one of them could we find.

I remembered that when I saw them last Amos had them in his hand.

"I'm awful 'fraid for him—ayes I be!" said Aunt Deel. "I'm 'fraid Rovin' Kate was right about him—ayes!"

"What did she say?" I asked.

"That he was goin' to be hung—ayes! You can't play with him no more. Boys that take what don't belong to `em—which I hope he didn't—ayes I hope it awful—are apt to be hung by their necks until they are dead—jest as he was goin' to hang ol' Shep—ayes!—they are!"

Again I saw the dark figure of old Kate standing in the sunlight and her ragged garments and bony hands and heard the hiss of her flying pencil point. I clung to my aunt's dress for a moment and then I found old Shep and sat down beside him with my arm around his neck. I did not speak of the story because I had promised not to and felt sure that Amos would do something to me if I did.

Uncle Peabody seemed to feel very badly when he learned how Amos had turned out.

"Don't say a word about it," said he. "Mebbe you lost the pennies. Don't mind 'em."

Soon after that, one afternoon, Aunt Deel came down in the field where we were dragging. While she was talking with Uncle Peabody an idea occurred to me and the dog and I ran for the house. There was a pan of honey on the top shelf of the pantry and ever since I had seen it put there I had cherished secret designs.

I ran into the deserted house, and with the aid of a chair climbed to the first shelf and then to the next, and reached into the pan and drew out a comb of honey, and with no delay whatever it went to my mouth. Suddenly it seemed to me that I had been hit by lightning. It was the sting of a bee. I felt myself going and made a wild grab and caught the edge of the pan and down we came to the floor—the pan and I—with a great crash.

I discovered that I was in desperate pain and trouble and I got to my feet and ran. I didn't know where I was going. It seemed to me that any other place would be better than that. My feet took me toward the barn and I crawled under it and hid there. My lip began to feel better, by and by, but big and queer. It stuck out so that I could see it. I heard my uncle coming with the horses. I concluded that I would stay where I was, but the dog came and sniffed and barked at the hole through which I had crawled as if saying, "Here he is!" My position was untenable. I came out. Shep began trying to clean my clothes with his tongue. Uncle Peabody stood near with the horses. He looked at me. He stuck his finger into the honey on my coat and smelt it.

"Well, by—" he stopped and came closer and asked.

"What's happened?"

"Bee stung me," I answered.

"Where did ye find so much honey that ye could go swimmin' in it?" he asked.

I heard the door of the house open suddenly and the voice of Aunt Deel.

"Peabody! Peabody! come here quick," she called.

Uncle Peabody ran to the house, but I stayed out with the dog.

Through the open door I heard Aunt Deel saying: "I can't stan' it any longer and I won't—not another day—ayes, I can't stan' it. That boy is a reg'lar pest."

They came out on the veranda. Uncle Peabody said nothing, but I could see that he couldn't stand it either. My brain was working fast.

"Come here, sir," Uncle Peabody called.

I knew it was serious, for he had never called me "sir" before. I went slowly to the steps.

"My lord!" Aunt Deel exclaimed. "Look at that lip and the honey all over him—ayes! I tell ye—I can't stan' it."

"Say, boy, is there anything on this place that you ain't tipped over?" Uncle Peabody asked in a sorrowful tone. "Wouldn't ye like to tip the house over?"

I was near breaking down in this answer:

"I went into the but'ry and that pan jumped on to me."

"Didn't you taste the honey?"

"No," I drew in my breath and shook my head.

"Liar, too!" said Aunt Deel. "I can't stan' it an' I won't."

Uncle Peabody was sorely tried, but he was keeping down his anger. His voice trembled as he said:

"Boy, I guess you'll have to—"

Uncle Peabody stopped. He had been driven to the last ditch, but he had not stepped over it. However, I knew what he had started to say and sat down on the steps in great dejection. Shep followed, working at my coat with his tongue.

I think that the sight of me must have touched the heart of Aunt Deel.

"Peabody Baynes, we mustn't be cruel," said she in a softer tone, and then she brought a rag and began to assist Shep in the process of cleaning my coat. "Good land! He's got to stay here—ayes!—he ain't got no other place to go to."

"But if you can't stan' it," said Uncle Peabody.

"I've got to stan' it—ayes!—I can't stan' it, but I've got to—ayes! So have you."

Aunt Deel put me to bed although it was only five o'clock. As I lay looking up at the shingles a singular resolution came to me. It was born of my longing for the companionship of my kind and of my resentment. I would go and live with the Dunkelbergs. I would go the way they had gone and find them. I knew it was ten miles away, but of course everybody knew where the Dunkelbergs lived and any one would show me. I would run and get there before dark and tell them that I wanted to live with them, and every day I would play with Sally Dunkelberg. Uncle Peabody was not half as nice to play with as she was.

I heard Uncle Peabody drive away. I watched him through the open window. I could hear Aunt Deel washing the dishes in the kitchen. I got out of bed very slyly and put on my Sunday clothes. I went to the open window. The sun had just gone over the top of the woods. I would have to hurry to get to the Dunkelbergs' before dark. I crept out on the top of the shed and descended the ladder that leaned against it. I stood a moment listening. The dooryard was covered with shadows and very still. The dog must have gone with Uncle Peabody. I ran through the garden to the road and down it as fast as my bare feet could carry me. In that direction the nearest house was almost a mile away. I remember I was out of breath, and the light growing dim before I got to it. I went on. It seemed to me that I had gone nearly far enough to reach my destination when I heard a buggy coming behind me.

"Hello!" a voice called.

I turned and looked up at Dug Draper, in a single buggy, dressed in his Sunday suit.

"Is it much further to where the Dunkelbergs live?" I asked.

"The Dunkelbergs? Who be they?"

It seemed to me very strange that he didn't know the Dunkelbergs.

"Where Sally Dunkelberg lives."

That was a clincher. He laughed and swore and said:

"Git in here, boy. I'll take ye there."

I got into the buggy, and he struck his horse with the whip and went galloping away in the dusk.

"I reckon you're tryin' to git away from that old pup of an aunt," said he. "I don't wonder. I rather live with a she bear."

I have omitted and shall omit the oaths and curses with which his talk was flavored.

"I'm gittin' out o' this country myself," said he. "It's too pious for me."

By and by we passed Rovin' Kate. I could just discern her ragged form by the roadside and called to her. He struck his horse and gave me a rude shake and bade me shut up.

It was dark and I felt very cold and began to wish myself home in bed.

"Ain't we most to the Dunkelbergs'?" I asked.

"No—not yet," he answered.

I burst into tears and he hit me a sounding whack in the face with his hand.

"No more whimperin'," he shouted. "Do ye hear me?"

He hurt me cruelly and I was terribly frightened and covered my face and smothered my cries and was just a little quaking lump of misery.

He shook me roughly and shoved me down on the buggy floor and said:

"You lay there and keep still; do you hear?"

"Yes," I sobbed.

I lay shaking with fear and fighting my sorrow and keeping as still as I could with it, until, wearied by the strain, I fell asleep.

What an angel of mercy is sleep! Down falls her curtain and away she leads us—delivered! free!—into some magic country where are the things we have lost—perhaps even joy and youth and strength and old friendships.

What befell me that night while I dreamed of playing with the sweet-faced girl I have wondered often. Some time in the night Dug Draper had reached the village of Canton, and got rid of me. He had probably put me out at the water trough. Kind hands had picked me up and carried me to a little veranda that fronted the door of a law office. There I slept peacefully until daylight, when I felt a hand on my face and awoke suddenly. I remember that I felt cold. A kindly faced man stood leaning over me.

"Hello, boy!" said he. "Where did you come from?"

I was frightened and confused, but his gentle voice reassured me.

"Uncle Peabody!" I called, as I arose and looked about me and began to cry.

The man lifted me in his arms and held me close to his breast and tried to comfort me. I remember seeing the Silent Woman pass while I was in his arms.

"Tell me what's your name," he urged.

"Barton Baynes," I said as soon as I could speak.

"Where is your father?"

"In Heaven," I answered, that being the place to which he had moved, as I understood it.

"Where do you live?"

"In Lickitysplit."

"How did you get here?"

"Dug Draper brought me. Do you know where Sally Dunkelberg lives?"

"Is she the daughter of Horace Dunkelberg?"

"Mr. and Mrs. Horace Dunkelberg," I amended.

"Oh, yes, I know her. Sally is a friend of mine. We'll get some breakfast and then we'll go and find her."

He carried me through the open door of his office and set me down at his desk. The cold air of the night had chilled me and I was shivering.

"You sit there and I'll have a fire going in a minute and get you warmed up."

He wrapped me in his coat and went into the back room and built a fire in a small stove and brought me in and set me down beside it. He made some porridge in a kettle while I sat holding my little hands over the stove to warm them, and a sense of comfort grew in me. Soon a boy came bringing a small pail of fresh milk and a loaf of bread. I remember how curiously the boy eyed me as he said to my new friend:

"Captain Moody wants to know if you'll come up to dinner?"

There was a note of dignity in the reply which was new to me, and for that reason probably I have always remembered it.

"Please present my thanks to the Captain and tell him that I expect to go up to Lickitysplit in the town of Ballybeen."

He dipped some porridge into bowls and put them on a small table. My eyes had watched him with growing interest and I got to the table about as soon as the porridge and mounted a chair and seized a spoon.

"One moment, Bart," said my host. "By jingo! We've forgotten to wash, and your face looks like the dry bed of a river. Come here a minute."

He led me out of the back door, where there were a wash-stand and a pail and a tin basin and a dish of soft soap. He dipped the pail in a rain barrel and filled the basin, and I washed myself and waited not upon my host, but made for the table and began to eat, being very hungry, after hastily drying my face on a towel. In a minute he came and sat down to his own porridge and bread and butter.

"Bart, don't dig so fast," said he. "You're down to hard pan now. Never be in a hurry to see the bottom of the bowl."

I have never forgotten the look of amusement in his big, smiling, gray eyes as they looked down upon me out of his full, ruddy, smooth-shaven face. It inspired confidence and I whispered timidly:

"Could I have some more?"

"All you want," he answered, as he put another ladle full in my bowl.

When we had finished eating he set aside the dishes and I asked:

"Now could I go and see Sally Dunkelberg?"

"What in the world do you want of Sally Dunkelberg?" he asked.

"Oh, just to play with her," I said as I showed him how I could sit on my hands and raise myself from the chair bottom.

"Haven't you any one to play with at home?"

"Only my Uncle Peabody."

"Don't you like to play with him?"

"Oh, some, but he can't stand me any longer. He's all tired out, and my Aunt Deel, too. I've tipped over every single thing on that place. I tipped over the honey yesterday—spillt it all over everything and rooend my clothes. I'm a reg'lar pest. So I want to play with Sally Dunkelberg. She knows all kinds o' riddles and games and all about grand ladies and gentlemen and she wears shiny shoes and her hair smells just like roses, and I want to play with her a little while—just a wee little while."

I had unburdened my soul. The above words are quoted not from my memory, but from his, which has always been most reliable. I remember well my thoughts and feelings but not many of my words on a day so distant.

"Forward, march!" said he and away we started for the home of the Dunkelbergs. The village interested me immensely. I had seen it only twice before. People were moving about in the streets. One thing I did not fail to notice. Every man we met touched his hat as he greeted my friend.

"Good morning, Sile," some said, as we passed them, or, "How are you, Comptroller?"

It was a square, frame house—that of the Dunkelbergs—large for that village, and had a big dooryard with trees in it. As we came near the gate I saw Sally Dunkelberg playing with other children among the trees. Suddenly I was afraid and began to hang back. I looked down at my bare feet and my clothes, both of which were dirty. Sally and her friends had stopped their play and were standing in a group looking at us. I heard Sally whisper:

"It's that Baynes boy. Don't he look dirty?"

I stopped and withdrew my hand from that of my guide.

"Come on, Bart," he said.

I shook my head and stood looking over at that little, hostile tribe near me.

"Go and play with them while I step into the house," he urged.

Again I shook my head.

"Well, then, you wait here a moment," said my new-found friend.

He left me and I sat down upon the ground, thoughtful and silent.

He went to the children and kissed Sally and whispered in her ear and passed on into the house. The children walked over to me.

"Hello, Bart!" said Sally.

"Hello!" I answered.

"Wouldn't you like to play with us?"

I shook my head.

Some of them began to whisper and laugh. I remember how beautiful the girls looked with their flowing hair and ribbons and pretty dresses. What happy faces they had! I wonder why it all frightened and distressed me so.

In a moment my friend came out with Mrs. Dunkelberg, who kissed me, and asked me to tell how I happened to be there.

"I just thought I would come," I said as I twisted a button on my coat, and would say no more to her.

"Mr. Wright, you're going to take him home, are you?" Mrs. Dunkelberg asked.

"Yes. I'll start off with him in an hour or so," said my friend. "I am interested in this boy and I want to see his aunt and uncle."

"Let him stay here with us until you're ready to go."

"I don't want to stay here," I said, seizing my friend's hand.

"Well, Sally, you go down to the office and stay with Bart until they go."

"You'd like that wouldn't you?" the man asked of me.

"I don't know," I said.

"That means yes," said the man.

Sally and another little girl came with us and passing a store I held back to look at many beautiful things in a big window.

"Is there anything you'd like there, Bart?" the man asked.

"I wisht I had a pair o' them shiny shoes with buttons on," I answered in a low, confidential tone, afraid to express, openly, a wish so extravagant.

"Come right in," he said, and I remember that when we entered the store I could hear my heart beating.

He bought a pair of shoes for me and I would have them on at once, and that made it necessary for him to buy a pair of socks also. After the shoes were buttoned on my feet I saw little of Sally Dunkelberg or the other people of the village, my eyes being on my feet most of the time.

The man took us into his office and told us to sit down until he could write a letter.

I remember how, as he wrote, I stood by his chair and examined the glazed brown buttons on his coat and bit one of them to see how hard it was, while Sally was feeling his gray hair and necktie. He scratched along with his quill pen as if wholly unaware of our presence.

Soon a horse and buggy came for us and I briefly answered Sally's good-by before the man drove away with me. I remember telling him as we went on over the rough road, between fields of ripened grain, of my watermelon and my dog and my little pet hen.

I shall not try to describe that home coming. We found Aunt Deel in the road five miles from home. She had been calling and traveling from house to house most of the night, and I have never forgotten her joy at seeing me and her tender greeting. She got into the buggy and rode home with us, holding me in her lap. Uncle Peabody and one of our neighbors had been out in the woods all night with pine torches. I recall how, although excited by my return, he took off his hat at the sight of my new friend and said:

"Mr. Wright, I never wished that I lived in a palace until now."

He didn't notice me until I held up both feet and called: "Look a' there, Uncle Peabody."

Then he came and took me out of the buggy and I saw the tears in his eyes when he kissed me.

The man told of finding me on his little veranda, and I told of my ride with Dug Draper, after which Uncle Peabody said:

"I'm goin' to put in your hoss and feed him, Comptroller."

"And I'm goin' to cook the best dinner I ever cooked in my life," said Aunt Deel.

I knew that my new friend must be even greater than the Dunkelbergs, for there was a special extravagance in their tone and manner toward him which I did not fail to note. His courtesy and the distinction of his address, as he sat at our table, were not lost upon me, either. During the meal I heard that Dug Draper had run off with a neighbor's horse and buggy and had not yet returned. Aunt Deel said that he had taken me with him out of spite, and that he would probably never come back—a suspicion justified by the facts of history.

When the great man had gone Uncle Peabody took me in his lap and said very gently and with a serious look:

"You didn't think I meant it, did ye?—that you would have to go 'way from here?"

"I don't know," was my answer.

"Course I didn't mean that. I just wanted ye to see that it wa'n't goin' to do for you to keep on tippin' things over so."

I sat telling them of my adventures and answering questions, flattered by their tender interest, until milking time. I thoroughly enjoyed all that. When I rose to go out with Uncle Peabody, Aunt Deel demanded my shoes.

"Take 'em right off," said she. "It ain't a goin' to do to wear 'em common—no, sir-ee! They're for meetin' or when company comes—ayes!"

I regretfully took off the shoes and gave them to her, and thereafter the shoes were guarded as carefully as the butternut trousers.

That evening as I was about to go up-stairs to bed, Aunt Deel said to my uncle:

"Do you remember what ol' Kate wrote down about him? This is his first peril an' he has met his first great man an' I can see that Sile Wright is kind o' fond o' him."

I went to sleep that night thinking of the strange, old, ragged, silent woman.

CHAPTER III

WE GO TO MEETING AND SEE MR. WRIGHT AGAIN

I had a chill that night and in the weeks that followed I was nearly burned up with lung fever. Doctor Clark came from Canton to see me every other day for a time, and one evening Mr. Wright came with him and watched all night near my bedside. He gave me medicine every hour, and I remember how gently he would speak and raise my head when he came with the spoon and the draft. It grieved me to hear him say, as he raised me in his arms, that I wasn't bigger than "a cock mosquito."

I would lie and watch him as he put a stick on the fire and tiptoed to his armchair by the table, on which three lighted candles were burning. Then he would adjust his spectacles, pick up his book, and begin to read, and I would see him smile or frown or laugh until I wondered what was between the black covers of the book to move him so. In the morning he said that he could come the next Tuesday night, if we needed him, and set out right after breakfast, in the dim dawn light, to walk to Canton.

"Peabody Baynes," said my Aunt Deel as she stood looking out of the window at Mr. Wright, "that is one of the grandest, splendidest men that I ever see or heard of. He's an awful smart man, an' a day o' his time is worth more'n a month of our'n, but he comes away off here to set up with a sick young one and walks back. Does beat all—don't it?—ayes!"

"If any one needs help Sile Wright is always on hand," said Uncle Peabody.

I was soon out of bed and he came no more to sit up with me.

When I was well again Aunt Deel said one day "Peabody Baynes, I ain't heard no preachin' since Mr Pangborn died. I guess we better go down to Canton to meetin' some Sunday. If there ain't no minister Sile Wright always reads a sermon, if he's home, and the paper says he don't go 'way for a month yit. I kind o' feel the need of a good sermon—ayes!"

"All right. I'll hitch up the hosses and we'll go. We can start at eight o'clock and take a bite with us an' git back here by three."

"Could I wear my new shoes and trousers?" I asked joyfully.

"Ayes I guess ye can if you're a good boy—ayes!" said Aunt Deel.

I had told Aunt Deel what Sally had said of my personal appearance.

"Your coat is good enough for anybody—ayes!" said she. "I'll make you a pair o' breeches an' then I guess you won't have to be 'shamed no more."

She had spent several evenings making them out of an old gray flannel petticoat of hers and had put two pockets in them of which I was very proud. They came just to the tops of my shoes, which pleased me, for thereby the glory of my new shoes suffered no encroachment.

The next Sunday after they were finished we had preaching in the schoolhouse and I was eager to go and wear my wonderful trousers. Uncle Peabody said that he didn't know whether his leg would hold out or not "through a whole meetin'." His left leg was lame from a wrench and pained him if he sat long in one position. I greatly enjoyed this first public exhibition of my new trousers. I remember praying in silence, as we sat down, that Uncle Peabody's leg would hold out. Later, when the long sermon had begun to weary me, I prayed that it would not.

I decided that meetin's were not a successful form of entertainment. Indeed, Sunday was for me a lost day. It was filled with shaving and washing and reading and an overwhelming silence. Uncle Peabody always shaved after breakfast and then he would sit down to read the *St. Lawrence Republican.* Both occupations deprived him utterly of his usefulness as an uncle. I remember that I regarded the razor and the *Republican* as my worst enemies. The *Republican* earned my keenest dislike, for it always put my uncle to sleep and presently he would stretch out on the lounge and begin to puff and snore and then Aunt Deel always went around on her tiptoes and said sh-h-h! She spent the greater part of the forenoon in her room washing and changing her clothes and reading the Bible. How loudly the clock ticked that day! How defiantly the cock crew! It seemed as if he were making special efforts to start up the life of the farm. How shrill were the tree crickets! Often Shep and I would steal off into the back lot trying to scare up a squirrel and I would look longingly down the valley, and could dimly see the roofs of houses where there were other children. I would gladly have made friends with the Wills boy, but he would have nothing to do with me, and soon his people moved away. My uncle said that Mr. Grimshaw had foreclosed their mortgage.

The fields were so still that I wondered if the grass grew on Sunday. The laws of God and nature seemed to be in conflict, for our livers got out of order and some one of us always had a headache in the afternoon. It was apt to be Uncle Peabody, as I had reason to know, for I always begged him to go in swimmin' with me in the afternoon.

It was a beautiful summer morning as we drove down the hills and from the summit of the last high ridge we could see the smoke of a steamer looming over the St. Lawrence and the big buildings of Canton on the distant flats below us. My heart beat fast when I reflected that I should soon see Mr. Wright and the Dunkelbergs. I had lost a little of my interest in Sally. Still I felt sure that when she saw my new breeches she would conclude that I was a person not to be trifled with.

When we got to Canton people were flocking to the big stone Presbyterian Church. We drove our horses under the shed of the tavern and Uncle Peabody brought them water from the pump and fed them, out of our own bag under the buggy seat, before we went to the church.

It was what they called a "deacon meeting." I remember that Mr. Wright read from the Scriptures, and having explained that there was no minister in the village, read one of Mr. Edwards' sermons, in the course of which I went to sleep on the arm of my aunt. She awoke me when the service had ended, and whispered:

"Come, we're goin' down to speak to Mr. Wright."

We saw Mr. and Mrs. Horace Dunkelberg in the aisle, who said that they would wait for us outside the church.

I remember that Mr. Wright kissed me and said:

"Hello! Here's my boy in a new pair o' trousers!"

"Put yer hand in there," I said proudly, as I took my own out of one of my pockets, and pointed the way.

He did not accept the invitation, but laughed heartily and gave me a little hug.

When we went out of the church there stood Mr. and Mrs. Horace Dunkelberg, and Sally and some other children. It was a tragic moment for me when Sally laughed and ran behind her mother. Still worse was it when a couple of boys ran away crying, "Look at the breeches!"

I looked down at my breeches and wondered what was wrong with them. They seemed very splendid to me and yet I saw at once that they were not popular. I went close to my Aunt Deel and partly hid myself in her cloak. I heard Mrs. Dunkelberg say:

"Of course you'll come to dinner with us?"

For a second my hopes leaped high. I was hungry and visions of jelly cake and preserves rose before me. Of course there were the trousers, but perhaps Sally would get used to the trousers and ask me to play with her.

"Thank ye, but we've got a good ways to go and we fetched a bite with us—ayes!" said Aunt Deel.

Eagerly I awaited an invitation from the great Mrs. Dunkelberg that should be decisively urgent, but she only said:

"I'm very sorry you can't stay."

My hopes fell like bricks and vanished like bubbles.

The Dunkelbergs left us with pleasant words. They had asked me to shake hands with Sally, but I had clung to my aunt's cloak and firmly refused to make any advances. Slowly and without a word we walked across the park toward the tavern sheds. Hot tears were flowing down my cheeks—silent tears! for I did not wish to explain them. Furtively I brushed them away with my hand. The odor of frying beef steak came out of the open doors of the tavern. It was more than I could stand. I hadn't tasted fresh meat since Uncle Peabody had killed a deer in midsummer. He gave me a look of understanding, but said nothing for a minute. Then he proposed:

"Mebbe we better git dinner here?"

Aunt Deel hesitated at the edge of the stable yard, surrounded as she was by the aroma of the fleshpots, then:

"I guess we better go right home and save our money, Peabody—ayes!" said she. "We told Mr. and Mrs. Horace Dunkelberg that we was goin' home and they'd think we was liars."

"We orto have gone with `em," said Uncle Peabody as he unhitched the horses.

"Well, Peabody Baynes, they didn't appear to be very anxious to have us," Aunt Deel answered with a sigh.

We had started away up the South road when, to my surprise, Aunt Deel mildly attacked the Dunkelbergs.

"These here village folks like to be waited on—ayes!—an' they're awful anxious you should come to see 'em when ye can't—ayes!—but when ye git to the village they ain't nigh so anxious—no they ain't!"

Uncle Peabody made no answer, but sat looking forward thoughtfully and tapping the dashboard with his whipstock, and we rode on in a silence broken only by the creak of the evener and the sound of the horses' hoofs in the sand.

In the middle of the great cedar swamp near Little River Aunt Deel got out the lunch basket and I sat down on the buggy bottom between their legs and leaning against the dash. So disposed we ate our luncheon of fried cakes and bread and butter and maple sugar and cheese. The road was a straight alley through the evergreen forest, and its grateful shadow covered us. When we had come out into the hot sunlight by the Hale farm both my aunt and uncle complained of headache. What an efficient cure for good health were the doughnuts and cheese and sugar, especially if they were mixed with the idleness of a Sunday. I had a headache also and soon fell asleep.

The sun was low when they awoke me in our dooryard.

"Hope it'll be some time 'fore ye feel the need of another sermon," said Uncle Peabody as Aunt Deel got out of the buggy. "I ain't felt so wicked in years."

I was so sick that Aunt Deel put me to bed and said that she would feed the pigs and the chickens. Sick as he was, Uncle Peabody had to milk the cows. How relentless were the cows!

I soon discovered that the Dunkelbergs had fallen from their high estate in our home and that Silas Wright, Jr., had taken their place in the conversation of Aunt Deel.

CHAPTER IV

OUR LITTLE STRANGE COMPANION

In the pathless forest we had a little companion that always knew its way. No matter how strange and remote the place might be or how black the night its tiny finger always pointed in the same direction. By the light of the torch at midnight, in blinding darkness, I have seen it sway and settle toward its beloved goal. It seemed to be thinking of some far country which it desired to recommend to us.

It seemed to say: "Look! I know not which way is yours, but this—this is my way and all the little cross roads lead off it."

What a wonderful wisdom it had! I remember it excited a feeling of awe in me as if it were a spirit and not a tool.

The reader will have observed that my uncle spoke of the compass as if it directed plant and animal in achieving their purposes. From the beginning in the land of my birth it had been a thing as familiar as the dial and as necessary. The farms along our road were only stumpy recesses in the wilderness, with irregular curving outlines of thick timber—beech and birch and maple and balsam and spruce and pine and tamarack—forever whispering of the unconquered lands that rolled in great billowy ridges to the far horizon.

We were surrounded by the gloom and mystery of the forest. If one left the road or trail for even a short walk he needed a compass to guide him. That little brass box with its needle, swaying and seeming to quiver with excitement as it felt its way to the north side of the circle and pointed unerringly at last toward its favorite star, filled me with wonder.

"Why does it point toward the north star?" I used to ask.

"That's a secret," said Uncle Peabody. "I wouldn't wonder if the gate o' heaven was up there. Maybe it's a light in God's winder. Who knows? I kind o' mistrust it's the direction we're all goin' in."

"You talk like one o' them Universalists," said Aunt Deel. "They're gettin' thick as flies around here."

"Wal, I kind o' believe—" he paused at the edge of what may have been a dangerous opinion.

I shook the box and the needle swung and quivered back and forth and settled with its point in the north again. Oh, what a mystery! My eyes grew big at the thought of it.

"Do folks take compasses with 'em when they die?" I asked.

"No, they don't need 'em then," said Uncle Peabody. "Everybody has a kind of a compass in his own heart—same as watermelons and chickens have. It shows us the way to be useful, and I guess the way o' usefulness is the way to heaven every time."

"An' the way o' uselessness is the way to hell," Aunt Deel added.

One evening in the early summer the great Silas Wright had come to our house from the village of Russell, where he had been training a company of militia.

I remember that as he entered our door he spoke in this fashion: "Baynes, le's go fishing. All the way down the road I've heard the call o' the brooks. I stopped on the Dingley Bridge and looked down at the water. The trout were jumping so I guess they must 'a' got sunburnt and freckled and sore. I can't stand too much o' that kind o' thing. It riles me. I heard, long ago, that you were a first-class fisherman, so I cut across lots and here I am."

His vivid words touched my imagination and I have often recalled them.

"Well, now by mighty! I—" Uncle Peabody drew the rein upon his imagination at the very brink of some great extravagance and after a moment's pause added: "We'll start out bright an' early in the mornin' an' go up an' git Bill Seaver. He's got a camp on the Middle Branch, an' he can cook almost as good as my sister."

"Is your spring's work done?"

"All done, an' I was kind o' thinkin'," said Uncle Peabody with a little shake of his head. He didn't say of what he had been thinking, that being unnecessary.

"Bart, are you with us?" said Mr. Wright as he gave me a playful poke with his hand.

"May I go?" I asked my uncle.

"I wouldn't wonder—go an' ask yer aunt," said Uncle Peabody.

My soul was afire with eagerness. My feet shook the floor and I tipped over a chair in my hurry to get to the kitchen, whither my aunt had gone soon after the appearance of our guest. She was getting supper for Mr. Wright.

"Aunt Deel, I'm goin' fishin'," I said.

"Fishin'! I guess not—ayes I do," she answered.

It was more than I could stand. A roar of distress and disappointment came from my lips.

Uncle Peabody hurried into the kitchen.

"The Comptroller wants him to go," said he.

"He does?" she repeated as she stood with her hands on her hips looking up at her brother.

"He likes Bart and wants to take him along."

"Wal, then, you'll have to be awful careful of him," said Aunt Deel. "I'm 'fraid he'll plague ye—ayes!"

"No, he won't—we'll love to have him."

"Wal, I guess you could git Mary Billings to come over and stay with me an' help with the chores—ayes, I wouldn't wonder!"

I could contain my joy no longer, but ran into the other room on tiptoe and announced excitedly that I was going. Then I rushed out of the open door and rolled and tumbled in the growing grass, with the dog barking at my side. In such times of joyful excitement I always rolled and tumbled in the grass. It was my way of expressing inexpressible delight.

I felt sorry for the dog. Poor fellow! He couldn't go fishing. He had to stay home always. I felt sorry for the house and the dooryard and the cows and the grindstone and Aunt Deel. The glow of the candles and the odor of ham and eggs drew me into the house. Wistfully I watched the great man as he ate his supper. I was always hungry those days. Mr. Wright asked me to have an egg, but I shook my head and said "No, thank you" with sublime self-denial. At the first hint from Aunt Deel I took my candle and went up to bed.

"I ain't afraid o' bears," I heard myself whispering as I undressed. I whispered a good deal as my imagination ran away into the near future.

Soon I blew out my candle and got into bed. The door was open at the foot of the stairs. I could see the light and hear them talking. It had been more than a year since Uncle Peabody had promised to take me into the woods fishing, but most of our joys were enriched by long anticipation filled with talk and fancy.

I lay planning my behavior in the woods. It was to be helpful and polite and generally designed to show that I could be a man among men. I lay a long time whispering over details. There was to be no crying, even if I did get hurt a little once in a while. Men never cried. Only babies cried. I could hear Mr. Wright talking about Bucktails and Hunkers below stairs and I could hear the peepers down in the marsh.

Peepers and men who talked politics were alike to me those days. They were beyond my understanding and generally put me to sleep—especially the peepers. In my childhood the peepers were the bells of dream-land calling me to rest. The sweet sound no sooner caught my ear than my thoughts began to steal away on tiptoe and in a moment the house of my brain was silent and deserted, and thereafter, for a time, only fairy feet came into it. So even those happy thoughts of a joyous holiday soon left me and I slept.

I was awakened by a cool, gentle hand on my brow. I opened my eyes and saw the homely and beloved face of Uncle Peabody smiling down at me. What a face it was! It welcomed me, always, at the gates of the morning and I saw it in the glow of the candle at night as I set out on my lonely, dreaded voyage into dream-land. Do you wonder that I stop a moment and wipe my glasses when I think of it?

"Hello, Bart!" said he. "It's to-morrer."

I sat up. The delicious odor of frying ham was in the air. The glow of the morning sunlight was on the meadows.

"Come on, ol' friend! By mighty! We're goin' to—" said Uncle Peabody.

Happy thoughts came rushing into my brain again. What a tumult! I leaped out of bed.

"I'll be ready in a minute, Uncle Peabody," I said as, yawning, I drew on my trousers.

"Don't tear yer socks," he cautioned as I lost patience with their unsympathetic behavior.

He helped me with my boots, which were rather tight, and I flew down-stairs with my coat half on and ran for the wash-basin just outside the kitchen door.

"Hello, Bart! If the fish don't bite to-day they ought to be ashamed o' themselves," said Mr. Wright, who stood in the dooryard in an old suit of clothes which belonged to Uncle Peabody.

The sun had just risen over the distant tree-tops and the dew in the meadow grass glowed like a net of silver and the air was chilly. The chores were done. Aunt Deel appeared in the open door as I was wiping my face and hands and said in her genial, company voice:

"Breakfast is ready."

Aunt Deel never shortened her words when company was there. Her respect was always properly divided between her guest and the English language.

How delicious were the ham, smoked in our own barrels, and the eggs fried in its fat and the baked potatoes and milk gravy and the buckwheat cakes and maple syrup, and how we ate of them! Two big pack baskets stood by the window filled with provisions and blankets, and the black bottom of Uncle Peabody's spider was on the top of one of them, with its handle reaching down into the depths of the basket. The musket and the powder horn had been taken down from the wall and the former leaned on the window-sill.

"If we see a deer we ain't goin' to let him bite us," said Uncle Peabody.

Aunt Deel kept nudging me under the table and giving me sharp looks to remind me of my manners, for now it seemed as if a time had come when eating was a necessary evil to be got through with as soon as possible. Even Uncle Peabody tapped his cup lightly with his teaspoon, a familiar signal of his by which he indicated that I was to put on the brakes.

To Aunt Deel men-folks were a careless, irresponsible and mischievous lot who had to be looked after all the time or there was no telling what would happen to them. She slipped some extra pairs of socks and a bottle of turpentine into the pack basket and told us what we were to do if we got wet feet or sore throats or stomach ache.

Aunt Deel kissed me lightly on the cheek with a look that seemed to say, "There, I've done it at last," and gave me a little poke with her hand (I remember thinking what an extravagant display of affection it was) and many cautions before I got into the wagon with Mr. Wright, and my uncle. We drove up the hills and I heard little that the men said for my thoughts were busy. We arrived at the cabin of Bill Seaver that stood on the river bank just above Rainbow Falls. Bill stood in his dooryard and greeted us with a loud "Hello, there!"

"Want to go fishin'?" Uncle Peabody called.

"You bet I do. Gosh! I ain't had no fun since I went to Joe Brown's funeral an' that day I enjoyed myself—damned if I didn't! Want to go up the river?"

"We thought we'd go up to your camp and fish a day or two."

"All right! We'll hitch in the hosses. My wife'll take care of 'em 'til we git back. Say it looks as fishy as hell, don't it?"

"This is Mr. Silas Wright—the Comptroller," said Uncle Peabody.

"It is! Gosh almighty! I ought to have knowed it," said Bill Seaver, his tone and manner having changed like magic to those of awed respect. "I see ye in court one day years ago. If I'd knowed 'twas you I wouldn't 'a' swore as I did." The men began laughing and then he added: "Damned if I would!"

"It won't hurt me any—the boy is the one," said Mr. Wright as he took my hand and strolled up the river bank with me. I rather feared and dreaded those big roaring men like Bill Seaver.

The horses were hitched in and the canoes washed out. Then we all turned to and dug some angle-worms. The poles were brought—lines, hooks and sinkers were made ready and in an hour or so we were on our way up the river, Mr. Wright and I and Uncle Peabody being in one of the canoes, the latter working the paddle.

I remember how, as we went along, Mr. Wright explained the fundamental theory of his politics. I gave strict attention because of my pride in the fact that he included me in the illustration of his point. This in substance is what he said, for I can not pretend to quote his words with precision although I think they vary little from his own, for here before me is the composition entitled "The Comptroller," which I wrote two years later and read at a lyceum in the district schoolhouse.

"We are a fishing party. There are four of us who have come together with one purpose—that of catching fish and having a good time. We have elected Bill guide because he knows the river and the woods and the fish better than we do. It's Bill's duty to give us the benefit of his knowledge, and to take us to and from camp and out of the woods at our pleasure and contribute in all reasonable ways to our comfort. He is the servant of his party. Now if Bill, having approved our aim and accepted the job from us, were to try to force a new aim upon the party and insist that we should all join him in the sport of catching butterflies, we would soon break up. If we could agree on the butterfly program that would be one thing, but if we held to our plan and Bill stood out, he would be a traitor to his party and a fellow of very bad manners. As long as the aims of my party are, in the main, right, I believe its commands are sacred. Always in our country the will of the greatest number ought to prevail—right or wrong. It has a right even to make mistakes, for through them it should learn wisdom and gradually adjust itself to the will of its greatest leaders."

It is remarkable that the great commoner should have made himself understood by a boy of eight, but in so doing he exemplified the gift that raised him above all the men I have met—that of throwing light into dark places so that all could see the truth that was hidden there.

Now and then we came to noisy water hills slanting far back through rocky timbered gorges, or little foamy stairways in the river leading up to higher levels. The men carried the canoes around these places while I followed gathering wild flowers and watching the red-winged black birds that flew above us calling hoarsely across the open spaces. Now and then, a roaring veering cloud of pigeons passed in the upper air. The breath of the river was sweet with the fragrance of pine and balsam.

We were going around a bend when we heard the voice of Bill shouting just above us. He had run the bow of his canoe on a gravel beach just below a little waterfall and a great trout was flopping and tumbling about in the grass beside him.

"Yip!" he shouted as he held up the radiant, struggling fish that reached from his chin to his belt. "I tell ye boys they're goin' to be sassy as the devil. Jump out an' go to work here."

With what emotions I leaped out upon the gravel and watched the fishing! A new expression came into the faces of the men. Their mouths opened. There was a curious squint in their eyes. Their hands trembled as they baited their hooks. The song of the river, tumbling down a rocky slant, filled the air. I saw the first bite. How the pole bent! How the line hissed as it went rushing through the water out among the spinning bubbles! What a splash as the big fish in his coat of many colors broke through the ripples and rose aloft and fell at my feet throwing a spray all over me as he came down! That was the way they fished in those days. They angled with a stout pole of seasoned tamarack and no reel, and catching a fish was like breaking a colt to halter.

While he was fishing Mr. Wright slipped off the rock he stood on and sank shoulder deep in the water. I ran and held out my hand crying loudly. Uncle Peabody helped him ashore with his pole. Tears were flowing down my cheeks while I stood sobbing in a kind of juvenile hysterics.

"What's the matter?" Uncle Peabody demanded.

"I was 'fraid—Mr. Wright—was goin' to be drownded," I managed to say.

The Comptroller shook his arms and came and knelt by my side and kissed me.

"God bless the dear boy!" he exclaimed. "It's a long time since any one cried for me. I love you, Bart."

When Bill swore after that the Comptroller raised his hand and shook his head and uttered a protesting hiss.

We got a dozen trout before we resumed our journey and reached camp soon after one o'clock very hungry. It was a rude bark lean-to, and we soon made a roaring fire in front of it. What a dinner we had! the bacon and the fish fried in its fat and the boiled potatoes and the flapjacks and maple sugar! All through my long life I have sought in vain for a dinner like it. I helped with the washing of the dishes and, that done, Bill made a back for his fire of green beech logs, placed one upon the other and held in place by stakes driven in the ground. By and by Mr. Wright asked me if I would like to walk over to Alder Brook with him.

"The fish are smaller there and I guess you could catch 'em," said he.

The invitation filled me with joy and we set out together through the thick woods. The leaves were just come and their vivid, glossy green sprinkled out in the foliage of the little beeches and the woods smelt of new things. The trail was overgrown and great trees had fallen into it and we had to pick our way around them. The Comptroller carried me on his back over the wet places and we found the brook at last and he baited my hook while I caught our basket nearly full of little trout. Coming back we lost the trail and presently the Comptroller stopped and said:

"Bart, I'm 'fraid we're going wrong. Let's sit down here and take a look at the compass."

He took out his compass and I stood by his knee and watched the quivering needle.

"Yes, sir," he went on. "We just turned around up there on the hill and started for Alder Brook again."

As we went on he added: "When you're in doubt look at the compass. It always knows its way."

"How does it know?" I asked.

"It couldn't tell ye how and I couldn't. There are lots o' things in the world that nobody can understand."

The needle now pointed toward its favorite star.

"My uncle says that everything and everybody has compasses in 'em to show 'em the way to go," I remarked thoughtfully.

"He's right," said the Comptroller. "I'm glad you told me for I'd never thought of it. Every man has a compass in his heart to tell which way is right. I shall always remember that, partner."

He gave me a little hug as we sat together and I wondered what a partner might be, for the word was new to me.

"What's partner?" I asked.

"Somebody you like to have with you."

Always when we were together after that hour the great man called me "partner."

We neared camp in the last light of the day. Mr. Wright stopped to clean our fish at a little murmuring brook and I ran on ahead for I could hear the crackling of the camp-fire and the voice of Bill Seaver. I thought in whispers what I should say to my Uncle Peabody and they were brave words. I was close upon the rear of the camp when I checked my eager pace and approached on tiptoe. I was going to surprise and frighten my uncle and then embrace him. Suddenly my heart stood still, for I heard him saying words fit only for the tongue of a Dug Draper or a Charley Boyce—the meanest boy in school—low, wicked words which Uncle Peabody himself had taught me to fear and despise. My Uncle Peabody! Once I heard a man telling of a doomful hour in which his fortune won by years of hard work, broke and vanished like a bubble. The dismay he spoke of reminded me of my own that day. My Aunt Deel had told me that the devil used bad words to tempt his victims into a lake of fire where they sizzled and smoked and yelled forever and felt worse, every minute, than one sitting on a hot griddle. To save me from such a fate my uncle had nearly blistered me with his slipper. How was I to save him? I stood still for a moment of confusion and anxiety, with my hand over my mouth, while a strange sickness came upon me. A great cold wave had swept in off the uncharted seas and flooded my little beach, and covered it with wreckage. What was I to do? I knew that I couldn't punish him. I couldn't bear to speak to him even, so I turned and walked slowly away.

My dear, careless old uncle was in great danger. As I think of it now, what a whited sepulchre he had become in a moment! Had I better consult Mr. Wright? No. My pride in my uncle and my love for him would not permit it. I must bear my burden alone until I could tell Aunt Deel. She would know what to do. Mr. Wright came along and found me sitting in deep dejection on a bed of vivid, green moss by an old stump at the trail-side.

"What ye doing here?" he asked in surprise.

"Nothing," I answered gravely.

The Comptroller must have observed the sorrow in my face, for he asked:

"What's the matter?"

"Nothing," I lied, and then my conscience caught up with my tongue and I added: "It's a secret."

Fearing that my uncle would disgrace himself in the hearing of Mr. Wright, I said something—I do not remember what, save that it related to the weather—in a loud voice by way of warning.

They noticed the downcast look of me when we entered camp.

"Why, Bub, you look tired," said Uncle Peabody as he gave me that familiar hug of his.

I did not greet him with the cheerful warmth which had characterized our meetings, and seeing the disappointment in his look I kissed him rather flippantly.

"Lay down on this old sheep skin and take a nap," said he. "It's warm in here."

He spread the sheep skin on the balsam boughs back under the lean-to and I lay down upon it and felt the glow of the fire and heard the talk of the men but gave no heed to it. I turned my face away from them and lay as if asleep, but with a mind suddenly estranged and very busy.

Now I know what I knew not then, that my soul was breaking camp on the edge of the world and getting ready to move over the line. Still no suspicion of the truth reached me that since I came to live with him my uncle had been bitting and breaking his tongue. It occurred to me that Bill Seaver, whom I secretly despised, had spoilt him and that I had done wrong in leaving him all the afternoon defenseless in bad company.

I wondered if he were beyond hope or if he would have to fry and smoke and yell forever. But I had hope. My faith in Aunt Deel as a corrector and punisher was very great. She would know what to do. I heard the men talking in low voices as they cooked the supper and the frying of the fish and bacon. It had grown dark. Uncle Peabody came and leaned over me with a lighted candle and touched my face with his hand. I lay still with closed eyes. He left me and I heard him say to the others:

"He's asleep and his cheeks are wet. Looks as if he'd been cryin' all to himself there. I guess he got too tired."

Then Mr. Wright said: "Something happened to the boy this afternoon. I don't know what. I stopped at the brook to clean the fish and he ran on toward the camp to surprise you. I came along soon and found him sitting alone by the trail out there. He looked as if he hadn't a friend in the world. I asked him what was the matter and he said it was a secret."

"Say, by—" Uncle Peabody paused. "He must a stole up here and heard me tellin' that—" he paused again and went on: "Say, I wouldn't 'a' had him hear that for a thousan' dollars. I don't know how to behave myself when I get in the woods. If you're goin' to travel with a boy like that you've got to be good all the time—ye can't take no rest or vacation at all whatever."

"You've got to be sound through and through or they'll find it out," said the Comptroller. "You can't fool 'em long."

"He's got a purty keen edge on him," said Bill Seaver.

"On the whole I think he's the most interesting child I ever saw," said Mr. Wright.

I knew that these words were compliments but their meaning was not quite clear to me. The words, however, impressed and pleased me deeply and I recalled them often after that night. I immediately regretted them, for I was hungry and wanted to get up and eat some supper but had to lie a while longer now so they would not know that my ears had been open. Nothing more was said and I lay and listened to the wind in the tree-tops and the crackling of the fire, and suddenly the day ended.

I felt the gentle hand of Uncle Peabody on my face and I heard him speak my name very tenderly. I opened my eyes. The sun was shining. It was a new day. Bill Seaver had begun to cook the breakfast. I felt better and ran down to the landing and washed. My uncle's face had a serious look in it. So had Mr. Wright's. I was happy but dimly conscious of a change.

I remember how Bill beat the venison steak, which he had brought in his pack basket, with the head of his ax, adding a strip of bacon and a pinch of salt, now and then, until the whole was a thick mass of pulp which he broiled over the hot coals. I remember, too, how delicious it was.

We ate and packed and got into the boats and fished along down the river. At Seaver's we hitched up our team and headed homeward. When we drove into the dooryard Aunt Deel came and helped me out of the buggy and kissed my cheek and said she had been "terrible lonesome." Mr. Wright changed his clothes and hurried away across country with his share of the fish on his way to Canton.

"Well, I want to know!—ayes! ain't they beautiful! ayes!" Aunt Deel exclaimed as Uncle Peabody spread the trout in rows on the wash-stand by the back door.

"I've got to tell you something," I said.

"What is it?" she asked.

"I heard him say naughty words."

"What words?"

"I—I can't say `em. They're wicked. I'm—I'm 'fraid he's goin' to be burnt up," I stammered.

"It's so. I said 'em," my uncle confessed.

Aunt Deel turned to me and said: "Bart, you go right down to the barn and bring me a strap—ayes!—you bring me a strap—right away."

I walked slowly toward the barn. For the moment, I was sorry that I had told on my uncle. Scalding tears began to flow down my cheeks. I sat on the steps to the hay loft for a moment to collect my thoughts.

Then I heard Aunt Deel call to me: "Hurry up, Bart."

I rose and picked out the smallest strap I could find and walked slowly back to the house. I said, in a trembling voice, as I approached them, "I—I don't think he meant it."

"He'll have to be punished—just the same—ayes—he will."

We went into the house together, I sniffling, but curious to see what was going to happen. Uncle Peabody, by prearrangement, as I know now, lay face downward on the sofa, and Aunt Deel began to apply the strap. It was more than I could bear, and I threw myself between my beloved friend and the strap and pleaded with loud cries for his forgiveness.

Uncle Peabody rose and walked out of the house without a word and with a sterner look in his face than I had ever seen there. I searched for him as soon as my excitement had passed, but in vain. I went out back of the cow barn and looked away down across the stumpy flats. Neither he nor Shep were in sight. All that lonely afternoon I watched for him. The sun fell warm but my day was dark. Aunt Deel found me in tears sitting on the steps of the cheese house and got her Indian book out of her trunk and, after she had cautioned me to be very careful of it, let me sit down with it by myself alone, and look at the pictures.

I had looked forward to the time when I could be trusted to sit alone with the Indian book. In my excitement over the picture of a red man tomahawking a child I turned a page so swiftly that I put a long tear in it. My pleasure was gone. I carefully joined the torn edges and closed the book and put it on the table and ran and hid behind the barn.

By and by I saw Uncle Peabody coming down the lane with the cows, an ax on his shoulder. I ran to meet him with a joy in my heart as great as any I have ever known. He greeted me with a cheerful word and leaned over me and held me close against his legs and looked into my eyes and asked:

"Are you willin' to kiss me?"

I kissed him and then he said:

"If ye ever hear me talk like that ag'in, I'll let the stoutest man in Ballybeen hit me with his ax."

I was not feeling well and went to bed right after supper. As I was undressing I heard Aunt Deel exclaim: "My heavens! See what that boy has done to my Indian book—ayes! Ain't that awful!—ayes!"

"Pretend ye ain't noticed it," said Uncle Peabody. "He's had trouble enough for one day."

A deep silence followed in which I knew that Aunt Deel was probably wiping tears from her eyes. I went to bed feeling better.

Next day the stage, on its way to Ballybeen, came to our house and left a box and a letter from Mr. Wright, addressed to my uncle, which read:

"DEAR SIR—I send herewith a box of books and magazines in the hope that you or Miss Baynes will read them aloud to my little partner and in doing so get some enjoyment and profit for yourselves.

"Yours respectfully,
S. WRIGHT, JR.

"P.S.—When the contents of the box has duly risen into your minds, will you kindly see that it does a like service to your neighbors in School District No. 7? S.W., JR."

"I guess Bart has made a friend o' this great man—sartin ayes!" said Aunt Deel. "I wonder who'll be the next one."

CHAPTER V

IN THE LIGHT OF THE CANDLES

I remember that I tried to walk and talk like Silas Wright after that day. He had a way of twisting little locks of his hair between his thumb and finger when he sat thinking. I practised that trick of his when I was alone and unobserved.

One day I was walking up and down, as I had seen Mr. Wright do, and talking to my friend "Baynes," when Aunt Deel called to me that I should bring the candle molds from the shed. I was keeper of the molds and greatly enjoyed the candle-making. First we strung the wicks on slender wooden rods—split and whittled by Uncle Peabody and me as we sat down by the stove in the evening. Then the wicks were let down into tin molds, each of which ended in a little inverted cone with a hole through its point. We carefully worked the wick ends through these perforations and drew them tight. When the mold was ready we poured in the melted tallow, which hardened in a few minutes. Later, by pulling the wooden rods, we loosened the candles and drew them out of the molds. They were as smooth and white as polished alabaster. With shears we trimmed the wick ends. The iron candlesticks were filled and cleaned of drippings and set on the little corner shelf above the sink.

When night fell again and the slender white shaft, rising above its base of iron, was crowned with yellow flame, I can think of nothing more beautiful in color, shape and symbolism. It was the torch of liberty and learning in the new world—a light-house on the shore of the great deep.

The work of the day ended, the candles were grouped near the edge of the table and my aunt's armchair was placed beside them. Then I sat on Uncle Peabody's lap by the fire or, as time went on, in my small chair beside him, while Aunt Deel adjusted her spectacles and began to read.

At last those of wearied bones and muscles had sat down to look abroad with the mind's eye. Their reason began to concern itself with problems beyond the narrow limits of the house and farm; their imaginations took the wings of the poet and rose above all their humble tasks.

I recall how, when the candles were lighted, storyteller, statesman, explorer, poet and preacher came from the far ends of the earth and poured their souls into ours. It was a dim light—that of the candles—but even to-day it shines through the long alley of these many years upon my pathway. I see now what I saw not then in the candle-light, a race marching out of darkness, ignorance and poverty with our little party in the caravan. Crowding on, they widened the narrow way of their stern religion.

At first we had only *The Horse Farrier, The Cattle Book, The Story of the Indian Wars*—a book which had been presented to Aunt Deel by her grandmother, and which in its shroud of white linen lay buried in her trunk most of the time for fear harm would come to it, as it did, indeed, when in a moment of generosity she had loaned it to me. The Bible and the *St. Lawrence Republican* were always with us.

Many a night, when a speech of Daniel Webster or Henry Clay or Dewitt Clinton had pushed me to the edge of unconsciousness, while I resisted by counting the steel links in the watch chain of Uncle Peabody—my rosary in every time of trouble—I had been bowled over the brink by some account of horse colic and its remedy, or of the proper treatment of hoof disease in sheep. I suffered keenly from the horse colic and like troubles and from the many hopes and perils of democracy in my childhood. I found the Bible, however, the most joyless book of all, Samson being, as I thought, the only man in it who amounted to much. A shadow lay across its pages which came, I think, from the awful solemnity of my aunt when she opened them. It reminded me of a dark rainy day made fearful by thunder and lightning. It was not the cheerful thing, illumined by the immortal faith of man which, since then, I have found it to be. The box of books changed the whole current of our lives.

I remember vividly that evening when we took out the books and tenderly felt their covers and read their titles. There were *Cruikshanks' Comic Almanac* and *Hood's Comic Annual*; tales by Washington Irving and James K. Paulding and Nathaniel Hawthorne and Miss Mitford and Miss Austin; the poems of John Milton and Felicia Hemans. Of the treasures in the box I have now; in my possession: A life of Washington, *The Life and Writings of Doctor Duckworth*, *The Stolen Child*, by "John Galt, Esq."; *Rosine Laval*, by "Mr. Smith"; *Sermons and Essays*, by William Ellery Channing. We found in the box, also, thirty numbers of the *United States Magazine and Democratic Review* and sundry copies of the *New York Mirror.*

"Ayes! I declare! What do you think o' this, Peabody Baynes!" Aunt Deel exclaimed as she sat turning the pages of a novel. "Ye know Aunt Minervy used to say that a novel was a fast horse on the road to perdition—ayes!"

"Well she wasn't—" Uncle Peabody began and stopped suddenly. What he meant to say about her will never be definitely known. In half a moment he added:

"I guess if Sue Wright recommends 'em they won't hurt us any."

"Ayes! I ain't afraid—we'll wade into 'em," she answered recklessly. "Ayes! we'll see what they're about."

Aunt Deel began with *The Stolen Child.* She read slowly and often paused for comment or explanation or laughter or to touch the corner of an eye with a corner of her handkerchief in moments when we were all deeply moved by the misfortunes of our favorite characters, which were acute and numerous. Often she stopped to spell out phrases of French or Latin, whereupon Uncle Peabody would exclaim:

"Call it 'snags' and go on."

The "snags" were numerous in certain of the books we read, in which case Uncle Peabody would exclaim:

"Say, that's purty rough plowin'. Mebbe you better move into another field."

How often I have heard Aunt Deel reading when the effect was like this:

"The Duchess exclaimed with an accent which betrayed the fact that she had been reared in the French Capital: 'Snags!' Whereupon Sir Roger rejoined in French equally patrician: 'Snags!"

Those days certain authors felt it necessary to prove that their education had not been neglected or forgotten. Their way was strewn with fragments of classic lore intended to awe and mystify the reader, while evidences of correct religious sentiment were dropped, here and there, to reassure him. The newspapers and magazines of the time, like certain of its books, were salted with little advertisements of religion, and virtue and honesty and thrift.

In those magazines we read of the great West—"the poor man's paradise"—"the stoneless land of plenty"; of its delightful climate, of the ease with which the farmer prospered on its rich soil. Uncle Peabody spoke playfully of going West, after that, but Aunt Deel made no answer and concealed her opinion on that subject for a long time. As for myself, the reading had deepened my interest in east and west and north and south and in the skies above them. How mysterious and inviting they had become!

One evening a neighbor had brought the *Republican* from the post-office. I opened it and read aloud these words, in large type at the top of the page:

Silas Wright Elected to the U.S. Senate.

"Well I want to know!" Uncle Peabody exclaimed. "That would make me forgit it if I was goin' to be hung. Go on and read what it says."

I read of the choosing of our friend for the seat made vacant by the resignation of William L. Marcy, who had been elected governor, and the part which most impressed us were these words from a letter of Mr. Wright to Azariah Flagg of Albany, written when the former was asked to accept the place:

"I am too young and too poor for such an elevation. I have not had the experience in that great theater of politics to qualify me for a place so exalted and responsible. I prefer therefore the humbler position which I now occupy."

"That's his way," said Uncle Peabody. "They had hard work to convince him that he knew enough to be Surrogate."

"Big men have little conceit—ayes!" said Aunt Deel with a significant glance at me.

The candles had burned low and I was watching the shroud of one of them when there came a rap at the door. It was unusual for any one to come to our door in the evening and we were a bit startled. Uncle Peabody opened it and old Kate entered without speaking and nodded to my aunt and uncle and sat down by the fire. Vividly I remembered the day of the fortune-telling. The same gentle smile lighted her face as she looked at me. She held up her hand with four fingers spread above it.

"Ayes," said Aunt Deel, "there are four perils."

My aunt rose and went into the but'ry while I sat staring at the ragged old woman. Her hair was white now and partly covered by a worn and faded bonnet. Forbidding as she was I did not miss the sweetness in her smile and her blue eyes when she looked at me. Aunt Deel came with a plate of doughnuts and bread and butter and head cheese and said in a voice full of pity:

"Poor ol' Kate—ayes! Here's somethin' for ye—ayes!"

She turned to, my uncle and said:

"Peabody Baynes, what'll we do—I'd like to know—ayes! She can't rove all night."

"I'll git some blankets an' make a bed for her, good 'nough for anybody, out in the hired man's room over the shed," said my uncle.

He brought the lantern—a little tower of perforated tin—and put a lighted candle inside of it. Then he beckoned to the stranger, who followed him out of the front door with the plate of food in her hands.

"Well I declare! It's a long time since she went up this road—ayes!" said Aunt Deel, yawning as she resumed her chair.

"Who is ol' Kate?" I asked.

"Oh, just a poor ol' crazy woman—wanders all 'round—ayes!"

"What made her crazy?"

"Oh, I guess somebody misused and deceived her when she was young—ayes! It's an awful wicked thing to do. Come, Bart—go right up to bed now. It's high time—ayes!"

"I want to wait 'til Uncle Peabody comes back," said I.

"Why?"

"I—I'm afraid she'll do somethin' to him."

"Nonsense! Ol' Kate is just as harmless as a kitten. You take your candle and go right up to bed—this minute—ayes!"

I went up-stairs with the candle and undressed very slowly and thoughtfully while I listened for the footsteps of my uncle. I did not get into bed until I heard him come in and blow out his lantern and start up the stairway. As he undressed he told me how for many years the strange woman had been roving in the roads "up hill and down dale, thousands an' thousands o' miles," and never reaching the end of her journey.

In a moment we heard a low wail above the sound of the breeze that shook the leaves of the old "popple" tree above our roof.

"What's that?" I whispered.

"I guess it's ol' Kate ravin'," said Uncle Peabody.

It touched my heart and I lay listening for a time but heard only the loud whisper of the popple leaves.

CHAPTER VI

THE GREAT STRANGER

Some strangers came along the road those days—hunters, peddlers and the like—and their coming filled me with a joy which mostly went away with them, I regret to say. None of these, however, appealed to my imagination as did old Kate. But there was one stranger greater than she—greater, indeed, than any other who came into Rattleroad. He came rarely and would not be long detained. How curiously we looked at him, knowing his fame and power! This great stranger was Money.

I shall never forget the day that my uncle showed me a dollar bill and a little shiny, gold coin and three pieces of silver, nor can I forget how carefully he watched them while they lay in my hands and presently put them back into his wallet. That was long before the time of which I am writing. I remember hearing him say, one day of that year, when I asked him to take us to the Caravan of Wild Beasts which was coming to the village:

"I'm sorry, but it's been a hundred Sundays since I had a dollar in my wallet for more than ten minutes."

I have his old account book for the years of 1837 and 1838. Here are some of the entries:

"Balanced accounts with J. Dorothy and gave him my note for $2.15, to be paid in salts January 1, 1838. Sold ten bushels of wheat to E. Miner at 90 cents, to be paid in goods.

"Sold two sheep to Flavius Curtis and took his note for $6, payable in boots on or before March the first."

Only one entry in more than a hundred mentions money, and this was the sum of eleven cents received in balance from a neighbor.

So it will be seen that a spirit of mutual accommodation served to help us over the rough going. Mr. Grimshaw, however, demanded his pay in cash and that I find was, mainly, the habit of the money-lenders.

We were poor but our poverty was not like that of these days in which I am writing. It was proud and cleanly and well-fed. We had in us the best blood of the Puritans. Our fathers had seen heroic service in the wars and we knew it.

There were no farmer-folk who thought more of the virtue of cleanliness. On this subject my aunt was a deep and tireless thinker. She kept a watchful eye upon us. In her view men-folks were like floors, furniture and dishes. They were in the nature of a responsibility—a tax upon women as it were. Every day she reminded me of the duty of keeping my body clean. Its members had often suffered the tyranny of the soaped hand at the side of the rain barrel. I suppose that all the waters of this world have gone up in the sky and come down again since those far days, but even now the thought of my aunt brings back the odor of soft soap and rain barrels.

She did her best, also, to keep our minds in a cleanly state of preservation—a work in which the teacher rendered important service. He was a young man from Canton.

One day when I had been kept after hours for swearing in a fight and then denying it, he told me that there was no reason why I shouldn't be a great man if I stuck to my books and kept my heart clean. I heard with alarm that there was another part of me to be kept clean. How was it to be done?

"Well, just make up your mind that you'll never lie, whatever else you do," he said. "You can't do anything bad or mean unless you intend to cover it up with lies."

What a simple rule was this of the teacher!—and yet—well the very next thing he said was:

"Where did you hear all that swearing?"

How could I answer his question truthfully? I was old enough to know that the truth would disgrace my Uncle Peabody. I could not tell the truth, therefore, and I didn't. I put it all on Dug Draper, although his swearing had long been a dim, indefinite and useless memory.

As a penalty I had to copy two maxims of Washington five times in my writing-book. In doing so I put them on the wall of my memory where I have seen them every day of my life and from which I read as I write.

"Speak no evil of the absent for it is unjust."

"Labor to keep alive in your breast that little spark of celestial fire called conscience."

The boys in the school were a sturdy big-boned lot with arms and legs like the springing bow. Full-lunged, great-throated fellows, they grew to be, calling the sheep and cattle in the land of far-reaching pastures. There was an undersized boy three years older who often picked on me and with whom I would have no peaceful commerce.

I copy from an old memorandum book a statement of my daily routine just as I put it down one of those days:

"My hardest choar is to get up after uncle calls me. I scramble down stairs and pick up my boots and socks and put them on. Then I go into the setting room and put on my jacket. I get some brand for the sheep. Then I put on my cap and mittens and go out and feed the sheep. Then I get my breakfast. Then I put on my frock, cap, mittens and fetch in my wood. Then I feed the horses their oats. Then I lay away my old clothes until night. I put on my best coat and mittens and tippet and start for school. By the time I get to Joe's my toes are cold and I stop and warm them. When I get to school I warm me at the stove. Then I go to my seat and study my reader, then I take out my arithmetic, then my spelling book, then comes the hardest study that ever landed on Plymouth Rock. It is called geography. After the spelling lesson comes noon. The teacher plays with me cos the other boys are so big. I am glad when I go home. Then I do my choars again, and hear my aunt read until bedtime."

There were girls in the school, but none like Sally. They whispered together with shy glances in our direction, as if they knew funny secrets about us, and would then break into noisy jeers. They did not interest me, and probably because I had seen the lightness and grace and beauty of Sally Dunkelberg and tasted the sweetness of her fancies.

There were the singing and spelling schools and the lyceums, but those nights were few and far between. Not more than four or five in the whole winter were we out of the joyful candle-light of our own home. Even then our hands were busy making lighters or splint brooms, or paring and quartering and stringing the apples or cracking butternuts while Aunt Deel read.

After the sheep came we kept only two cows. The absence of cattle was a help to the general problem of cleanliness. The sheep were out in the fields and I kept away from them for fear the rams would butt me. I remember little of the sheep save the washing and shearing and the lambs which Uncle Peabody brought to our fireside to be warmed on cold mornings of the early spring. I remember asking where the lambs came from when I was a small boy, and that Uncle Peabody said they came from "over the river"—a place regarding which his merry ignorance provoked me. In the spring they were driven to the deep hole and dragged, one by one, into the cold water to have their fleeces washed. When the weather had warmed men came to shear them and their oily white fleeces were clipped close to the skin and each taken off in one piece like a coat and rolled up and put on the wool pile.

I was twelve years old when I began to be the reader for our little family. Aunt Deel had long complained that she couldn't keep up with her knitting and read so much. We had not seen Mr. Wright for nearly two years, but he had sent us the novels of Sir Walter Scott and I had led them heart deep into the creed battles of Old Mortality.

Then came the evil days of 1837, when the story of our lives began to quicken its pace and excite our interest in its coming chapters. It gave us enough to think of, God knows.

Wild speculations in land and the American paper-money system had brought us into rough going. The banks of the city of New York had suspended payment of their notes. They could no longer meet their engagements. As usual, the burden fell heaviest on the poor. It was hard to get money even for black salts.

Uncle Peabody had been silent and depressed for a month or more. He had signed a note for Rodney Barnes, a cousin, long before and was afraid that he would have to pay it. I didn't know what a note was and I remember that one night, when I lay thinking about it, I decided that it must be something in the nature of horse colic. My uncle told me that a note was a trouble which attacked the brain instead of the stomach. I was with Uncle Peabody so much that I shared his feeling but never ventured to speak of it or its cause. He didn't like to be talked to when he felt badly. At such times he used to say that he had the brain colic. He told me that notes had an effect on the brain like that of green apples on the stomach.

One autumn day in Canton Uncle Peabody traded three sheep and twenty bushels of wheat for a cook stove and brought it home in the big wagon. Rodney Barnes came with him to help set up the stove. He was a big giant of a man with the longest nose in the township. I had often wondered how any one would solve the problem of kissing Mr. Barnes in the immediate region of his nose, the same being in the nature of a defense.

I remember that I regarded it with a kind of awe because I had been forbidden to speak of it. The command invested Mr. Barnes' nose with a kind of sanctity. Indeed it became one of the treasures of my imagination.

That evening I was chiefly interested in the stove. What a joy it was to me with its damper and griddles and high oven and the shiny edge on its hearth! It rivaled, in its novelty and charm, any tin peddler's cart that ever came to our door. John Axtell and his wife, who had seen it pass their house, hurried over for a look at it. Every hand was on the stove as we tenderly carried it into the house, piece by piece, and set it up. Then they cut a hole in the upper floor and the stone chimney and fitted the pipe.

How keenly we watched the building of the fire! How quickly it roared and began to heat the room!

When the Axtells had gone away Aunt Deel said:

"It's grand! It is sartin—but I'm 'fraid we can't afford it—ayes I be!"

"We can't afford to freeze any longer. I made up my mind that we couldn't go through another winter as we have," was my uncle's answer.

"How much did it cost?" she asked.

"Not much differ'nt from thirty-four dollars in sheep and grain," he answered.

Rodney Barnes stayed to supper and spent a part of the evening with us.

Like other settlers there, Mr. Barnes was a cheerful optimist. Everything looked good to him until it turned out badly. He stood over the stove with a stick of wood and made gestures with it as he told how he had come from Vermont with a team and a pair of oxen and some bedding and furniture and seven hundred dollars in money. He flung the stick of wood into the box with a loud thump as he told how he had bought his farm of Benjamin Grimshaw at a price which doubled its value. True it was the price which other men had paid in the neighborhood, but they had all paid too much. Grimshaw had established the price and called it fair. He had taken Mr. Barnes to two or three of the settlers on the hills above Lickitysplit.

"Tell this man what you think about the kind o' land we got here," Grimshaw had demanded.

The tenant recommended it. He had to. They were all afraid of Grimshaw. Mr. Barnes picked up a flat iron and felt its bottom and waved it in the air as he alleged that it was a rocky, stumpy, rooty, God-forsaken region far from church or market or school on a rough road almost impassable for a third of the year. Desperate economy and hard work had kept his nose to the grindstone but, thank God, he had nose enough left.

Now and then Grimshaw (and others like him) loaned money to people, but he always had some worthless hay or a broken-down horse which you had to buy before you could get the money.

Mr. Barnes put down the flat iron and picked up the poker and tried its strength on his knee as he told how he had heard that it was a growing country near the great water highway of the St. Lawrence. Prosperous towns were building up in it. There were going to be great cities in Northern New York. What they called a railroad was coming. There were rich stores of lead and iron in the rocks. Mr. Barnes had bought two hundred acres at ten dollars an acre. He had to pay a fee of five per cent. to

Grimshaw's lawyer for the survey and the papers. This left him owing fourteen hundred dollars on his farm—much more than it was worth. One hundred acres of the land had been roughly cleared by Grimshaw and a former tenant. The latter had toiled and struggled and paid tribute and given up.

Our cousin twisted the poker in his great hands until it squeaked as he stood before my uncle and said:

"My wife and I have chopped and burnt and pried and hauled rocks an' shoveled dung an' milked an' churned until we are worn out. For almost twenty years we've been workin' days an' nights an' Sundays. My mortgage was over-due, I owed six hundred dollars on it. I thought it all over one day an' went up to Grimshaw's an' took him by the back of the neck and shook him. He said he would drive me out o' the country. He gave me six months to pay up. I had to pay or lose the land. I got the money on the note that you signed over in Potsdam. Nobody in Canton would 'a' dared to lend it to me."

The poker broke and he threw the pieces under the stove.

"Why?" my uncle asked.

Mr. Barnes got hold of another stick of wood and went on.

"'Fraid o' Grimshaw. He didn't want me to be able to pay it. The place is worth more than six hundred dollars now—that's the reason. I intended to cut some timber an' haul it to the village this winter so I could pay a part o' the note an' git more time as I told ye, but the roads have been so bad I couldn't do any haulin'."

My uncle went and took a drink at the water pail. I saw by his face that he was unusually wrought up.

"My heavens an' earth!" he exclaimed as he sat down again.

"It's the brain colic," I said to myself as I looked at him.

Mr. Barnes seemed to have it also.

"Too much note," I whispered.

"I'm awful sorry, but I've done everything I could," said Mr. Barnes.

"Ain't there somebody that'll take another mortgage?—it ought to be safe now," my uncle suggested.

"Money is so tight it can't be done. The bank has got all the money an' Grimshaw owns the bank. I've tried and tried, but I'll make you safe. I'll give you a mortgage until I can turn 'round."

So I saw how Rodney Barnes, like other settlers in Lickitysplit, had gone into bondage to the landlord.

"How much do you owe on this place?" Barnes asked.

"Seven hundred an' fifty dollars," said my uncle.

"Is it due?"

"It's been due a year an' if I have to pay that note I'll be short my interest."

"God o' Israel! I'm scairt," said Barnes.

Down crashed the stick of wood into the box.

"What about?"

Mr. Barnes tackled a nail that stuck out of the woodwork and tried to pull it between his thumb and finger while I watched the process with growing interest.

"It would be like him to put the screws on you now," he grunted, pulling at the nail. "You've got between him an' his prey. You've taken the mouse away from the cat."

I remember the little panic that fell on us then. I could see tears in the eyes of Aunt Deel as she sat with her head leaning wearily on her hand.

"If he does I'll do all I can," said Barnes, "whatever I've got will be yours."

The nail came out of the wall.

"I had enough saved to pay off the mortgage," my uncle answered. "I suppose it'll have to go for the note."

Mr. Barnes' head was up among the dried apples on the ceiling. A movement of his hand broke a string of them. Then he dropped his huge bulk into a chair which crashed to the floor beneath him. He rose blushing and said:

"I guess I better go or I'll break everything you've got here. I kind o' feel that way."

Rodney Barnes left us.

I remember how Uncle Peabody stood in the middle of the floor and whistled the merriest tune he knew.

"Stand right up here," he called in his most cheerful tone. "Stand right up here before me, both o' ye."

I got Aunt Deel by the hand and led her toward my uncle. We stood facing him. "Stand straighter," he demanded. "Now, altogether. One, two, three, ready, sing."

He beat time with his hand in imitation of the singing master at the schoolhouse and we joined him in singing an old tune which began: "O keep my heart from sadness, God."

This irresistible spirit of the man bridged a bad hour and got us off to bed in fairly good condition.

A few days later the note came due and its owner insisted upon full payment. There was such a clamor for money those days! I remember that my aunt had sixty dollars which she had saved, little by little, by selling eggs and chickens. She had planned to use it to buy a tombstone for her mother and father—a long-cherished ambition. My uncle needed the most of it to help pay the note. We drove to Potsdam on that sad errand and what a time we had getting there and back in deep mud and sand and jolting over corduroys!

"Bart," my uncle said the next evening, as I took down the book to read. "I guess we'd better talk things over a little to-night. These are hard times. If we can find anybody with money enough to buy 'em I dunno but we better sell the sheep."

"If you hadn't been a fool," my aunt exclaimed with a look of great distress—"ayes! if you hadn't been a fool."

"I'm just what I be an' I ain't so big a fool that I need to be reminded of it," said my uncle.

"I'll stay at home an' work," I proposed bravely.

"You ain't old enough for that," sighed Aunt Deel.

"I want to keep you in school," said Uncle Peabody, who sat making a splint broom.

While we were talking in walked Benjamin Grimshaw—the rich man of the hills. He didn't stop to knock but walked right in as if the house were his own. It was common gossip that he held a mortgage on every acre of the countryside. I had never liked him, for he was a stern-eyed man who was always scolding somebody, and I had not forgotten what his son had said of him.

"Good night!" he exclaimed curtly, as he sat down and set his cane between his feet and rested his hands upon it. He spoke hoarsely and I remember the curious notion came to me that he looked like our old ram. The stern and rugged face of Mr. Grimshaw and the rusty gray of his homespun and the hoarseness of his tone had suggested this thought to me. The long silvered tufts above his keen, gray eyes moved a little as he looked at my uncle. There were deep lines upon his cheeks and chin and forehead. He wore a thin, gray beard under his chin. His mouth was shut tight in a long line curving downward a little at the ends. My uncle used to say that his mouth was made to keep his thoughts from leaking and going to waste. He had a big body, a big chin, a big mouth, a big nose and big ears and hands. His eyes lay small in this setting of bigness.

"Why, Mr. Grimshaw, it's years since you've been in our house—ayes!" said Aunt Deel.

"I suppose it is," he answered rather sharply. "I don't have much time to get around. I have to work. There's some people seem to be able to git along without it."

He drew in his breath quickly and with a hissing sound after every sentence.

"How are your folks?" my aunt asked.

"So's to eat their allowance—there's never any trouble about that," said Mr. Grimshaw. "I see you've got one o' these newfangled stoves," he added as he looked it over. "Huh! Rich folks can have anything they want."

Uncle Peabody had sat splintering the long stick of yellow birch. I observed that the jackknife trembled in his hand. His tone had a touch of unnaturalness, proceeding no doubt from his fear of the man before him, as he said:

"When I bought that stove I felt richer than I do now. I had almost enough to settle with you up to date, but I signed a note for a friend and had to pay it."

"Ayuh! I suppose so," Grimshaw answered in a tone of bitter irony which cut me like a knife-blade, young as I was. "What business have you signin' notes an' givin' away money which ain't yours to give—I'd like to know? What business have you actin' like a rich man when you can't pay yer honest debts? I'd like to know that, too?"

"If I've ever acted like a rich man it's been when I wa'n't lookin'," said Uncle Peabody.

"What business have you got enlargin' yer family—takin' another mouth to feed and another body to spin for? That costs money. I ain't no objection if a man can afford it, but the money it costs ain't yours to give. It looks as if it belonged to me. You spend yer nights readin' books when ye ought to be to work an' you've scattered that kind o' foolishness all over the neighborhood. I want to tell you one thing, Baynes, you've got to pay up or git out o' here."

He raised his cane and shook it in the air as he spoke.

"Oh, I ain't no doubt o' that," said Uncle Peabody. "You'll have to have yer money—that's sure; an' you will have it if I live, every cent of it. This boy is goin' to be a great help to me—you don't know what a good boy he is and what a comfort he's been to us!"

I had understood that reference to me in Mr. Grimshaw's complaint and these words of my beloved uncle uncovered my emotions so that I put my elbow on the wood-box and leaned my head upon it and sobbed.

"I tell ye I'd rather have that boy than all the money you've got, Mr. Grimshaw," Uncle Peabody added.

My aunt came and patted my shoulder and said: "Sh—sh—sh! Don't you care, Bart! You're just the same as if you was our own boy—ayes!—you be."

"I ain't goin' to be hard on ye, Baynes," said Mr. Grimshaw as he rose from his chair; "I'll give ye three months to see what you can do. I wouldn't wonder if the boy would turn out all right. He's big an' cordy of his age an' a purty likely boy they tell me. He'd 'a' been all right at the county house until he was old enough to earn his livin', but you was too proud for that—wasn't ye? I don't mind pride unless it keeps a man from payin' his honest debts. You ought to have better sense."

"An' you ought to keep yer breath to cool yer porridge," said Uncle Peabody.

Mr. Grimshaw opened the door and stood for a moment looking at us and added in a milder tone: "You've got one o' the best farms in this town an' if ye work hard an' use common sense ye ought to be out o' debt in five years—mebbe less."

He closed the door and went away.

Neither of us moved or spoke as we listened to his footsteps on the gravel path that went down to the road and to the sound of his buggy as he drove away. Then Uncle Peabody broke the silence by saying:

"He's the dam'dest—"

He stopped, set the half-splintered stick aside, closed his jackknife and went to the water-pail to cool his emotions with a drink.

Aunt Deel took up the subject where he had dropped it, as if no half-expressed sentiment would satisfy her, saying:

"—old skinflint that ever lived in this world, ayes! I ain't goin' to hold down my opinion o' that man no longer, ayes! I can't. It's too powerful—ayes!"

Having recovered my composure I repeated that I should like to give up school and stay at home and work.

Aunt Deel interrupted me by saying:

"I have an idee that Sile Wright will help us—ayes! He's comin' home an' you better go down an' see him—ayes! Hadn't ye?"

"Bart an' I'll go down to-morrer," said Uncle Peabody.

I remember well our silent going to bed that night and how I lay thinking and praying that I might grow fast and soon be able to take the test of manhood—that of standing in a half-bushel measure and shouldering two bushels of corn. By and by a wind began to shake the popple leaves above us and the sound soothed me like the whispered "hush-sh" of a gentle mother.

We dressed with unusual care in the morning. After the chores were done and we had had our breakfast we went up-stairs to get ready.

Aunt Deel called at the bottom of the stairs in a generous tone:

"Peabody, if I was you I'd put on them butternut trousers—ayes! an' yer new shirt an' hat an' necktie, but you must be awful careful of 'em—ayes."

The hat and shirt and necktie had been stored in the clothes press for more than a year but they were nevertheless "new" to Aunt Deel. Poor soul! She felt the importance of the day and its duties. It was that ancient, Yankee dread of the poorhouse that filled her heart I suppose. Yet I wonder, often, why she wished us to be so proudly adorned for such a crisis.

Some fourteen months before that day my uncle had taken me to Potsdam and traded grain and salts for what he called a "rip roarin' fine suit o' clothes" with boots and cap and shirt and collar and necktie to match, I having earned them by sawing and cording wood at three shillings a cord. How often we looked back to those better days! The clothes had been too big for me and I had had to wait until my growth had taken up the "slack" in my coat and trousers before I could venture out of the neighborhood. I had tried them on every week or so for a long time. Now my stature filled them handsomely and they filled me with a pride and satisfaction which I had never known before. The collar was too tight, so that Aunt Deel had to sew one end of it to the neckband, but my tie covered the sewing.

Since that dreadful day of the petticoat trousers my wonder had been regarding all integuments, what Sally Dunkelberg would say to them. At last I could start for Canton with a strong and capable feeling. If I chanced to meet Sally Dunkelberg I need not hide my head for shame as I had done that memorable Sunday.

"Now may the Lord help ye to be careful—awful, terrible careful o' them clothes every minute o' this day," Aunt Deel cautioned as she looked at me. "Don't git no horse sweat nor wagon grease on 'em."

To Aunt Deel wagon grease was the worst enemy of a happy and respectable home.

We hitched our team to the grasshopper spring wagon and set out on our journey. It was a warm, hazy Indian-summer day in November. My uncle looked very stiff and sober in his "new" clothes. Such breathless excitement as that I felt when we were riding down the hills and could see the distant spires of Canton, I have never known since that day. As we passed "the mill" we saw the Silent Woman looking out of the little window of her room above the blacksmith shop—a low, weather-stained, frame building, hard by the main road, with a narrow hanging stair on the side of it.

"She keeps watch by the winder when she ain't travelin'," said Uncle Peabody. "Knows all that's goin' on—that woman—knows who goes to the village an' how long they stay. When Grimshaw goes by they say she hustles off down the road in her rags. She looks like a sick dog herself, but I've heard that she keeps that room o' hers just as neat as a pin."

Near the village we passed a smart-looking buggy drawn by a spry-footed horse in shiny harness. Then I noticed with a pang that our wagon was covered with dry mud and that our horses were rather bony and our harnesses a kind of lead color. So I was in an humble state of mind when we entered the village. Uncle Peabody had had little to say and I had kept still knowing that he sat in the shadow of a great problem.

There was a crowd of men and women in front of Mr. Wright's office and through its open door I saw many of his fellow townsmen. We waited at the door for a few minutes. I crowded in while Uncle Peabody stood talking with a villager. The Senator caught sight of me and came to my side and put his hand on my head and said:

"Hello, Bart! How you've grown! and how handsome you look! Where's your uncle?"

"He's there by the door," I answered.

"Well, le's go and see him."

Then I followed him out of the office.

Mr. Wright was stouter and grayer and grander than when I had seen him last. He was dressed in black broadcloth and wore a big beaver hat and high collar and his hair was almost white. I remember vividly his clear, kindly, gray eyes and ruddy cheeks.

"Baynes, I'm glad to see you," he said heartily. "Did ye bring me any jerked meat?"

"Didn't think of it," said Uncle Peabody. "But I've got a nice young doe all jerked an' if you're fond o' jerk I'll bring ye down some to-morrer."

"I'd like to take some to Washington but I wouldn't have you bring it so far."

"I'd like to bring it—I want a chance to talk with ye for half an hour or such a matter," said my uncle. "I've got a little trouble on my hands."

"There's a lot of trouble here," said the Senator. "I've got to settle a quarrel between two neighbors and visit a sick friend and make a short address to the Northern New York Conference at the Methodist Church and look over a piece of land that I'm intending to buy, and discuss the plans for my new house with the carpenter. I expect to get through about six o'clock and right after supper I could ride up to your place with you and walk back early in the morning. We could talk things over on the way up."

"That's first rate," said my uncle. "The chores ain't much these days an' I guess my sister can git along with 'em."

The Senator took us into his office and introduced us to the leading men of the county. There were: Minot Jenison, Gurdon Smith, Ephraim Butterfield, Lemuel Buck, Baron S. Doty, Richard N. Harrison, John L. Russell, Silas Baldwin, Calvin Hurlbut, Doctor Olin, Thomas H. Conkey and Preston King. These were names with which, the *Republican* had already made us familiar.

"Here," said the Senator as he put his hand on my head, "is a coming man in the Democratic party."

The great men laughed at my blushes and we came away with a deep sense of pride in us. At last I felt equal to the ordeal of meeting the Dunkelbergs. My uncle must have shared my feeling for, to my delight, he went straight to the basement store above which was the modest sign: "H. Dunkelberg, Produce." I trembled as we walked down the steps and opened the door. I saw the big gold watch chain, the handsome clothes, the mustache and side whiskers and the large silver ring approaching us, but I was not as scared as I expected to be. My eyes were more accustomed to splendor.

"Well I swan!" said the merchant in the treble voice which I remembered so well. "This is Bart and Peabody! How are you?"

"Pretty well," I answered, my uncle being too slow of speech to suit my sense of propriety. "How is Sally?"

The two men laughed heartily much to my embarrassment.

"He's getting right down to business," said my uncle.

"That's right," said Mr. Dunkelberg. "Why, Bart, she's spry as a cricket and pretty as a picture. Come up to dinner with me and see for yourself."

Uncle Peabody hesitated, whereupon I gave him a furtive nod and he said "All right," and then I had a delicious feeling of excitement. I had hard work to control my impatience while they talked. I walked on some butter tubs in the back room and spun around on a whirling stool that stood in front of a high desk and succeeded in the difficult feat of tipping over a bottle of ink without getting any on myself. I covered the multitude of my sins on the desk with a newspaper and sat down quietly in a chair.

By and by I asked, "Are you 'most ready to go?"

"Yes—come on—it's after twelve o'clock," said Mr. Dunkelberg. "Sally will be back from school now."

My conscience got the better of me and I confessed about the ink bottle and was forgiven.

So we walked to the big house of the Dunkelbergs and I could hear my heart beating when we turned in at the gate—the golden gate of my youth it must have been, for after I had passed it I thought no more as a child. That rude push which Mr. Grimshaw gave me had hurried the passing.

I was a little surprised at my own dignity when Sally opened the door to welcome us. My uncle told Aunt Deel that I acted and spoke like Silas Wright, "so nice and proper." Sally was different, too—less playful and more beautiful with long yellow curls covering her shoulders.

"How nice you look!" she said as she took my arm and led me into her playroom.

"These are my new clothes," I boasted. "They are very expensive and I have to be careful of them."

I remember not much that we said or did but I could never forget how she played for me on a great shiny piano—I had never seen one before—and made me feel very humble with music more to my liking than any I have heard since—crude and simple as it was—while her pretty fingers ran up and down the keyboard.

O magic ear of youth! I wonder how it would sound to me now—the rollicking lilt of *Barney Leave the Girls Alone*—even if a sweet maid flung its banter at me with flashing fingers and well-fashioned lips.

I behaved myself with great care at the table—I remember that—and, after dinner, we played in the dooryard and the stable, I with a great fear of tearing my new clothes. I stopped and cautioned her more than once: "Be careful! For gracious sake! be careful o' my new suit!"

As we were leaving late in the afternoon she said:

"I wish you would come here to school."

"I suppose he will sometime," said Uncle Peabody.

A new hope entered my breast, that moment, and began to grow there.

"Aren't you going to kiss her?" said Mr. Dunkelberg with a smile.

I saw the color in her cheeks deepen as she turned with a smile and walked away two or three steps while the grown people laughed, and stood with her back turned looking in at the window.

"You're looking the wrong way for the scenery," said Mr. Dunkelberg.

She turned and walked toward me with a look Of resolution in her pretty face and said:

"I'm not afraid of him."

We kissed each other and, again, that well-remembered touch of her hair upon my face! But the feel of her warm lips upon my own—that was so different and so sweet to remember in the lonely days that followed! Fast flows the river to the sea when youth is sailing on it. They had shoved me out of the quiet cove into the swift current—those dear, kindly, thoughtless people! Sally ran away into the house as their laughter continued and my uncle and I walked down the street. How happy I was!

We went to the Methodist Church where Mr. Wright was speaking but we couldn't get in. There were many standing at the door who had come too late. We could hear his voice and I remember that he seemed to be talking to the people just as I had heard him talk to my aunt and uncle, sitting by our fireside, only louder. We were tired and went down to the tavern and waited for him on its great porch. We passed a number of boys playing three-old-cat in the school yard. How I longed to be among them!

I observed with satisfaction that the village boys did not make fun of me when I passed them as they did when I wore the petticoat trousers. Mr. and Mrs. Wright came along with the crowd, by and by, and Colonel Medad Moody. We had supper with them at the tavern and started away in the dark with the Senator on the seat with us. He and my uncle began to talk about the tightness of money and the banking laws and I remember a remark of my uncle, for there was that in his tone which I could never forget:

"We poor people are trusting you to look out for us—we poor people are trusting you to see that we get treated fair. We're havin' a hard time."

This touched me a little and I was keen to hear the Senator's answer. I remember so well the sacred spirit of democracy in his words. Long afterward I asked him to refresh my memory of them and so I am able to quote him as he would wish.

"I know it," he answered. "I lie awake nights thinking about it. I am poor myself, almost as poor as my father before me. I have found it difficult to keep my poverty these late years but I have not failed. I'm about as poor as you are, I guess. I could enjoy riches, but I want to be poor so I may not forget what is due to the people among whom I was born—you who live in small houses and rack your bones with toil. I am one of you, although I am racking my brain instead of my bones in our common interest. There are so many who would crowd us down we must stand together and be watchful or we shall be reduced to an overburdened, slavish peasantry, pitied and despised. Our danger will increase as wealth accumulates and the cities grow. I am for the average man—like myself. They've lifted me out of the crowd to an elevation which I do not deserve. I have more reputation than I dare promise to keep. It frightens me. I am like a child clinging to its father's hand in a place of peril. So I cling to the crowd. It is my father. I know its needs and wrongs and troubles. I had other things to do to-night. There were people who wished to discuss their political plans and ambitions with me. But I thought I would rather go with you and learn about your troubles. What are they?"

My uncle told him about the note and the visit of Mr. Grimshaw and of his threats and upbraidings.

"Did he say that in Bart's hearing?" asked the Senator.

"Ayes!—right out plain."

"Too bad! I'm going to tell you frankly, Baynes, that the best thing I know about you is your conduct toward this boy. I like it. The next best thing is the fact that you signed the note. It was bad business but it was good Christian conduct to help your friend. Don't regret it. You were poor and of an age when the boy's pranks were troublesome to both of you, but you took him in. I'll lend you the interest and try to get another holder for the mortgage on one condition. You must let me attend to Bart's schooling. I want to be the boss about that. We have a great schoolmaster in Canton and when Bart is a little older I want him to go there to school. I'll try to find him a place where he can work for his board."

"We'll miss Bart but we'll be tickled to death—there's no two ways about that," said Uncle Peabody.

I had been getting sleepy, but this woke me up. I no longer heard the monotonous creak of harness and whiffletrees and the rumble of wheels; I saw no longer the stars and the darkness of the night. My mind had scampered off into the future. I was playing with Sally or with the boys in the school yard.

The Senator tested my arithmetic and grammar and geography as we rode along in the darkness and said by and by:

"You'll have to work hard, Bart. You'll have to take your book into the field as I did. After every row of corn I learned a rule of syntax or arithmetic or a fact in geography while I rested, and my thought and memory took hold of it as I plied the hoe. I don't want you to stop the reading, but from now on you must spend half of every evening on your lessons."

We got home at half past eight and found my aunt greatly worried. She had done the chores and been standing in her hood and shawl on the porch listening for the sound of the wagon. She had kept our suppers warm but I was the only hungry one.

As I was going to bed the Senator called me to him and said:

"I shall be gone when you are up in the morning. It may be a long time before I see you; I shall leave something for you in a sealed envelope with your name on it. You are not to open the envelope until you go away to school. I know how you will feel that first day. When night falls you will think of your aunt and uncle and be very lonely. When you go to your room for the night I want you to sit down all by yourself and open the envelope and read what I shall write. They will be, I think, the most impressive words ever written. You will think them over but you will not understand them for a long time. Ask every wise man you meet to explain them to you, for all your happiness will depend upon your understanding of these few words in the envelope."

In the morning Aunt Deel put it in my hands.

"I wonder what in the world he wrote there—ayes!" said she. "We must keep it careful—ayes!—I'll put it in my trunk an' give it to ye when ye go to Canton to school."

"Has Mr. Wright gone?" I asked rather sadly.

"Ayes! Land o' mercy! He went away long before daylight with a lot o' jerked meat in a pack basket—ayes! Yer uncle is goin' down to the village to see 'bout the mortgage this afternoon, ayes!"

It was a Saturday and I spent its hours cording wood in the shed, pausing now and then for a look into my grammar. It was a happy day, for the growing cords expressed in a satisfactory manner my new sense of obligation to those I loved. Imaginary conversations came into my brain as I worked and were rehearsed in whispers.

"Why, Bart, you're a grand worker," my uncle would say in my fancy. "You're as good as a hired man."

"Oh, that's nothing," I would answer modestly. "I want to be useful so you won't be sorry you took me and I'm going to study just as Mr. Wright did and be a great man if I can and help the poor people. I'm going to be a better scholar than Sally Dunkelberg, too."

What a day it was!—the first of many like it. I never think of those days without saying to myself: "What a God's blessing a man like Silas Wright can be in the community in which his heart and soul are as an open book!"

As the evening came on I took a long look at my cords. The shed was nearly half full of them. Four rules of syntax, also, had been carefully stored away in my brain. I said them over as I hurried down into the pasture with old Shep and brought in the cows. I got through milking just as Uncle Peabody came. I saw with joy that his face was cheerful.

"Yip!" he shouted as he stopped his team at the barn door where Aunt Deel and I were standing. "We ain't got much to worry about now. I've got the interest money right here in my pocket."

We unhitched and went in to supper. I was hoping that Aunt Deel would speak of my work but she seemed not to think of it.

"Had a grand day!" said Uncle Peabody, as he sat down at the table and began to tell what Mr. Wright and Mr. Dunkelberg had said to him.

I, too, had had a grand day and probably my elation was greater than his. I tarried at the looking-glass hoping that Aunt Deel would give me a chance modestly to show my uncle what I had done. But the talk about interest and mortgages continued. I went to my uncle and tried to whisper in his ear a hint that he had better go and look into the wood-shed. He stopped me before I had begun by saying:

"Don't bother me now, Bub. I'll git that candy for ye the next time I go to the village."

Candy! I was thinking of no such trivial matter as candy. He couldn't know how the idea shocked me in the exalted state of mind into which I had risen. He didn't know then of the spiritual change in me and how generous and great I was feeling and how sublime and beautiful was the new way in which I had set my feet.

I went out on the porch and stood looking down with a sad countenance. Aunt Deel followed me.

"W'y, Bart!" she exclaimed, "you're too tired to eat—ayes! Be ye sick?"

I shook my head.

"Peabody," she called, "this boy has worked like a beaver every minute since you left—ayes he has! I never see anything to beat it—never! I want you to come right out into the wood-shed an' see what he's done—this minute—ayes!"

I followed them into the shed.

"W'y of all things!" my uncle exclaimed. "He's worked like a nailer, ain't he?"

There were tears in his eyes when he took my hand in his rough palm and squeezed it and said:

"Sometimes I wish ye was little ag'in so I could take ye up in my arms an' kiss ye just as I used to. Horace Dunkelberg says that you're the best-lookin' boy he ever see."

"Stop!" Aunt Deel exclaimed with a playful tap on his shoulder. "W'y! ye mustn't go on like that."

"I'm tellin' just what he said," my uncle answered.

"I guess he only meant that Bart looked clean an' decent—that's all—ayes! He didn't mean that Bart was purty. Land sakes!—no."

I observed the note of warning in the look she gave my uncle.

"No, I suppose not," he answered, as he turned away with a smile and brushed one of his eyes with a rough finger.

I repeated the rules I had learned as we went to the table.

"I'm goin' to be like Silas Wright if I can," I added.

"That's the idee!" said Uncle Peabody. "You keep on as you've started an' everybody'll milk into your pail."

I kept on—not with the vigor of that first day with its new inspiration—but with growing strength and effectiveness. Nights and mornings and

Saturdays I worked with a will and my book in my pocket or at the side of the field and was, I know, a help of some value on the farm. My scholarship improved rapidly and that year I went about as far as I could hope to go in the little school at Leonard's Corners.

"I wouldn't wonder if ol' Kate was right about our boy," said Aunt Deel one day when she saw me with my book in the field.

I began to know then that ol' Kate had somehow been at work in my soul—subconsciously as I would now put it. I was trying to put truth into the prophecy. As I look at the whole matter these days I can see that Mr. Grimshaw himself was a help no less important to me, for it was a sharp spur with which he continued to prod us.

CHAPTER VII

MY SECOND PERIL

We always thank God for men like Purvis: we never thank them. They are without honor in their own time, but how they brighten the pages of memory! How they stimulated the cheerfulness of the old countryside and broke up its natural reticence!

Mr. Franklin Purvis was our hired man—an undersized bachelor. He had a Roman nose, a face so slim that it would command interest and attention in any company, and a serious look enhanced by a bristling mustache and a retreating chin. At first and on account of his size I had no very high opinion of Mr. Purvis. That first evening after his arrival I sat with him on the porch surveying him inside and out.

"You don't look very stout," I said.

"I ain't as big as some, but I'm all gristle from my head to my heels, inside an' out," he answered.

I surveyed him again as he sat looking at the ledges. He was not more than a head taller than I, but if he were "all gristle" he might be entitled to respect and I was glad to learn of his hidden resources—glad and a bit apprehensive as they began to develop.

"I'm as full o' gristle as a goose's leg," he went on. "God never made a man who could do more damage when he lets go of himself an' do it faster. There ain't no use o' talkin'."

There being no use of talking, our new hired man continued to talk while I listened with breathless interest and growing respect. He took a chew of tobacco and squinted his eyes and seemed to be studying the wooded rock ledges across the road as he went on:

"You'll find me wide awake, I *guess*. I ain't afraid o' anythin' but lightnin'—no, sir!—an' I can hurt hard an' do it rapid when I begin, but I can be jest as harmless as a kitten. There ain't no man that can be more harmlesser when he wants to be an' there's any decent chance for it—none whatsomever! No, sir! I'd rather be harmless than not—a good deal."

This relieved, and was no doubt calculated to relieve, a feeling of insecurity which his talk had inspired. He blew out his breath and shifted his quid as he sat with his elbows resting on his knees and took another look at the ledges as if considering how much of his strength would be required to move them.

"Have you ever hurt anybody?" I asked.

"Several," he answered.

"Did you kill 'em?"

"No, I never let myself go too fur. Bein' so stout, I have to be kind o' careful."

After a moment's pause he went on:

"A man threatened to lick me up to Seaver's t'other day. You couldn't blame him. He didn't know me from a side o' sole leather. He just thought I was one o' them common, every-day cusses that folks use to limber up on. But he see his mistake in time. I tell ye God was good to him when he kept him away from me."

Aunt Deel called us to supper.

"Le's go in an' squench our hunger," Mr. Purvis proposed as he rose and shut his jackknife.

I was very much impressed and called him "Mr. Purvis" after that. I enjoyed and believed many tales of adventure in which he had been the hero as we worked together in the field or stable. I told them to my aunt and uncle one evening, whereupon the latter said:

"He's a good man to work, but Jerusalem—!"

He stopped. He always stopped at the brink of every such precipice. I had never heard him finish an uncomplimentary sentence.

I began to have doubts regarding the greatness of our hired man. I still called him "Mr. Purvis," but all my fear of him had vanished.

One day Mr. Grimshaw came out in the field to see my uncle. They walked away to the shade of a tree while "Mr. Purvis" and I went on with the hoeing. I could hear the harsh voice of the money-lender speaking in loud and angry tones and presently he went away.

"What's the rip?" I asked as my uncle returned looking very sober.

"We won't talk about it now," he answered.

That look and the fears it inspired ruined my day which had begun with eager plans for doing and learning. In the candle-light of the evening Uncle Peabody said:

"Grimshaw has demanded his mortgage money an' he wants it in gold coin. We'll have to git it some way, I dunno how."

"W'y of all things!" my aunt exclaimed. "How are we goin' to git all that money—these hard times?—ayes! I'd like to know?"

"Well, I can't tell ye," said Uncle Peabody. "I guess he can't forgive us for savin' Rodney Barnes."

"What did he say?" I asked.

"Why, he says we hadn't no business to hire a man to help us. He says you an' me ought to do all the work here. He thinks I ought to took you out o' school long ago."

"I can stay out o' school and keep on with my lessons," I said.

"Not an' please him. He was mad when he see ye with a book in yer hand out there in the corn-field."

What were we to do now? I spent the first sad night of my life undoing the plans which had been so dear to me but not so dear as my aunt and uncle. I decided to give all my life and strength to the saving of the farm. I would still try to be great, but not as great as the Senator. Purvis stayed with us through the summer and fall.

After the crops were in we cut and burned great heaps of timber and made black salts of the ashes by leaching water through them and boiling down the lye. We could sell the salts at three dollars and a half a hundred pounds. The three of us working with a team could produce from one hundred and twenty to one hundred and forty pounds a week. Yet we thought it paid—there in Lickitysplit. All over the hills men and women were turning their efforts and strength into these slender streams of money forever flowing toward the mortgagee.

Mr. Dunkelberg had seen Benjamin Grimshaw and got him to give us a brief extension. They had let me stay out of school to work. I was nearly thirteen years old and rather strong and capable. I think that I got along in my books about as well as I could have done in our little school.

One day in December of that year, I had my first trial in the full responsibility of man's work. I was allowed to load and harness and hitch up and go to mill without assistance. My uncle and Purvis were busy with the chopping and we were out of flour and meal. It took a lot of them to keep the axes going. So I filled two sacks with corn and two with wheat and put them into the box wagon, for the ground was bare, and hitched up my horses and set out. Aunt Deel took a careful look at the main hitches and gave me many a caution before I drove away. She said it was a shame that I had to be "Grimshawed" into a man's work at my age. But I was elated by my feeling of responsibility. I knew how to handle horses and had driven at the drag and plow and once, alone, to the post-office, but this was my first long trip without company. I had taken my ax and a chain, for one found a tree in the road now and then those days, and had to trim and cut and haul it aside. It was a drive of six miles to the nearest mill, over a bad road. I sat on two cleated boards placed across the box, with a blanket over me and my new overcoat and mittens on, and was very comfortable and happy.

I had taken a little of my uncle's chewing tobacco out of its paper that lay on a shelf in the cellarway, for I had observed that my uncle generally chewed when he was riding. I tried a little of it and was very sick for a few minutes.

Having recovered, I sang all the songs I knew, which were not many, and repeated the names of the presidents and divided the world into its parts and recited the principal rivers with all the sources and emptyings of the latter and the boundaries of the states and the names and locations of their capitals. It amused me in the midst of my loneliness to keep my tongue busy and I exhausted all my knowledge, which included a number of declamations from the speeches of Otis, Henry and Webster, in the effort. Before the journey was half over I had taken a complete inventory of my mental effects. I repeat that it was amusement—of the only kind available—and not work to me.

I reached the mill safely and before the grain was ground the earth and the sky above it were white with snow driving down in a cold, stiff wind out of the northwest. I loaded my grists and covered them with a blanket and hurried away. The snow came so fast that it almost blinded me. There were times when I could scarcely see the road or the horses. The wind came colder and soon it was hard work to hold the reins and keep my hands from freezing.

Suddenly the wheels began jumping over rocks. The horses were in the ditch. I knew what was the matter, for my eyes had been filling with snow and I had had to brush them often. Of course the team had suffered in a like manner. Before I could stop I heard the crack of a felly and a front wheel dropped to its hub. I checked the horses and jumped out and went to their heads and cleared their eyes. The snow was up to my knees then.

It seemed as if all the clouds in the sky were falling to the ground and stacking into a great, fleecy cover as dry as chaff.

We were there where the road drops into a rocky hollow near the edge of Butterfield's woods. They used to call it Moosewood Hill because of the abundance of moosewood around the foot of it. How the thought of that broken wheel smote me! It was our only heavy wagon, and we having to pay the mortgage. What would my uncle say? The query brought tears to my eyes.

I unhitched and led my horses up into the cover of the pines. How grateful it seemed, for the wind was slack below but howling in the tree-tops! I knew that I was four miles from home and knew, not how I was to get there. Chilled to the bone, I gathered some pitch pine and soon had a fire going with my flint and tinder. I knew that I could mount one of the horses and lead the other and reach home probably. But there was the grist. We needed that; I knew that we should have to go hungry without the grist. It would get wet from above and below if I tried to carry it on the back of a horse. I warmed myself by the fire and hitched my team near it so as to thaw the frost out of their forelocks and eyebrows. I felt in my coat pockets and found a handful of nails—everybody carried nails in one pocket those days—and I remember that my uncle's pockets were a museum of bolts and nuts and screws and washers.

The idea occurred to me that I would make a kind of sled which was called a jumper.

So I got my ax out of the wagon and soon found a couple of small trees with the right crook for the forward end of a runner and cut them and hewed their bottoms as smoothly as I could. Then I made notches in them near the top of their crooks and fitted a stout stick into the notches and secured it with nails driven by the ax-head. Thus I got a hold for my evener. That done, I chopped and hewed an arch to cross the middle of the runners and hold them apart and used all my nails to secure and brace it. I got the two boards which were fastened together and constituted my wagon seat and laid them over the arch and front brace. How to make them fast was my worst problem. I succeeded in splitting a green stick to hold the bolt of the evener just under its head while I heated its lower end in the fire and kept its head cool with snow. With this I burnt a hole in the end of each board and fastened them to the front brace with withes of moosewood.

It was late in the day and there was no time for the slow process of burning more holes, so I notched the other ends of the boards and lashed them to the rear brace with a length of my reins. Then I retempered my bolt and brought up the grist and chain and fastened the latter between the boards in the middle of the front brace, hitched my team to the chain and set out again, sitting on the bags.

It was, of course, a difficult journey, for my jumper was narrow. The snow heaped up beneath me and now and then I and my load were rolled off the jumper. When the drifts were more than leg deep I let down the fence and got around them by going into the fields. Often I stopped to clear the eyes of the horses—a slow task to be done with the bare hand—or to fling my palms against my shoulders and thus warm myself a little.

It was pitch dark and the horses wading to their bellies and the snow coming faster when we turned into Rattleroad. I should not have known the turn when we came to it, but a horse knows more than a man in the dark. Soon I heard a loud halloo and knew that it was the voice of Uncle Peabody. He had started out to meet me in the storm and Shep was with him.

"Thank God I've found ye!" he shouted. "I'm blind and tired out and I couldn't keep a lantern goin' to save me. Are ye froze?"

"I'm all right, but these horses are awful tired. Had to let 'em rest every few minutes."

I told him about the wagon—and how it relieved me to hear him say:

"As long as you're all right, boy, I ain't goin' to worry 'bout the ol' wagon—not a bit. Where'd ye git yer jumper?"

"Made it with the ax and some nails," I answered.

I didn't hear what he said about it for the horses were wallowing and we had to stop and paw and kick the snow from beneath them as best we could before it was possible to back out of our trouble. Soon we found an entrance to the fields—our own fields not far from the house—where Uncle Peabody walked ahead and picked out the best wading. After we got to the barn door at last he went to the house and lighted his lantern and came back with it wrapped in a blanket and Aunt Deel came with him.

How proud it made me to hear him say:

"Deel, our boy is a man now—made this jumper all 'lone by himself an' has got through all right."

She came and held the lantern up to my face and looked at my hands.

"Well, my stars, Bart!" she exclaimed in a moment. "I thought ye would freeze up solid—ayes—poor boy!"

The point of my chin and the lobes of my ears and one finger were touched and my aunt rubbed them with snow until the frost was out.

We carried the grist in and Aunt Deel made some pudding. How good it was to feel the warmth of the fire and of the hearts of those who loved me! How I enjoyed the pudding and milk and bread and butter!

"I guess you've gone through the second peril that ol' Kate spoke of," said Aunt Deel as I went up-stairs.

Uncle Peabody went out to look at the horses.

When I awoke in the morning I observed that Uncle Peabody's bed had not been slept in. I hurried down and heard that our off-horse had died in the night of colic. Aunt Deel was crying. As he saw me Uncle Peabody began to dance a jig in the middle of the floor.

"Balance yer partners!" he shouted. "You an' I ain't goin' to be discouraged if all the hosses die—be we, Bart?"

"Never," I answered.

"That's the talk! If nec'sary we'll hitch Purvis up with t'other hoss an' git our haulin' done."

He and Purvis roared with laughter and the strength of the current swept me along with them.

"We're the luckiest folks in the world, anyway," Uncle Peabody went on. "Bart's alive an' there's three feet o' snow on the level an' more comin' an' it's colder'n Greenland."

It was such a bitter day that we worked only three hours and came back to the house and played Old Sledge by the fireside.

Rodney Barnes came over that afternoon and said that he would lend us a horse for the hauling.

When we went to bed that night Uncle Peabody whispered:

"Say, ol' feller, we was in purty bad shape this mornin'. If we hadn't 'a' backed up sudden an' took a new holt I guess Aunt Deel would 'a' caved in complete an' we'd all been a-bellerin' like a lot o' lost cattle."

We had good sleighing after that and got our bark and salts to market and earned ninety-eight dollars. But while we got our pay in paper "bank money," we had to pay our debts in wheat, salts or corn, so that our earnings really amounted to only sixty-two and a half dollars, my uncle said. This more than paid our interest. We gave the balance and ten bushels of wheat to Mr. Grimshaw for a spavined horse, after which he agreed to give us at least a year's extension on the principal.

We felt easy then.

CHAPTER VIII

MY THIRD PERIL

"Mr. Purvis" took his pay in salts and stayed with us until my first great adventure cut him off. It came one July day when I was in my sixteenth year. He behaved badly, and I as any normal boy would have done who had had my schooling in the candle-light. We had kept Grimshaw from our door by paying interest and the sum of eighty dollars on the principal. It had been hard work to live comfortably and carry the burden of debt. Again Grimshaw had begun to press us. My uncle wanted to get his paper and learn, if possible, when the Senator was expected in Canton.

So he gave me permission to ride with Purvis to the post-office—a distance of three miles—to get the mail. Purvis rode in our only saddle and I bareback, on a handsome white filly which my uncle had given me soon after she was foaled. I had fed and petted and broken and groomed her and she had grown so fond of me that my whistled call would bring her galloping to my side from the remotest reaches of the pasture. A chunk of sugar or an ear of corn or a pleasant grooming always rewarded her fidelity. She loved to have me wash her legs and braid her mane and rub her coat until it glowed, and she carried herself proudly when I was on her back. I had named her Sally because that was the only name which seemed to express my fondness.

"Mr. Purvis" was not an experienced rider. My filly led him at a swift gallop over the hills and I heard many a muttered complaint behind me, but she liked a free head when we took the road together and I let her have her way.

Coming back we fell in with another rider who had been resting at Seaver's little tavern through the heat of the day. He was a traveler on his way to Canton and had missed the right trail and wandered far afield. He had a big military saddle with bags and shiny brass trimmings and a pistol in a holster, all of which appealed to my eye and interest. The filly was a little tired and the stranger and I were riding abreast at a walk while Purvis trailed behind us. The sun had set and as we turned the top of a long hill the dusk was lighted with a rich, golden glow on the horizon far below us.

We heard a quick stir in the bushes by the roadside.

"What's that?" Purvis demanded in a half-whisper of excitement. We stopped.

Then promptly a voice—a voice which I did not recognize—broke the silence with these menacing words sharply spoken:

"Your money or your life!"

"Mr. Purvis" whirled his horse and lashed him up the hill. Things happened quickly in the next second or two. Glancing backward I saw him lose a stirrup and fall and pick himself up and run as if his life depended on it. I saw the stranger draw his pistol. A gun went off in the edge of the bushes close by. The flash of fire from its muzzle leaped at the stranger. The horses reared and plunged and mine threw me in a clump of small poppies by the roadside and dashed down the hill. All this had broken into the peace of a summer evening on a lonely road and the time in which it had happened could be measured, probably, by ten ticks of the watch.

My fall on the stony siding had stunned me and I lay for three or four seconds, as nearly as I can estimate it, in a strange and peaceful dream. Why did I dream of Amos Grimshaw coming to visit me, again, and why, above all, should it have seemed to me that enough things were said and done in that little flash of a dream to fill a whole day—enough of talk and play and going and coming, the whole ending with a talk on the haymow. Again and again I have wondered about that dream. I came to and lifted my head and my consciousness swung back upon the track of memory and took up the thread of the day, the briefest remove from where it had broken.

I peered through the bushes. The light was unchanged. I could see quite clearly. The horses were gone. It was very still. The stranger lay helpless in the road and a figure was bending over him. It was a man with a handkerchief hanging over his face with holes cut opposite his eyes. He had not seen my fall and thought, as I learned later, that I had ridden away.

His gun lay beside him, its stock toward me. I observed that a piece of wood had been split off the lower side of the stock. I jumped to my feet and seized a stone to hurl at him. As I did so the robber fled with gun in hand. If the gun had been loaded I suppose that this little history would never have been written. Quickly I hurled the stone at the robber. I remember it was a smallish stone about the size of a hen's egg. I saw it graze the side of his head. I saw his hand touch the place which the stone had grazed. He reeled and nearly fell and recovered himself and ran on, but the little stone had put the mark of Cain upon him.

The stranger lay still in the road. I lifted his head and dropped it quickly with a strange sickness. The feel of it and the way it fell back upon the ground when I let go scared me, for I knew that he was dead. The dust around him was wet. I ran down the hill a few steps and stopped and whistled to my filly. I could hear her answering whinny far down the dusty road and then her hoofs as she galloped toward me. She came within a few feet of me and stood snorting. I caught and mounted her and rode to the nearest house for help. On the way I saw why she had stopped. A number of horses were feeding on the roadside near the log house where Andrew Crampton lived. Andrew had just unloaded some hay and was backing out of his barn. I hitched my filly and jumped on the rack saying:

"Drive up the road as quick as you can. A man has been murdered."

What a fearful word it was that I had spoken! What a panic it made in the little dooryard! The man gasped and jerked the reins and shouted to his horses and began swearing. The woman uttered a little scream and the children ran crying to her side. Now for the first time I felt the dread significance of word and deed. I had had no time to think of it before. I thought of the robber fleeing, terror-stricken, in the growing darkness.

The physical facts which are further related to this tragedy are of little moment to me now. The stranger was dead and we took his body to our home and my uncle set out for the constable. Over and over again that night I told the story of the shooting. We went to the scene of the tragedy with lanterns and fenced it off and put some men on guard there.

How the event itself and all that hurrying about in the dark had shocked and excited me! The whole theater of life had changed. Its audience had suddenly enlarged and was rushing over the stage and a kind of terror was in every face and voice. There was a red-handed villain behind the scenes, now, and how many others, I wondered. Men were no longer as they had been. Even the God to whom I prayed was different. As I write the sounds and shadows of that night are in my soul again. I see its gathering gloom. I hear its rifle shot which started all the galloping hoofs and swinging lanterns and flitting shadows and hysterical profanity. In the morning they found the robber's footprints in the damp dirt of the road and measured them. The whole countryside was afire with excitement and searching the woods and fields for the highwayman.

"Mr. Purvis," who had lost confidence suddenly in the whole world, had been found, soon after daylight next morning, under a haycock in the field of a farmer who was getting in his hay. Our hired man rose up and reported in fearful tones. A band of robbers—not one, or two, even, but a band of them—had chased him up the road and one of their bullets had torn the side of his trousers, in support of which assertion he showed the tear. With his able assistance we see at a glance both the quality and the state of mind prevailing among the humbler citizens of the countryside. They were, in a way, children whose cows had never recovered from the habit of jumping over the moon and who still worshiped at the secret shrine of Jack the Giant Killer.

The stranger was buried. There was nothing upon him to indicate his name or residence. Weeks passed with no news of the man who had slain him. I had told of the gun with a piece of wood broken out of its stock, but no one knew of any such weapon in or near Lickitysplit.

One day Uncle Peabody and I drove up to Grimshaw's to make a payment of money. I remember it was gold and silver which we carried in a little sack. I asked where Amos was and Mrs. Grimshaw—a timid, tired-looking, bony little woman who was never seen outside of her own house—said that he was working out on the farm of a Mr. Beekman near Plattsburg. He had gone over on the stage late in June to hire out for the haying. I observed that my uncle looked very thoughtful as we rode back home and had little to say.

"You never had any idee who that robber was, did ye?" he asked by and by.

"No—I could not see plain—it was so dusk," I said.

"I think Purvis lied about the gang that chased him," he said. "Mebbe he thought they was after him. In my opinion he was so scairt he couldn't 'a' told a hennock from a handsaw anyway. I think it was just one man that did that job."

How well I remember the long silence that followed and the distant voices that flashed across it now and then—the call of the mire drum in the marshes and the songs of the winter wren and the swamp robin. It was a solemn silence.

The swift words, "Your money or your life," came out of my memory and rang in it. I felt its likeness to the scolding demands of Mr. Grimshaw, who was forever saying in effect:

"Your money or your home!"

That was like demanding our lives because we couldn't live without our home. Our all was in it. Mr. Grimshaw's gun was the power he had over us, and what a terrible weapon it was! I credit him with never realizing how terrible.

We came to the sand-hills and then Uncle Peabody broke the silence by saying:

"I wouldn't give fifty cents for as much o' this land as a bird could fly around in a day."

Then for a long time I heard only the sound of feet and wheels muffled in the sand, while my uncle sat looking thoughtfully at the siding. When I spoke to him he seemed not to hear me.

Before we reached home I knew what was in his mind, but neither dared to speak of it.

People came from Canton and all the neighboring villages to see and talk with me and among them were the Dunkelbergs. Unfounded tales of my bravery had gone abroad.

Sally seemed to be very glad to see me. We walked down to the brook and up into the maple grove and back through the meadows.

The beauty of that perfect day was upon her. I remember that her dress was like the color of its fire-weed blossoms and that the blue of its sky was in her eyes and the yellow of its sunlight in her hair and the red of its clover in her cheeks. I remember how the August breezes played with her hair, flinging its golden curving strands about her neck and shoulders so that it touched my face, now and then, as we walked! Somehow the rustle of her dress started a strange vibration in my spirit. I put my arm around her waist and she put her arm around mine as we ran along. A curious feeling came over me. I stopped and loosed my arm.

"It's very warm!" I said as I picked a stalk of fire-weed.

What was there about the girl which so thrilled me with happiness?

She turned away and felt the ribbon by which her hair was gathered at the back of her head.

I wanted to kiss her as I had done years before, but I was afraid.

She turned suddenly and said to me:

"A penny for your thoughts."

"You won't laugh at me?"

"No."

"I was thinking how beautiful you are and how homely I am."

"You are not homely. I like your eyes and your teeth are as white and even as they can be and you are a big, brave boy, too."

Oh, the vanity of youth! I had never been so happy as then.

"I don't believe I'm brave," I said, blushing as we walked along beside the wheat-fields that were just turning yellow. "I was terribly scared that night—honest I was!"

"But you didn't run away."

"I didn't think of it or I guess I would have."

After a moment of silence I ventured:

"I guess you've never fallen in love."

"Yes, I have."

"Who with?"

"I don't think I dare tell you," she answered, slowly, looking down as she walked.

"I'll tell you who I love if you wish," I said.

"Who?"

"You." I whispered the word and was afraid she would laugh at me, but she didn't. She stopped and looked very serious and asked:

"What makes you think you love me?"

"Well, when you go away I shall think an' think about you an' feel as I do when the leaves an' the flowers are all gone an' I know it's going to be winter, an' I guess next Sunday Shep an' I will go down to the brook an' come back through the meadow, an' I'll kind o' think it all over—what you said an' what I said an' how warm the sun shone an' how purty the wheat looked, an' I guess I'll hear that little bird singing."

We stopped and listened to the song of a bird—I do not remember what bird it was—and then she whispered:

"Will you love me always and forever?"

"Yes," I answered in the careless way of youth.

She stopped and looked into my eyes and I looked into hers.

"May I kiss you?" I asked, and afraid, with cheeks burning.

She turned away and answered: "I guess you can if you want to."

Now I seem to be in Aladdin's tower and to see her standing so red and graceful and innocent in the sunlight, and that strange fire kindled by our kisses warms my blood again.

It was still play, although not like that of the grand ladies and the noble gentlemen in which we had once indulged, but still it was play—the sweetest and dearest kind of play which the young may enjoy, and possibly, also, the most dangerous.

She held my hand very tightly as we went on and I told her of my purpose to be a great man.

My mind was in a singular condition of simplicity those days. It was due to the fact that I had had no confidant in school and had been brought up in a home where there was neither father nor mother nor brother.

That night I heard a whispered conference below after I had gone up-stairs. I knew that something was coming and wondered what it might be. Soon Uncle Peabody came up to our little room looking highly serious. He sat down on the side of his bed with his hands clasped firmly under one knee, raising his foot below it well above the floor. He reminded me of one carefully holding taut reins on a horse of a bad reputation. I sat, half undressed and rather fearful, looking into his face. As I think of the immaculate soul of the boy, I feel a touch of pathos in that scene. I think that he felt it, for I remember that his whisper trembled a little as he began to tell me why men are strong and women are beautiful and given to men in marriage.

"You'll be falling in love one o' these days," he said. "It's natural ye should. You remember Rovin' Kate?" he asked by and by.

"Yes," I answered.

"Some day when you're a little older I'll tell ye her story an' you'll see what happens when men an' women break the law o' God. Here's Mr. Wright's letter. Aunt Deel asked me to give it to you to keep. You're old enough now an' you'll be goin' away to school before long, I guess."

I took the letter and read again the superscription on its envelope:

To Master Barton Baynes—
(To be opened when he leaves home to
go to school.)

I put it away in the pine box with leather hinges on its cover which Uncle Peabody had made for me and wondered again what it was all about, and again that night I broke camp and moved further into the world over the silent trails of knowledge.

Uncle Peabody went away for a few days after the harvesting. He had gone afoot, I knew not where. He returned one afternoon in a buggy with the great Michael Hacket of the Canton Academy. Hacket was a big, brawny, red-haired, kindly Irishman with a merry heart and tongue, the latter having a touch of the brogue of the green isle which he had never seen, for he had been born in Massachusetts and had got his education in Harvard. He was then a man of forty.

"You're coming to me this fall," he said as he put his hand on my arm and gave me a little shake. "Lad! you've got a big pair of shoulders! Ye shall live in my house an' help with the chores if ye wish to."

"That'll be grand," said Uncle Peabody, but, as to myself, just then, I knew not what to think of it.

We were picking up potatoes in the field.

"Without 'taters an' imitators this world would be a poor place to live in," said Mr. Hacket. "Some imitate the wise—thank God!—some the foolish—bad 'cess to the devil!"

As he spoke we heard a wonderful bird song in a tall spruce down by the brook.

"Do ye hear the little silver bells in yon tower?" he asked.

As we listened a moment he whispered: "It's the song o' the Hermit Thrush. I wonder, now, whom he imitates. I think the first one o' them must 'a' come on Christmas night an' heard the angels sing an' remembered a little o' it so he could give it to his children an' keep it in the world."

I looked up into the man's face and liked him, and after that I looked forward to the time when I should know him and his home.

Shep was rubbing his neck fondly on the schoolmaster's boot.

"That dog couldn't think more o' me if I were a bone," he said as he went away.

END OF BOOK ONE

BOOK TWO

Which is the Story of the Principal Witness

CHAPTER IX

IN WHICH I MEET OTHER GREAT MEN

It was a sunny day in late September on which Aunt Deel and Uncle Peabody took me and my little pine chest with all my treasures in it to the village where I was to go to school and live with the family of Mr. Michael Hacket, the schoolmaster. I was proud of the chest, now equipped with iron hinges and a hasp and staple. Aunt Deel had worked hard to get me ready, sitting late at her loom to weave cloth for my new suit, which a traveling tailor had fitted and made for me. I remember that the breeches were of tow and that they scratched my legs and made me very uncomfortable, but I did not complain. My uncle used to say that nobody with tow breeches on him could ride a horse without being thrown—they pricked so.

The suit which I had grown into—"the Potsdam clothes," we called them often, but more often "the boughten clothes"—had been grown out of and left behind in a way of speaking. I had an extra good-looking pair of cowhide boots, as we all agreed, which John Wells, the cobbler, had made for me. True, I had my doubts about them, but we could afford no better.

When the chest was about full, I remember that my aunt brought something wrapped in a sheet of the *St. Lawrence Republican* and put it into my hands.

"There are two dozen cookies an' some dried meat," said she. "Ayes, I thought mebbe you'd like 'em—if you was hungry some time between meals. Wait a minute."

She went to her room and Uncle Peabody and I waited before we shut the hasp with a wooden peg driven into its staple.

Aunt Deel returned promptly with the Indian Book in her hands.

"There," said she, "you might as well have it—ayes!—you're old enough now. You'll enjoy readin' it sometimes in the evenin', mebbe—ayes! Please be awful careful of it, Bart, for it was a present from my mother to me—ayes it was!"

How tenderly she held and looked at the sacred heirloom so carefully stitched into its cover of faded linen. It was her sole legacy. Tears came to my eyes as I thought of her generosity—greater, far greater than that which has brought me gifts of silver and gold—although my curiosity regarding the Indian Book had abated, largely, for I had taken many a sly peek at it. Therein I had read how Captain Baynes—my great grandfather—had been killed by the Indians.

I remember the sad excitement of that ride to the village and all the words of advice and counsel spoken by my aunt.

"Don't go out after dark," said she. "I'm 'fraid some o' them rowdies'll pitch on ye."

"If they do I guess they'll be kind o' surprised," said Uncle Peabody.

"I don't want him to fight."

"If it's nec'sary, I believe in fightin' tooth an' nail," my uncle maintained.

I remember looking in vain for Sally as we passed the Dunkelbergs'. I remember my growing loneliness as the day wore on and how Aunt Deel stood silently buttoning my coat with tears rolling down her cheeks while I leaned back upon the gate in front of the Hacket house, on Ashery Lane, trying to act like a man and rather ashamed of my poor success. It reminded me of standing in the half-bushel measure and trying in vain, as I had more than once, to shoulder the big bag of corn. Uncle Peabody stood surveying the sky in silence with his back toward us. He turned and nervously blew out his breath. His lips trembled a little as he said.

"I dunno but what it's goin' to rain."

I watched them as they walked to the tavern sheds, both looking down at the ground and going rather unsteadily. Oh, the look of that beloved pair as they walked away from me!—the look of their leaning heads! Their silence and the sound of their footsteps are, somehow, a part of the picture which has hung all these years in my memory.

Suddenly I saw a man go reeling by in the middle of the road. His feet swung. They did not rise and reach forward and touch the ground according to the ancient habit of the human foot. They swung sideways and rose high and each crossed the line of his flight a little, as one might say, when it came to the ground, for the man's movements reminded me of the aimless flight of a sporting swallow. He zig-zagged from one side of the street to the other. He caught my eye just in time and saved me from breaking down. I watched him until he swung around a corner. Only once before had I seen a man drunk and walking, although I had seen certain of our neighbors riding home drunk—so drunk that I thought their horses were ashamed of them, being always steaming hot and in a great hurry.

Sally Dunkelberg and her mother came along and said that they were glad I had come to school. I could not talk to them and seeing my trouble, they went on, Sally waving her hand to me as they turned the corner below. I felt ashamed of myself. Suddenly I heard the door open behind me and the voice of Mr. Hacket:

"Bart," he called, "I've a friend here who has something to say to you. Come in."

I turned and went into the house.

"Away with sadness—laddie buck!" he exclaimed as he took his violin from its case while I sat wiping my eyes. "Away with sadness! She often raps at my door, and while I try not to be rude, I always pretend to be very busy. Just a light word o' recognition by way o' common politeness! Then laugh, if ye can an' do it quickly, lad, an' she will pass on."

The last words were spoken in a whisper, with one hand on my breast.

He tuned the strings and played the *Fisher's Hornpipe*. What a romp of merry music filled the house! I had never heard the like and was soon smiling at him as he played. His bow and fingers flew in the wild frolic of the Devil's Dream. It led me out of my sadness into a world all new to me.

"Now, God bless your soul, boy!" he exclaimed, by and by, as he put down his instrument. "We shall have a good time together—that we will. Not a stroke o' work this day! Come, I have a guide here that will take us down to the land o' the fairies."

Then with his microscope he showed me into the wonder world of littleness of which I had had no knowledge.

"The microscope is like the art o' the teacher," he said. "I've known a good teacher to take a brain no bigger than a fly's foot an' make it visible to the naked eye."

One of the children, of which there were four in the Hacket home, called us to supper. Mrs. Hacket, a stout woman with a red and kindly face, sat at one end of the table, and between them were the children—Mary, a pretty daughter of seventeen years; Maggie, a six-year-old; Ruth, a delicate girl of seven, and John, a noisy, red-faced boy of five. The chairs were of plain wood—like the kitchen chairs of to-day. In the middle of the table was an empty one—painted green. Before he sat down Mr. Hacket put his hand on the back of this chair and said:

"A merry heart to you, Michael Henry."

I wondered at the meaning of this, but dared not to ask. The oldest daughter acted as a kind of moderator with the others.

"Mary is the constable of this house, with power to arrest and hale into court for undue haste or rebellion or impoliteness," Mr. Hacket explained.

"I believe that Sally Dunkelberg is your friend," he said to me presently.

"Yes, sir," I answered.

"A fine slip of a girl that and a born scholar. I saw you look at her as the Persian looks at the rising sun."

I blushed and Mary and her mother and the boy John looked at me and laughed.

"*Puer pulcherrime!*" Mr. Hacket exclaimed with a kindly smile.

Uncle Peabody would have called it a "stout snag." The schoolmaster had hauled it out of his brain very deftly and chucked it down before me in a kind of challenge.

"What does that mean?" I asked.

"You shall know in a week, my son," he answered. "I shall put you into the Latin class Wednesday morning, and God help you to like it as well as you like Sally."

Again they laughed and again I blushed.

"Hold up yer head, my brave lad," he went on. "Ye've a perfect right to like Sally if ye've a heart to."

He sang a rollicking ballad of which I remember only the refrain:

A lad in his teens will never know beans if he hasn't an eye for the girls.

It was a merry supper, and when it ended Mr. Hacket rose and took the green chair from the table, exclaiming:

"Michael Henry, God bless you!"

Then he kissed his wife and said:

"Maggie, you wild rose of Erin! I've been all day in the study. I must take a walk or I shall get an exalted abdomen. One is badly beaten in the race o' life when his abdomen gets ahead of his toes. Children, keep our young friend happy here until I come back, and mind you, don't forget the good fellow in the green chair."

Mary helped her mother with the dishes, while I sat with a book by the fireside. Soon Mrs. Hacket and the children came and sat down with me.

"Let's play backgammon," Mary proposed.

"I don't want to," said John.

"Don't forget Michael Henry," she reminded.

"Who is Michael Henry?" I asked.

"Sure, he's the boy that has never been born," said Mrs. Hacket. "He was to be the biggest and noblest one o' them—kind an' helpful an' cheery hearted an' beloved o' God above all the others. We try to live up to him."

He seemed to me a very strange and wonderful creature—this invisible occupant of the green chair.

I know now what I knew not then that Michael Henry was the spirit of their home—an ideal of which the empty green chair was a constant reminder.

We played backgammon and Old Maid and Everlasting until Mr. Hacket returned.

He sat down and read aloud from the *Letters of an Englishwoman in America.*

"Do you want to know what sleighing is?" she wrote. "Set your chair out on the porch on a Christmas day. Put your feet in a pail-full of powdered ice. Have somebody jingle a bell in one ear and blow into the other with a bellows and you will have an exact idea of it."

When she told of a lady who had been horned by a large insect known as a snapdragon, he laughed loudly and closed the book and said:

"They have found a new peril of American life. It is the gory horn of the snapdragon. Added to our genius for boastfulness and impiety, it is a crowning defect. Ye would think that our chief aim was the cuspidor. Showers of expectoration and thunder claps o' profanity and braggart gales o' Yankee dialect!—that's the moral weather report that she sends back to England. We have faults enough, God knows, but we have something else away beneath them an' none o' these writers has discovered it."

The sealed envelope which Mr. Wright had left at our home, a long time before that day, was in my pocket. At last the hour had come when. I could open it and read the message of which I had thought much and with a growing interest.

I rose and said that I should like to go to my room. Mr. Hacket lighted a candle and took me up-stairs to a little room where my chest had been deposited. There were, in the room, a bed, a chair, a portrait of Napoleon Bonaparte and a small table on which were a dictionary, a Bible and a number of school books.

"These were Mary's books," said Mr. Hacket. "I told yer uncle that ye could use them an' welcome. There's another book here which ye may study if ye think it worth the bother. It's a worn an' tiresome book, my lad, but I pray God ye may find no harm in it. Use it as often as ye will. It is the book o' my heart. Ye will find in it some kind o' answer to every query in the endless flight o' them that's coming on, an' may the good God help us to the truth."

He turned and bade me good night and went away and closed the door.

I sat down and opened the sealed envelope with trembling hands, and found in it this brief note:

"DEAR PARTNER: I want you to ask the wisest man you know to explain these words to you. I suggest that you commit them to memory and think often of their meaning. They are from Job:

"'His bones are full of the sin of his youth, which shall lie down with him in the dust.'

"I believe that they are the most impressive in all the literature I have read.

"Yours truly,
SILAS WRIGHT, JR."

I read the words over and over again, but knew not their meaning. Sadly and slowly I got ready for bed. I missed the shingles and the familiar rustle of the popple leaves above my head and the brooding silence of the hills. The noises of the village challenged my ear after I had put out my candle. There were many barking dogs. Some horsemen passed, with a creaking of saddle leather, followed by a wagon. Soon I heard running feet and eager voices. I rose and looked out of the open window. Men were hurrying down the street with lanterns.

"He's the son o' Ben Grimshaw," I heard one of them saying. "They caught him back in the south woods yesterday. The sheriff said that he tried to run away when he saw 'em coming."

What was the meaning of this? What had Amos Grimshaw been doing? I trembled as I got back into bed—I can not even now explain why, but long ago I gave up trying to fathom the depths of the human spirit with an infinite sea beneath it crossed by subtle tides and currents. We see only the straws on the surface.

I was up at daylight and Mr. Hacket came to my door while I was dressing.

"A merry day to you!" he exclaimed. "I'll await you below and introduce you to the humble herds and flocks of a schoolmaster."

I went with him while he fed his chickens and two small shoats. I milked the cow for him, and together we drove her back to the pasture. Then we split some wood and filled the boxes by the fireplace and the kitchen stove and raked up the leaves in the dooryard and wheeled them away.

"Now you know the duties o' your office," said the schoolmaster as we went in to breakfast.

We sat down at the table with the family and I drew out my letter from the Senator and gave it to Mr. Hacket to read.

"The Senator! God prosper him! I hear that he came on the Plattsburg stage last night," he said as he began the reading—an announcement which caused me and the children to clap our hands with joy.

Mr. Hacket thoughtfully repeated the words from Job with a most impressive intonation.

He passed the letter back to me and said:

"All true! I have seen it sinking into the bones o' the young and I have seen it lying down with the aged in the dust o' their graves. It is a big book—the one we are now opening. God help us! It has more pages than all the days o' your life. Just think o' your body, O brave and tender youth! It is like a sponge. How it takes things in an' holds 'em an' feeds upon 'em! A part o' every apple ye eat sinks down into yer blood an' bones. Ye can't get it out. It's the same way with the books ye read an' the thoughts ye enjoy. They go down into yer bones an' ye can't get 'em out. That's why I like to think o' Michael Henry. His food is good thoughts and his wine is laughter. I had a long visit with M.H. last night when ye were all abed. His face was a chunk o' laughter. Oh, what a limb he is! I wish I could tell ye all the good things he said."

"There comes Colonel Hand," said Mrs. Hacket as she looked out of the window. "The poor lonely Whig! He has nothing to do these days but sit around the tavern."

"Ye might as well pity a goose for going bare-footed," the schoolmaster remarked.

In the midst of our laughter Colonel Hand rapped at the door and Mr. Hacket admitted him.

"I tell you the country is going to the dogs," I heard the Colonel saying as he came into the house.

"You inhuman Hand!" said the schoolmaster. "I should think you would be tired of trying to crush that old indestructible worm."

Colonel Hand was a surly looking man beyond middle age with large eyes that showed signs of dissipation. He had a small dark tuft beneath his lower lip and thin, black, untidy hair.

"What do ye think has happened?" he asked as he looked down upon us with a majestic movement of his hand.

He stood with a stern face, like an orator, and seemed to enjoy our suspense.

"What do you think has happened?" he repeated.

"God knows! It may be that Bill Harriman has swapped horses again or that somebody has been talked to death by old Granny Barnes—which is it?" asked the schoolmaster.

"It is neither, sir," Colonel Hand answered sternly. "The son o' that old Buck-tail, Ben Grimshaw, has been arrested and brought to jail for murder."

"For murder?" asked Mr. and Mrs. Hacket in one breath.

"For bloody murder, sir," the Colonel went on. "It was the shooting of that man in the town o' Ballybeen a few weeks ago. Things have come to a pretty pass in this country, I should say. Talk about law and order, we don't know what it means here and why should we? The party in power is avowedly opposed to it—yes, sir. It has fattened upon bribery and corruption. Do you think that the son o' Ben Grimshaw will receive his punishment even if he is proved guilty? Not at all. He will be protected—you mark my words."

He bowed and left us. When the door had closed behind him Mr. Hacket said:

"Another victim horned by the Snapdragon! If a man were to be slain by a bear back in the woods Colonel Hand would look for guilt in the Democratic party. He will have a busy day and people will receive him as the ghost of Creusa received the embraces of Æneas—unheeding. Michael Henry, whatever the truth may be regarding the poor boy in jail, we are in no way responsible. Away with sadness! What is that?"

Mr. Hacket inclined his ear and then added: "Michael Henry says that he may be innocent and that we had better go and see if we can help him. Now I hadn't thought o' that. Had you, Mary?"

"No," the girl answered.

"We mustn't be letting Mike get ahead of us always," said her father.

The news brought by the Colonel had shocked me and my thoughts had been very busy since his announcement. I had thought of the book which I had seen Amos reading in the haymow. Had its contents sunk into his bones?—for I couldn't help thinking of all that Mr. Hacket had just said about books and thoughts. My brain had gone back over the events of that tragic moment—the fall, the swift dream, the look of the robber in the dim light, the hurling of the stone. The man who fled was about the size of Amos, but I had never thought of the latter as the guilty man.

"You saw the crime, I believe," said Mr. Hacket as he turned to me.

I told them all that I knew of it.

"Upon my word, I like you, my brave lad," said the schoolmaster. "I heard of all this and decided that you would be a help to Michael Henry and a creditable student. Come, let us go and pay our compliments to the Senator. He rises betimes. If he stayed at the tavern he will be out and up at his house by now."

The schoolmaster and I went over to Mr. Wright's house—a white, frame building which had often been pointed out to me.

Mrs. Wright, a fine-looking lady who met us at the door, said that the Senator had gone over to the mill with his wheelbarrow.

Mr. Hacket asked for the time and she answered:

"It wants one minute of seven."

I quote her words to show how early the day began with us back in those times.

"We've plenty of time and we'll wait for him," said the schoolmaster.

"I see him!" said little John as he and Ruth ran to the gate and down the rough plank walk to meet him.

We saw him coming a little way down the street in his shirt-sleeves with his barrow in front of him. He stopped and lifted little John in his arms, and after a moment put him down and embraced Ruth.

"Well, I see ye still love the tender embrace o' the wheelbarrow," said Mr. Hacket as we approached the Senator.

"My embrace is the tenderer of the two," the latter laughed with a look at his hands.

He recognized me and seized my two hands and shook them as he said:

"Upon my word, here is my friend Bart. I was not looking for you here."

He put his hand on my head, now higher than his shoulder, and said: "I was not looking for you *here*."

He moved his hand down some inches and added: "I was looking for you down there. You can't tell where you'll find these youngsters if you leave them a while."

"We are all forever moving," said the schoolmaster. "No man is ever two days in the same altitude unless he's a Whig."

"Or a *born* fool," the Senator laughed with a subtlety which I did not then appreciate.

He asked about my aunt and uncle and expressed joy at learning that I was now under Mr. Hacket.

"I shall be here for a number of weeks," he said, "and I shall want to see you often. Maybe we'll go hunting some Saturday."

We bade him good morning and he went on with his wheelbarrow, which was loaded, I remember, with stout sacks of meal and flour.

We went to the school at half past eight. What a thrilling place it was with its seventy-eight children and its three rooms. How noisy they were as they waited in the school yard for the bell to ring! I stood by the door-side looking very foolish, I dare say, for I knew not what to do with myself. My legs encased in the tow breeches felt as if they were on fire. My timidity was increased by the fact that many were observing me and that my appearance seemed to inspire sundry, sly remarks. I saw that most of the village boys wore boughten clothes and fine boots. I looked down at my own leather and was a tower of shame on a foundation of greased cowhide. Sally Dunkelberg came in with some other girls and pretended not to see me. That was the hardest blow I suffered.

Among the handsome, well-dressed boys of the village was Henry Wills—the boy who had stolen my watermelon. I had never forgiven him for that or for the killing of my little hen. The bell rang and we marched into the big room, while a fat girl with crinkly hair played on a melodeon. Henry and another boy tried to shove me out of line and a big paper wad struck the side of my head as we were marching in and after we were seated a cross-eyed, freckled girl in a red dress made a face at me.

It was, on the whole, the unhappiest day of my life. It reminded me of Captain Cook's account of his first day with a barbaric tribe on one of the South Sea islands. During recess I slapped a boy's face for calling me a rabbit and the two others who came to help him went away full of fear and astonishment, for I had the strength of a young moose in me those days. After that they began to make friends with me.

In the noon hour a man came to me in the school yard with a subpoena for the examination of Amos Grimshaw and explained its meaning. He also said that Bishop Perkins, the district attorney, would call to see me that evening.

While I was talking with this man Sally passed me walking with another girl and said:

"Hello, Bart!"

I observed that Henry Wills joined them and walked down the street at the side of Sally. I got my first pang of jealousy then.

When school was out that afternoon Mr. Hacket said I could have an hour to see the sights of the village, so I set out, feeling much depressed. My self-confidence had vanished. I was homesick and felt terribly alone. I passed the jail and stopped and looked at its grated windows and thought of Amos and wondered if he were really a murderer.

I walked toward the house of Mr. Wright and saw him digging potatoes in the garden and went in. I knew that he was my friend.

"Well, Bart, how do you like school?" he asked.

"Not very well," I answered.

"Of course not! It's new to you now, and you miss your aunt and uncle. Stick to it. You'll make friends and get interested before long."

"I want to go home," I declared.

"Now let's look at the compass," he suggested. "You're lost for a minute and, like all lost people, you're heading the wrong way. Don't be misled by selfishness. Forget what you want to do and think of what we want you to do. We want you to make a man of yourself. You must do it for the sake of those dear people who have done so much for you. The needle points toward the schoolhouse yonder."

He went on with his work, and, as I walked away, I understood that the needle he referred to was my conscience.

As I neared the schoolmaster's the same drunken man that I had seen before went zigzagging up the road.

Mr. Hacket stood in his dooryard.

"Who is that?" I asked.

"Nick Tubbs—the village drunkard and sign o' the times," he answered. "Does chores at the tavern all day and goes home at night filled with his earnings an' a great sense o' proprietorship. He is the top flower on the bush."

I went about my chores. There was to be no more wavering in my conduct. At the supper table Mr. Hacket kept us laughing with songs and jests and stories. The boy John, having been reproved for rapid eating, hurled his spoon upon the floor.

"Those in favor of his punishment will please say aye?" said the schoolmaster.

I remember that we had a divided house on that important question.

The schoolmaster said: "Michael Henry wishes him to be forgiven on promise of better conduct, but for the next offense he shall ride the badger."

This meant lying for a painful moment across his father's knee.

The promise was given and our merry-making resumed. The district attorney, whom I had met before, came to see me after supper and asked more questions and advised me to talk with no one about the shooting without his consent. Soon he went away, and after I had learned my lessons Mr. Hacket said:

"Let us walk up to the jail and spend a few minutes with Amos."

We hurried to the jail. The sheriff, a stout-built, stern-faced man, admitted us.

"Can we see the Grimshaw boy?" Mr. Hacket inquired.

"I guess so," he answered as he lazily rose from his chair and took down a bunch of large keys which had been hanging on the wall. "His father has just left."

He spoke in a low, solemn tone which impressed me deeply as he put a lighted candle in the hand of the schoolmaster. He led us through a door into a narrow corridor. He thrust a big key into the lock of a heavy iron grating and threw it open and bade us step in. We entered an ill-smelling, stone-floored room with a number of cells against its rear wall. He locked the door behind us. I saw a face and figure in the dim candle-light, behind the grated door of one of these cells. How lonely and dejected and helpless was the expression of that figure! The sheriff went to the door and unlocked it.

"Hello, Grimshaw," he said sternly. "Step out here."

It all went to my heart—the manners of the sheriff so like the cold iron of his keys and doors—the dim candle-light, the pale, frightened youth who walked toward us. We shook his hand and he said that he was glad to see us. I saw the scar under his left ear and reaching out upon his cheek which my stone had made and knew that he bore the mark of Cain.

He asked if he could see me alone and the sheriff shook his head and said sternly:

"Against the rules."

"Amos, I've a boy o' my own an' I feel for ye," said the schoolmaster. "I'm going to come here, now and then, to cheer ye up and bring ye some books to read. If there's any word of advice I can give ye—let me know. Have ye a lawyer?"

"There's one coming to-morrow."

"Don't say a word about the case, boy, to any one but your lawyer—mind that."

We left him and went to our home and beds. I to spend half the night thinking of my discovery, since which, for some reason, I had no doubt of the guilt of Amos, but I spoke not of it to any one and the secret worried me.

Next morning on my way to school I passed a scene more strange and memorable than any in my long experience. I saw the shabby figure of old Benjamin Grimshaw walking in the side path. His hands were in his pockets, his eyes bent upon the ground, his lips moving as if he were in deep thought. Roving Kate, the ragged, silent woman who, for the fortune of Amos, had drawn a gibbet, the shadow of which was now upon him, walked slowly behind the money-lender pointing at him with her bony forefinger. Her stern eyes watched him as the cat watches when its prey is near it. She did not notice me. Silently, her feet wrapped in rags, she walked behind the man, always pointing at him. When he stopped she stopped. When he resumed his slow progress she followed. It thrilled me, partly because I had begun to believe in the weird, mysterious power of the Silent Woman. I had twenty minutes to spare and so I turned into the main street, behind and close by them. I saw him stop and buy some crackers and an apple and a piece of cheese. Meanwhile she stood pointing at him. He saw, but gave no heed to her. He walked along the street in front of the stores, she following as before. How patiently she followed!

"Why does she follow him that way?" I asked the storekeeper when they were gone.

"Oh, I dunno, boy!" he answered. "She's crazy an' I guess she dunno what she's doin'."

The explanation did not satisfy me. I knew, or thought I knew, better than he the meaning of that look in her eyes. I had seen it before.

I started for the big schoolhouse and a number of boys joined me with pleasant words.

"I saw you lookin' at ol' Kate," one of them said to me. "Don't ye ever make fun o' her. She's got the evil eye an' if she puts it on ye, why ye'll git drownded er fall off a high place er somethin'."

The boys were of one accord about that.

Sally ran past us with that low-lived Wills boy, who carried her books for her. His father had gone into the grocery business and Henry wore boughten clothes. I couldn't tell Sally how mean he was. I was angry and decided not to speak to her until she spoke to me. I got along better in school, although there was some tittering when I recited, probably because I had a broader dialect and bigger boots than the boys of the village.

CHAPTER X

I MEET PRESIDENT VAN BUREN AND AM CROSS-EXAMINED BY MR. GRIMSHAW

The days went easier after that. The boys took me into their play and some of them were most friendly. I had a swift foot and a good eye as well as a strong arm, and could hold my own at three-old-cat—a kind of baseball which we played in the school yard. Saturday came. As we were sitting down at the table that morning the younger children clung to the knees of Mr. Hacket and begged him to take them up the river in a boat.

"Good Lord! What wilt thou give me when I grow childless?" he exclaimed with his arms around them. "That was the question of Abraham, and it often comes to me. Of course we shall go. But hark! Let us hear what the green chair has to say."

There was a moment of silence and then he went on with a merry laugh. "Right ye are, Michael Henry! You are always right, my boy—God bless your soul! We shall take Bart with us an' doughnuts an' cheese an' cookies an' dried meat for all."

From that moment I date the beginning of my love for the occupant of the green chair in the home of Michael Hacket. Those good people were Catholics and I a Protestant and yet this Michael Henry always insisted upon the most delicate consideration for my faith and feelings.

"I promised to spend the morning in the field with Mr. Wright, if I may have your consent, sir," I said.

"Then we shall console ourselves, knowing that you are in better company," said Mr. Hacket.

Mr. Dunkelberg called at the house in Ashery Lane to see me after breakfast.

"Bart, if you will come with me I should like to order some store clothes and boots for you," he said in his squeaky voice.

For a moment I knew not how to answer him. Nettled as I had been by Sally's treatment of me, the offer was like rubbing ashes on the soreness of my spirit.

I blushed and surveyed my garments and said:

"I guess I look pretty badly, don't I?"

"You look all right, but I thought, maybe, you would feel better in softer raiment, especially if you care to go around much with the young people. I am an old friend of the family and I guess it would be proper for me to buy the clothes for you. When you are older you can buy a suit for me, sometime, if you care to."

It should be understood that well-to-do people in the towns were more particular about their dress those days than now.

"I'll ask my aunt and uncle about it," I proposed.

"That's all right," he answered. "I'm going to drive up to your house this afternoon and your uncle wishes you to go with me. We are all to have a talk with Mr. Grimshaw."

He left me and I went over to Mr. Wright's.

They told me that he was cutting corn in the back lot, where I found him.

"How do I look in these clothes?" I bravely asked.

"Like the son of a farmer up in the hills and that's just as you ought to look," he answered.

In a moment he added as he reaped a hill of corn with his sickle.

"I suppose they are making fun of you, partner."

"Some," I answered, blushing.

"Don't mind that," he advised, and then quoted the stanza:

"Were I as tall to reach the pole
Or grasp the ocean in a span,
I'd still me measured by my soul;
The mind's the standard of the man."

"Mr. Dunkelberg came this morning and wanted to buy me some new clothes and boots," I said.

"Good Lord! What wilt thou give me when I grow childless?"

The Senator stopped work and stood looking at me with his hands upon his hips.

"I wouldn't let him do it if I were you," he said thoughtfully.

Just then I saw a young man come running toward us in the distant field.

Mr. Wright took out his compass.

"Look here," he said, "you see the needle points due north."

He took a lodestone out of his pocket and holding it near the compass moved it back and forth. The needle followed it.

The young man came up to us breathing deeply. Perspiration was rolling off his face. He was much excited and spoke with some difficulty.

"Senator Wright," he gasped, "Mrs. Wright sent me down to tell you that President Van Buren is at the house."

I remember vividly the look of mild amusement in the Senator's face and the serene calmness with which he looked at the young man and said to him:

"Tell Mrs. Wright to make him comfortable in our easiest chair and to say to the President that I shall be up directly."

To my utter surprise he resumed his talk with me as the young man went away.

"You see all ways are north when you put this lodestone near the needle," he went on. "If it is to tell you the truth you must keep the lodestone away from the needle. It's that way, too, with the compass of your soul, partner. There the lodestone is selfishness, and with its help you can make any direction look right to you and soon—you're lost."

He put his hand on my arm and said in a low tone which made me to understand that it was for my ear only.

"What I fear is that they may try to tamper with your compass. Look out for lodestones."

He was near the end of a row and went on with his reaping as he said:

"I could take my body off this row any minute, but the only way to get my mind off it is to go to its end."

He bound the last bundle and then we walked together toward the house, the Senator carrying his sickle.

"I shall introduce you to the President," he said as we neared our destination. "Then perhaps you had better leave us."

At home we had read much about the new President and regarded him with deep veneration. In general I knew the grounds of it—his fight against the banks for using public funds for selfish purposes and "swapping mushrats for mink" with the government, as uncle put it, by seeking to return the same in cheapened paper money; his long battle for the extension of the right of suffrage in our state; his fiery eloquence in debate. Often I had heard Uncle Peabody say that Van Buren had made it possible for a poor man to vote in York State and hold up his head like a man. So I was deeply moved by the prospect of seeing him.

I could not remember that I had ever been "introduced" to anybody. I knew that people put their wits on exhibition and often flung down a "snag" by way of demonstrating their fitness for the honor, when they were introduced in books. I remember asking rather timidly:

"What shall I say when—when you—introduce me?"

"Oh, say anything that you want to say," he answered with a look of amusement.

"I'm kind o' scared," I said.

"You needn't be—he was once a poor boy just like you."

"Just like *me*!" I repeated, thoughtfully, for while I had heard a good deal of that kind of thing in our home, it had not, somehow, got under my jacket, as they used to say.

"Just like *you*—cowhide and all—the son of a small freeholder in Kinderhook on the Hudson," he went on. "But he was well fed in brain and body and kept his heart clean. So, of course, he grew and is still growing. That's a curious thing about men and women, Bart. If they are in good ground and properly cared for they never stop growing-never!—and that's a pretty full word—isn't it?"

I felt its fulness, but the Senator had a way of stopping just this side of the grave in all his talks with me, and so there was no sign of preaching in any of it.

"As time goes on you'll meet a good many great men, I presume," he continued. "They're all just human beings like you and me. Most of them enjoy beefsteak, and apple pie and good boys."

We had come in sight of the house. I lagged behind a little when I saw the great man sitting on the small piazza with Mrs. Wright. I shall never forget the grand clothes he wore—black, saving the gray waistcoat, with shiny, brass buttons—especially the great, white standing collar and cravat. I see vividly, too, as I write, the full figure, the ruddy, kindly face, the large nose, the gray eyes, the thick halo of silvered hair extending from his collar to the bald top of his head. He rose and said in a deep voice:

"He sows ill luck who hinders the reaper."

Mr. Wright hung his sickle on a small tree in the dooryard and answered.

"The plowman has overtaken the reaper, Mr. President. I bid you welcome to my humble home."

"It is a pleasure to be here and a regret to call you back to Washington," said the President as they shook hands.

"I suppose that means an extra session," the Senator answered.

"First let me reassure you. I shall get away as soon as possible, for I know that a President is a heavy burden for one to have on his hands."

"Don't worry. I can get along with almost any kind of a human being, especially if he likes pudding and milk as well as you do," said the Senator, who then introduced me in these words:

"Mr. President, this is my young friend Barton Baynes of the neighborhood of Lickitysplit in the town of Ballybeen—a coming man of this county."

"Come on," was the playful remark of the President as he took my hand. "I shall be looking for you."

I had carefully chosen my words and I remember saying, with some dignity, like one in a story book, although with a trembling voice:

"It is an honor to meet you, sir, and thank you for the right to vote—when I am old enough."

Vividly, too, I remember his gentle smile as he looked down at me and said in a most kindly tone:

"I think it a great honor to hear you say that."

He put his hands upon my shoulders and turning to the Senator said:

"Wright, I often wish that I had your modesty."

"I need it much more than you do," the Senator laughed.

Straightway I left them with an awkward bow and blushing to the roots of my hair. A number of boys and girls stood under the shade trees opposite looking across at the President. In my embarrassment I did not identify any one in the group. Numbers of men and women were passing the house and, as they did so, taking "a good look," in their way of speaking at the two great men. Not before had I seen so many people walking about—many in their best clothes.

As I neared the home of Mr. Hacket I heard hurrying footsteps behind me and the voice of Sally calling my name. I stopped and faced about.

How charming she looked as she walked toward me! I had never seen her quite so fixed up.

"Bart," she said. "I suppose you're not going to speak to me."

"If you'll speak to me," I answered.

"I love to speak to you," she said. "I've been looking all around for you. Mother wants you to come over to dinner with us at just twelve o'clock. You're going away with father as soon as we get through."

I wanted to go but got the notion all at once that the Dunkelbergs were in need of information about me and that the time had come to impart it. So then and there, that ancient Olympus of our family received notice as it were.

"I can't," I said. "I've got to study my lessons before I go away with your father."

It was a blow to her. I saw the shadow that fell upon her face. She was vexed and turned and ran away from me without another word and I felt a pang of regret as I went to the lonely and deserted home of the schoolmaster.

I had hoped that the Senator would ask me to dinner, but the coming of the President had upset the chance of it. It was eleven o'clock. Mrs. Hacket had put a cold bite on the table for me. I ate it—not to keep it waiting—and sat down with my eyes on my book and my mind at the Dunkelbergs'—where I heard in a way what Sally was saying and what "Mr. and Mrs. Horace Dunkelberg" were saying.

At twelve-thirty Mr. Dunkelberg came for me, with a high-stepping horse in a new harness and a shiny still-running buggy. He wore gloves and a beaver hat and sat very erect and had little to say.

"I hear you met the President," he remarked.

"Yes, sir. I was introduced to him this morning," I answered a bit too proudly, and wondering how he had heard of my good fortune, but deeply gratified at his knowledge of it.

"What did he have to say?"

I described the interview and the looks of the great man. Not much more was said as we sped away toward the deep woods and the high hills.

I was eager to get home but wondered why he should be going with me to talk with Mr. Grimshaw and my uncle. Of course I suspected that it had to do with Amos but how I knew not. He hummed in the rough going and thoughtfully nicked the bushes with his whip. I never knew a more persistent hummer.

What a thrill came to me when I saw the house and the popple tree and the lilac bushes—they looked so friendly! Old Shep came barking up the road to meet us and ran by the buggy side with joyful leaps and cries. With what affection he crowded upon me and licked my face and hands when my feet were on the ground at last! Aunt Deel and Uncle Peabody were coming in from the pasture lot with sacks of butternuts on a wheelbarrow. My uncle clapped his hands and waved his handkerchief and shouted "Hooray!"

Aunt Deel shook hands with Mr. Dunkelberg and then came to me and said:

"Wal, Bart Baynes! I never was so glad to see anybody in all the days o' my life—ayes! We been lookin' up the road for an hour—ayes! You come right into the house this minute—both o' you."

The table was spread with the things I enjoyed most—big brown biscuits and a great comb of honey surrounded with its nectar and a pitcher of milk and a plate of cheese and some jerked meat and an apple pie.

"Set right down an' eat—I just want to see ye eat—ayes I do!"

Aunt Deel was treating me like company and with just a pleasant touch of the old company finish in her voice and manner. It was for my benefit—there could be no doubt of that—for she addressed herself to me, chiefly, and not to Mr. Dunkelberg. My absence of a few days had seemed so long to them! It had raised me to the rank of company and even put me above the exalted Dunkelbergs although if Mrs. Horace Dunkelberg had been there in her blue silk and gold chain "big enough to drag a stone boat," as Aunt Deel used to say, she might have saved the day for them. Who knows? Aunt Deel was never much impressed by any man save Silas Wright, Jr.

Mr. Grimshaw came soon after we had finished our luncheon. He hitched his horse at the post and came in. He never shook hands with anybody. In all my life I have met no man of scanter amenities. All that kind of thing was, in his view, I think, a waste of time, a foolish encouragement to men who were likely to be seeking favors.

"Good day," he said, once and for all, as he came in at the open door. "Baynes, I want to have a talk with you and the boy."

I remember how each intake of his breath hissed through his lips as he sat down. How worn and faded were his clothes and hat, which was still on his head! The lines on his rugged brow and cheeks were deeper than ever.

"Tell me what you know about that murder," he demanded.

"Wal, I had some business over to Plattsburg," my uncle began. "While I was there I thought I'd go and see Amos. So I drove out to Beekman's farm. They told me that Amos had left there after workin' four days. They gave him fourteen shillin's an' he was goin' to take the stage in the mornin'. He left some time in the night an' took Beekman's rifle with him, so they said. There was a piece o' wood broke out o' the stock o' the rifle. That was the kind o' gun that was used in the murder."

It surprised me that my uncle knew all this. He had said nothing to me of his journey or its result.

"How do you know?" snapped Mr. Grimshaw.

"This boy see it plain. It was a gun with a piece o' wood broke out o' the stock."

"Is that so?" was the brusque demand of the money-lender as he turned to me.

"Yes, sir," I answered.

"The boy lies," he snapped, and turning to my uncle added: "Yer mad 'cause I'm tryin' to make ye pay yer honest debts—ain't ye now?"

We were stunned by this quick attack. Uncle Peabody rose suddenly and sat down again. Mr. Grimshaw looked at him with a strange smile and a taunting devilish laugh came out of his open lips.

Uncle Peabody, keeping his temper, shook his head and calmly said: "No I ain't anything ag'in' you or Amos, but it's got to be so that a man can travel the roads o' this town without gettin' his head blowed off."

Mr. Dunkelberg jumped into the breach then, saying:

"I told Mr. Grimshaw that you hadn't any grudge against him or his boy and that I knew you'd do what you could to help in this matter."

"Of course I'll help in any way I can," my uncle answered. "I couldn't harm him if I tried—not if he's innocent. All he's got to do is to prove where he was that night."

"Suppose he was lost in the woods?" Mr. Dunkelberg asked.

"The truth wouldn't harm him any," my uncle insisted. "Them tracks wouldn't fit his boots, an' they'd have to."

Mr. Dunkelberg turned to me and asked:

"Are you sure that the stock of the gun you saw was broken?"

"Yes, sir-and I'm almost sure it was Amos that ran away with it."

"Why?"

"I picked up a stone and threw it at him and it grazed the left side of his face, and the other night I saw the scar it made."

My aunt and uncle and Mr. Dunkelberg moved with astonishment as I spoke of the scar. Mr. Grimshaw, with keen eyes fixed upon me, gave a little grunt of incredulity.

"Huh!—Liar!" he muttered.

"I am not a liar," I declared with indignation, whereupon my aunt angrily stirred the fire in the stove and Uncle Peabody put his hand on my arm and said:

"Hush, Bart! Keep your temper, son."

"If you tell these things you may be the means of sending an innocent boy to his death," Mr. Dunkelberg said to me. "I wouldn't be too sure about 'em if I were you. It's so easy to be mistaken. You couldn't be sure in the dusk that the stone really hit him, could you?"

I answered: "Yes, sir—I saw the stone hit and I saw him put his hand on the place while he was running. I guess it hurt him some."

"Look a' here, Baynes," Mr. Grimshaw began in that familiar scolding tone of his. "I know what you want an' we might jest as well git right down to business first as last. You keep this boy still an' I'll give ye five years' interest."

Aunt Deel gave a gasp and quickly covered her mouth with her hand. Uncle Peabody changed color as he rose from his chair with a strange look on his face. He swung his big right hand in the air as he said:

"By the eternal jumpin'—"

He stopped, pulled down the left sleeve of his flannel shirt and walked to the water pail and drank out of the dipper.

"The times are hard," Grimshaw resumed in a milder tone. "These days the rich men dunno what's a-comin' to 'em. If you don't have no interest to pay you ought to git along easy an' give this boy the eddication of a Sile Wright."

There was that in his tone and face which indicated that in his opinion Sile had more "eddication" than any man needed.

"Say, Mr. Grimshaw, I'm awful sorry for ye," said my uncle as he returned to his chair, "but I've always learnt this boy to tell the truth an' the hull truth. I know the danger I'm in. We're gettin' old. It'll be hard to start over ag'in an' you can ruin us if ye want to an' I'm as scared o' ye as a mouse in a cat's paw, but this boy has got to tell the truth right out plain. I couldn't muzzle him if I tried—he's too much of a man. If you're scared o' the truth you mus' know that Amos is guilty."

Mr. Grimshaw shook his head with anger and beat the floor with the end of his cane.

"Nobody knows anything o' the kind, Baynes," said Mr. Dunkelberg. "Of course Amos never thought o' killing anybody. He's a harmless kind of a boy. I know him well and so do you. The only thing that anybody ever heard against him is that he's a little lazy. Under the circumstances Mr. Grimshaw is afraid that Bart's story will make it difficult for Amos to prove his innocence. Just think of it. That boy was lost and wandering around in the woods at the time o' the murder. As to that scar, Amos says that he ran into a stub when he was going through a thicket in the night."

Uncle Peabody shook his head with a look of firmness.

Again Grimshaw laughed between his teeth as he looked at my uncle. In his view every man had his price.

"I see that I'm the mouse an' you're the cat," he resumed, as that curious laugh rattled in his throat. "Look a' here, Baynes, I'll tell ye what I'll do. I'll cancel the hull mortgage."

Again Uncle Peabody rose from his chair with a look in his face which I have never forgotten. How his voice rang out!

"*No, sir!*" he shouted so loudly that we all jumped to our feet and Aunt Deel covered her face with her apron and began to cry. It was like the explosion of a blast. Then the fragments began falling with a loud crash:

"NO, SIR! YE CAN'T BUY THE NAIL ON MY LITTLE FINGER OR HIS WITH ALL YER MONEY—DAMN YOU!"

It was like the shout of Israel from the top of the mountains. Shep bounced into the house with hair on end and the chickens cackled and the old rooster clapped his wings and crowed with all the power of his lungs. Every member of that little group stood stock-still and breathless.

I trembled with a fear I could not have defined. Quick relief came when, straightway, my uncle went out of the room and stood on the stoop, back toward us, and blew his nose vigorously with his big red handkerchief. He stood still looking down and wiping his eyes. Mr. Grimshaw shuffled out of the door, his cane rapping the floor as if his arm had been stricken with palsy in a moment.

Mr. Dunkelberg turned to my aunt, his face scarlet, and muttered an apology for the disturbance and followed the money-lender.

I remember that my own eyes were wet as I went to my aunt and kissed her. She kissed me—a rare thing for her to do—and whispered brokenly but with a smile: "We'll go down to the poorhouse together, Bart, but we'll go honest."

"Come on, Bart," Uncle Peabody called cheerfully, as he walked toward the barnyard. "Le's go an' git in them but'nuts."

He paid no attention to our visitors—neither did my aunt, who followed us. The two men talked together a moment, unhitched their horses, got into their buggies and drove away. The great red rooster had stood on the fence eying them. As they turned their horses and drove slowly toward the gate, he clapped his wings and crowed lustily.

"Give it to 'em, ol' Dick," said Uncle Peabody with a clap of his hands. "Tell 'em what ye think of 'em."

At last the Dunkelbergs had fallen—the legendary, incomparable Dunkelbergs!

"Wal, I'm surprised at Mr. Horace Dunkelberg tryin' to come it over us like that—ayes! I be," said Aunt Deel.

"Wal, I ain't," said Uncle Peabody. "Ol' Grimshaw has got him under his thumb—that's what's the matter. You'll find he's up to his ears in debt to Grimshaw—prob'ly."

As we followed him toward the house, he pushing the wheelbarrow loaded with sacks of nuts, he added:

"At last Grimshaw has found somethin' that he can't buy an' he's awful surprised. Too bad he didn't learn that lesson long ago."

He stopped his wheelbarrow by the steps and we sat down together on the edge of the stoop as he added:

"I got mad—they kep' pickin' on me so—I'm sorry, but I couldn't help it. We'll start up ag'in somewheres if we have to. There's a good many days' work in me yet."

As we carried the bags to the attic room I thought of the lodestone and the compass and knew that Mr. Wright had foreseen what was likely to happen. When we came down Uncle Peabody said to me:

"Do you remember what you read out of a book one night about a man sellin' his honor?"

"Yes," I answered. "It's one o' the books that Mr. Wright gave us."

"It's somethin' purty common sense," he remarked, "an' we stopped and talked it over. I wish you'd git the book an' read it now."

I found the book and read aloud the following passage:

"Honor is a strange commodity. It can not be divided and sold in part. All or none is the rule of the market. While it can be sold in a way, it can not be truly bought. It vanishes in the transfer of its title and is no more. Who seeks to buy it gains only loss. It is the one thing which distinguishes manhood from property. Who sells his honor sells his manhood and becomes simply a thing of meat and blood and bones—a thing to be watched and driven and cudgelled like the ox—for he has sold that he can not buy, not if all the riches in the world were his."

A little silence followed the words. Then Uncle Peabody said:

"That's the kind o' stuff in our granary. We've been reapin' it out o' the books Mr. Grimshaw scolded about, a little here an' a little there for years, an' we knew it was good wheat. If he had books like that in his house mebbe Amos would 'a' been different. An' he'd 'a' been different. He wouldn't 'a' had to come here tryin' to buy our honor like you'd buy a hoss."

"Oh, dear!" Aunt Deel exclaimed wearily, with her hands over her eyes; "a boy has to have somethin' besides pigs an' cattle an' threats an' stones an' hoss dung an' cow manure to take up his mind."

Uncle Peabody voiced my own feeling when he said:

"I feel sorry, awful sorry, for that boy."

We spent a silent afternoon gathering apples. After supper we played Old Sledge and my uncle had hard work to keep us in good countenance. We went to bed early and I lay long hearing the autumn wind in the popple leaves and thinking of that great thing which had grown strong within us, little by little, in the candle-light.

CHAPTER XI

A PARTY AND—MY FOURTH PERIL?

"A dead fish can swim down-stream but only a live one can swim up it," said Uncle Peabody as we rode toward the village together. We had been talking of that strong current of evil which had tried to carry us along with it. I understood him perfectly.

It was a rainy Sunday. In the middle of the afternoon Uncle Peabody and I had set out in our spring buggy with the family umbrella—a faded but sacred implement, always carefully dried, after using, and hung in the clothes press. I remember that its folded skirt was as big around as my coat sleeve and that Uncle Peabody always grasped it in the middle, with hand about its waist, in a way of speaking, when he carried it after a shower. The rain came on again and with such violence that we were drenched to the skin in spite of the umbrella. It was still raining when we arrived at the familiar door in Ashery Lane. Uncle Peabody wouldn't stop.

"Water never scares a live fish," he declared with a chuckle as he turned around. "Good-by, Bart."

He hurried away. We pioneers rarely stopped or even turned out for the weather. Uncle Peabody used to say that the way to get sick was to change your clothes every time you got wet. It was growing dusk and I felt sorry for him.

"Come in," said the voice of the schoolmaster at the door. "There's good weather under this roof."

He saw my plight as I entered.

"I'm like a shaggy dog that's been in swimming," I said.

"Upon my word, boy, we're in luck," remarked the schoolmaster.

I looked up at him.

"Michael Henry's clothes!—sure, they're just the thing for you!"

"Will they go on me?" I asked, for, being large of my age, I had acquired an habitual shyness of things that were too small for me, and things, too, had seemed to have got the habit of being too small.

"As easily as Nick Tubbs goes on a spree, and far more becoming, for I do not think a spree ever looks worse than when Tubbs is on it. Come with me."

I followed him up-stairs, wondering how it had happened that Michael Henry had clothes.

He took me into his room and brought some handsome soft clothes out of a press with shirt, socks and boots to match.

"There, my laddie buck," said he, "put them on."

"These will soon dry on me," I said.

"Put them on—ye laggard! Michael Henry told me to give them to you. It's the birthday night o' little Ruth, my boy. There's a big cake with candles and chicken pie and jellied cookies and all the like o' that. Put them on. A wet boy at the feast would dampen the whole proceedings."

I put them on and with a great sense of relief and comfort. They were an admirable fit—too perfect for an accident, although at the time I thought only of their grandeur as I stood surveying myself in the looking-glass. They were of blue cloth and I saw that they went well with my blond hair and light skin. I was putting on my collar and necktie when Mr. Hacket returned.

"God bless ye, boy," said he. "There's not a bear in the township whose coat and trousers are a better fit. Sure if ye had on a beaver hat ye'd look like a lawyer or a statesman. Boy! How delighted Michael Henry will be! Come on now. The table is spread and the feast is waiting. Mind ye, give a good clap when I come in with the guest."

We went below and the table was very grand with its great frosted cake and its candles, in shiny brass sticks, and its jellies and preserves with the gleam of polished pewter among them. Mrs. Hacket and all the children, save Ruth, were waiting for us in the dining-room.

"Now sit down here, all o' ye, with Michael Henry," said the schoolmaster. "The little lady will be impatient. I'll go and get her and God help us to make her remember the day."

He was gone a moment, only, when he came back with Ruth in lovely white dress and slippers and gay with ribbons, and the silver beads of Mary on her neck. We clapped our hands and cheered and, in the excitement of the moment, John tipped over his drinking glass and shattered it on the floor.

"Never mind, my brave lad—no glass ever perished in a better cause. God bless you!"

What a merry time we had in spite of recurring thoughts of Uncle Peabody and the black horse toiling over the dark hills and flats in the rain toward the lonely farm and the lonelier, beloved woman who awaited him! There were many shadows in the way of happiness those days but, after all, youth has a way of speeding through them—hasn't it?

We ate and jested and talked, and the sound of our laughter drowned the cry of the wind in the chimney and the drumming of the rain upon the windows.

In the midst of it all Mr. Hacket arose and tapped his cup with his spoon.

"Oh you merry, God-blessed people," he said. "Michael Henry has bade me speak for him."

The schoolmaster took out of his pocketbook a folded sheet of paper. As he opened it a little, golden, black-tipped feather fell upon the table.

"Look! here is a plume o' the golden robin," the schoolmaster went on. "He dropped it in our garden yesterday to lighten ship, I fancied, before he left, the summer's work and play being ended. Ye should 'a' seen Michael Henry when he looked at the feather. How it tickled his fancy! I gave him my thought about it.

"'Nay, father,' he answered. 'Have ye forgotten that to-morrow is the birthday o' our little Ruth? The bird knew it and brought this gift to her. It is out o' the great gold mines o' the sky which are the richest in the world.'

"Then these lines came off his tongue, with no more hesitation about it than the bird has when he sings his song on a bright summer morning and I put them down to go with the feather. Here they are now:

"TO RUTH

"'Little lady, draw thy will
With this Golden Robin's quill—
Sun-stained, night-tipped, elfish thing—
Symbol of thy magic wing!

"'Give to me thy fairy lands
And palaces, on silver sands.
Oh will to me, my heart implores,
Their alabaster walls and floors!
Their gates that ope on Paradise
Or earth, or Eden in a trice.
Give me thy title to the hours
That pass in fair Aladdin towers.

But most I'd prize thy heavenly art
To win and lead the stony heart.
Give these to me that solemn day
Thou'rt done with them, I humbly pray.

"'Little lady, draw thy will
With this Golden Robin's quill.'"

He bowed to our young guest and kissed her hand and sat down in the midst of our cheering.

I remember well the delightful sadness that came into my heart on the musical voice of the reader. The lines, simple as they were, opened a new gate in my imagination beyond which I heard often the sound of music and flowing fountains and caught glimpses, now and then, of magic towers and walls of alabaster. There had been no fairies in Lickitysplit. Two or three times I had come upon fairy footprints in the books which Mr. Wright had sent to us, but neither my aunt nor my uncle could explain whence they came or the nature of their errand.

Mr. Hacket allowed me to write down the lines in my little diary of events and expenses, from which I have just copied them.

We sang and spoke pieces until nine o'clock and then we older members of the party fell to with Mrs. Hacket and washed and dried the dishes and put them away.

Next morning my clothes, which had been hung by the kitchen stove, were damp and wrinkled. Mr. Racket came to my room before I had risen.

"Michael Henry would rather see his clothes hanging on a good boy than on a nail in the closet," said he. "Sure they give no comfort to the nail at all."

"I guess mine are dry now," I answered.

"They're wet and heavy, boy. No son o' Baldur could keep a light heart in them. Sure ye'd be as much out o' place as a sunbeam in a cave o' bats. If ye care not for your own comfort think o' the poor lad in the green chair. He's that proud and pleased to see them on ye it would be a shame to reject his offer. Sure, if they were dry yer own garments would be good enough, God knows, but Michael Henry loves the look o' ye in these togs and then the President is in town."

That evening he discovered a big stain, black as ink, on my coat and trousers. Mr. Hacket expressed the opinion that it might have come from the umbrella but I am quite sure that he had spotted them to save me from the last home-made suit I ever wore, save in rough work, and keep Michael Henry's on my back. In any event I wore them no more save at chore time.

I began to make good progress in my studies that week and to observe the affection with which Mr. Hacket was regarded in the school and village. I remember that his eyes gave out and had to be bandaged but the boys and girls in his room behaved even better than before. It was curious to observe how the older ones controlled the younger in that emergency.

Sally came and went, with the Wills boy, and gave no heed to me. In her eyes I had no more substance than a ghost, it seemed to me, although I caught her, often, looking at me. I judged that her father had given her a bad report of us and had some regrets, in spite of my knowledge that we were right, although they related mostly to Amos.

Next afternoon I saw Mr. Wright and the President walking back and forth on the bridge as they talked together. A number of men stood in front of the blacksmith shop, by the river shore, watching them, as I passed, on my way to the mill on an errand. The two statesmen were in broadcloth and white linen and beaver hats. They stopped as I approached them.

"Well, partner, we shall be leaving in an hour or so," said Mr. Wright as he gave me his hand. "You may look for me here soon after the close of the session. Take care of yourself and go often to see Mrs. Wright and obey your captain and remember me to your aunt and uncle."

"See that you keep coming, my good boy," said the President as he gave me his hand, with playful reference, no doubt, to Mr. Wright's remark that I was a coming man.

"Bart, I've some wheat to be threshed in the barn on the back lot," said the Senator as I was leaving them. "You can do it Saturdays, if you care to, at a shilling an hour. Stack the straw out-of-doors until you've finished then put it back in the bay. Winnow the wheat carefully and sack it and bring it down to the granary and I'll settle with you when I return."

I remember that a number of men who worked in Grimshaw's saw-mill were passing as he spoke.

"Yes, sir," I answered, much elated by the prospect of earning money.

I left with a feeling of keen disappointment that I was to see so little of my distinguished friend and a thought of the imperious errands of men which put the broad reaches of the earth between friend and friend.

I remember repeating to myself the words of the Senator which began: "You may look for me here soon after the close of the session," in the tone in which he had said them. As of old, I admired and tried to imitate his dignity of speech and bearing.

When I returned from the mill they were gone.

The examination of Amos was set down for Monday and the people of the village were stirred and shaken by wildest rumors regarding the evidence to be adduced. Every day men and women stopped me in the Street to ask what I knew of the murder. I followed the advice of Bishop Perkins and kept my knowledge to myself.

My life went on at the same kindly, merry pace in the home of the schoolmaster. The bandages over his eyes had in no way clouded his spirit.

"Ah, now, I wish that I could see you," he said one evening when we were all laughing at some remark of his. "I love the look of a merry face."

I continued to wear the mysterious clothes of Michael Henry, save at chore time, when I put on the spotted suit of homespun. I observed that it made a great difference with my social standing. I was treated with a greater deference at the school, and Elizabeth Allen invited me to her party, to which, however, I had not the courage to go, having no idea what happened to one at a village party.

I asked a boy in my Latin class to tell me.

"Oh, ye just fly around an' kiss and git kissed till ye feel like a fool."

That settled it for me. Not that I would have failed to enjoy kissing Sally, but we were out, as they used to say, and it would have embarrassed both of us to meet at a party.

Saturday came and, when the chores were done, I went alone to the grain barn in the back lot of the Senator's farm with flail and measure and broom and fork and shovel and sacks and my luncheon, in a push cart, with all of which Mrs. Wright had provided me.

It was a lonely place with woods on three sides of the field and a road on the other. I kept laying down beds of wheat on the barn-floor and beating them out with the flail until the sun was well over the roof when I sat down to eat my luncheon. Then I swept up the grain and winnowed out the chaff and filled one of my sacks. That done, I covered the floor again and the thump of the flail eased my loneliness until in the middle of the afternoon two of my schoolmates came and asked me to go swimming, with them. The river was not forty rods away and a good trail led to the swimming hole. It was a warm bright day and I was hot and thirsty. The thought of cool waters and friendly companionship was too much for me. I went with them.

More ancient than the human form is that joy of the young in the feel of air and water on the naked skin, in the frog-like leap and splash and the monkey-chatter of the swimming hole. There were a number of the "swamp boys" in the water. They lived in cabins on the edges of the near swamp. I stayed with them longer than I intended. I remember saying as I dressed that I should have to work late and go without my supper in order to finish my stent.

It was almost dark when I was putting the last sack of wheat into my cart, in the gloomy barn, and getting ready to go.

A rustling in the straw near where I stood stopped me suddenly. My skin prickled and began to stir on my head and my feet and hands felt numb with a new fear. I heard stealthy footsteps in the darkness. I stood my ground and demanded:

"Who's there?"

I saw a form approaching in the gloom with feet as noiseless as a cat's. I took a step backward and, seeing that it was a woman, stopped.

"It's Kate," the answer came in a hoarse whisper as I recognized her form and staff.

"Run, boy—they have just come out o' the woods. I saw them. They will take you away. Run."

She had picked up the flail and now she put it in my hands and gave me a push toward the door. I ran, and none too quickly, for I had not gone fifty feet from the barn in the stubble when I heard them coming after me, whoever they were. I saw that they were gaining and turned quickly. I had time to raise my flail and bring it down upon the head of the leader, who fell as I had seen a beef fall under the ax. Another man stopped beyond the reach of my flail and, after a second's hesitation, turned and ran away in the darkness.

I could hear or see no other motion in the field. I turned and ran on down the slope toward the village. In a moment I saw some one coming out of the maple grove at the field's end, just ahead, with a lantern.

Then I heard the voice of the schoolmaster saying:

"Is it you, my lad?"

"Yes," I answered, as I came up to him and Mary, in a condition of breathless excitement.

I told them of the curious adventure I had had.

"Come quick," said the schoolmaster. "Let's go back and find the man in the stubble."

I remembered that I had struck the path in my flight just before stopping to swing the flail. The man must have fallen very near it. Soon we found where he had been lying and drops of fresh blood on the stubble.

"Hush," said the schoolmaster.

We listened and heard a wagon rattling at a wild pace down the road toward the river.

"There he goes," said Mr. Hacket. "His companions have carried him away. Ye'd be riding in that wagon now, yerself, my brave lad, if ye hadn't 'a' made a lucky hit with the flail—God bless ye!"

"What would they 'a' done with me?" I asked.

"Oh, I reckon they'd 'a' took ye off, lad, and kep' ye for a year or so until Amos was out o' danger," said Mr. Hacket. "Maybe they'd drowned ye in the river down there an' left yer clothes on the bank to make it look like an honest drowning. The devil knows what they'd 'a' done with ye, laddie buck. We'll have to keep an eye on ye now, every day until the trial is over—sure we will. Come, we'll go up to the barn and see if Kate is there."

Just then we heard the receding wagon go roaring over the bridge on Little River. Mary shuddered with fright. The schoolmaster reassured us by saying:

"Don't be afraid. I brought my gun in case we'd meet a painter. But the danger is past."

He drew a long pistol from his coat pocket and held it in the light of the lantern.

The loaded cart stood in the middle of the barn floor, where I had left it, but old Kate had gone. We closed the barn, drawing the cart along with us. When we came into the edge of the village I began to reflect upon the strange peril out of which I had so luckily escaped. It gave me a heavy sense of responsibility and of the wickedness of men.

I thought, of old Kate and her broken silence. For once I had heard her speak. I could feel my flesh tingle when I thought of her quick words and her hoarse passionate whisper. She must have come into the barn while I was swimming and hidden behind the straw heap in the rear end of it and watched the edge of the woods through the many cracks in the boarding.

I knew, or thought I knew, why she took such care of me. She was in league with the gallows and could not bear to see it cheated of its prey. For some reason she hated the Grimshaws. I had seen the hate in her eyes the day she dogged along behind the old money-lender through the streets of the village when her pointing finger had seemed to say to me: "There, there is the man who has brought me to this. He has put these rags upon my back, this fire in my heart, this wild look in my eyes. Wait and you shall see what I will put upon him."

I knew that old Kate was not the irresponsible, witless creature that people thought her to be. I had begun to think of her with a kind of awe as one gifted above all others. One by one the things she had said of the future seemed to be coming true.

When we had pulled the cart into the stable I tried to shift one of the bags of grain and observed that my hands trembled and that it seemed very heavy.

As we were going into the house the schoolmaster said:

"Now, Mary, you take this lantern and go across the street to the house o' Deacon Binks, the constable. You'll find him asleep by the kitchen stove. Arrest his slumbers, but not rudely, and, when he has come to, tell him that I have news o' the devil."

"This shows the power o' knowledge. Bart," he said to me when we entered the house.

I wondered what he meant and he went on:

"You have knowledge of the shooting that no other man has. You could sell it for any money ye would ask. Only ye can't sell it, now, because it's about an evil thing. But suppose ye knew more than any other man about the law o' contracts, or the science o' bridge building, or the history o' nations or the habits o' bugs or whatever. Then ye become the principal witness in a different kind o' case. Then it's proper to sell yer knowledge for the good o' the world and they'll be as eager to get it as they are what ye know about the shooting. And nobody'll want to kill ye. Every man o' them'll want to keep ye alive. But mind, ye must be the *principal witness*."

Deacon Binks arrived, a fat man with a big round body and a very wise and serious countenance between side whiskers bending from his temple to his neck and suggesting parentheses of hair, as if his head and its accessories were in the nature of a side issue. He and the schoolmaster went out-of-doors and must have talked together while I was eating a bowl of bread and milk which Mrs. Hacket had brought to me.

When I went to bed, by and by, I heard somebody snoring on the little porch under my window. The first sound that reached my ear at the break of dawn was the snoring of the same sleeper. I dressed and went below and found the constable in his coon-skin overcoat asleep on the porch with a long-barreled gun at his side. While I stood there the schoolmaster came around the corner of the house from the garden. He smiled as he saw the deacon.

"Talk about the placid rest of Egyptian gods!" he exclaimed. "Look at the watchful eye o' Justice. How well she sleeps in this peaceful valley! Sometimes ye can hardly wake her up at all, at all."

He put his hand on the deacon's shoulder and gave him a little shake.

"Awake, ye limb o' the law," he demanded. "Prayer is better than sleep."

The deacon arose and stretched himself and cleared his throat and assumed an air of alertness and said it was a fine morning, which it was not, the sky being overcast and the air dank and chilly. He removed his greatcoat and threw it on the stoop saying:

"Deacon, you lay there. From now on I'm constable and ready for any act that may be necessary to maintain the law. I can be as severe as Napoleon Bonaparte and as cunning as Satan, if I have to be."

I remember that through the morning's work the sleepy deacon and the alert constable contended over the possession of his stout frame.

The constable shouldered the gun and followed me into the pasture where I went to get the cow. I saw now that his intention was to guard me from further attacks. While I was milking, the deacon sat on a bucket in the doorway of the stable and snored until I had finished. He awoke when I loosed the cow and the constable went back to the pasture with me, yawning with his hand over his mouth much of the way. The deacon leaned his elbow on the top of the pen and snored again, lightly, while I mixed the feed for the pigs.

Mr. Hacket met us at the kitchen door, where Deacon Binks said to him:

"If you'll look after the boy to-day, I'll go home and get a little rest."

"God bless yer soul, ye had a busy night," said the schoolmaster with a smile.

He added as he went into the house:

"I never knew a man to rest with more energy and persistence. It was a perfect flood o' rest. It kept me awake until long after midnight."

CHAPTER XII

THE SPIRIT OF MICHAEL HENRY AND OTHERS

That last peril is one of the half-solved mysteries of my life. The following affidavit, secured by an assistant of the district attorney from a young physician in a village above Ballybeen, never a matter of record, heightened its interest for me and my friends.

"Deponent saith that about eleven o'clock on the evening of the, 24th of September (that on which the attack upon me was made) a man unknown to him called at his office and alleged that a friend of the stranger had been injured and was in need of surgical aid. He further alleged that his friend was in trouble and being sought after and that he, the caller, dared not, therefore, reveal the place where his friend had taken refuge. He offered the deponent the sum of ten dollars to submit to the process of blindfolding and of being conducted to I said place for the purpose of giving relief to the injured man. Whereupon the deponent declares that he submitted to said process and was conducted by wagon and trail to a bark shanty at some place in the woods unknown to him where the bandage was removed from his eyes. He declares further that he found there, a strong built, black-bearded man about thirty years of age, and a stranger to him, lying on a bed of boughs in the light of a fire and none other. This man was groaning in great pain from a wound made by some heavy weapon on the side of his head. The flesh of the cheek and ear were swollen and lacerated. Deponent further declares that he administered an opiate and dressed and put a number of stitches in the injured parts and bound them with a bandage soaked in liniment. Then deponent returned to his home, blindfolded as he had left it. He declares that the time consumed in the journey from the shanty to his home was one hour and ten minutes."

It should be said that, in the theory of the district attorney the effort to retire the principal witness, if, indeed, that were the intention of their pursuit of me, originated in the minds of lawless and irresponsible men. I know that there are those who find a joy in creating mysteries and defeating the law, but let it be set down here that I have never concurred in the views of that able officer.

At the examination of Amos Grimshaw my knowledge was committed to the records and ceased to be a source of danger to me. Grimshaw came to the village that day. On my way to the court room I saw him walking slowly, with bent head as I had seen him before, followed by old Kate. She carried her staff in her left hand while the forefinger of her right was pointing him out. Silent as a ghost and as unheeded—one would say—she followed his steps.

I remember when I went on the stand my eyes filled with tears. Amos gave me an appealing look that went to my heart. It was hard for me to tell the truth that day—never has it been so hard. If I had had the riches of Grimshaw himself I would have given them to be relieved. Was there nothing that I could do for Amos?

I observed that old Kate sat on a front seat with her hand to her ear and Grimshaw beside his lawyer at a big table and that when she looked at him her lips moved in a strange unuttered whisper of her spirit. Her face filled with joy as one damning detail after another came out in the evidence.

Aunt Deel and Uncle Peabody came to the village that day and sat in the court room. They had dinner with us at the schoolmaster's, but I had little chance to talk with them. Aunt Deel went up to my room with me and slyly gave me some fresh cookies wrapped in a piece of newspaper which she carried in a little basket bought from the Indians.

"Here's somethin' else," she said. "I was keepin' 'em for Chris'mas—ayes!—but it's so cold I guess ye better have 'em now—ayes!"

Then she gave me a pair of mittens with a red fringe around the wristbands, and two pairs of socks.

I remember that my uncle laughed at the jests of Mr. Hacket but said little and was not, I thought, in good spirits. They went home before the examination ended.

The facts hereinbefore alleged, and others, were proven, for the tracks fitted the shoes of Amos. The young man was held and presently indicted. The time of his trial was not determined.

I received much attention from young and old in the village after that, for I found soon that I had acquired a reputation for bravery, of the slender foundation for which the reader is well aware. I was invited to many parties, but had not much heart for them and went only to one at the home of Nettie Barrows. Sally was there. She came to me as if nothing had interrupted our friendship and asked if I would play Hunt the Squirrel with them. Of course I was glad to make this treaty of peace, which was sealed with many kisses as we played together in those lively games of the old time. I remember that I could think of nothing in this world with which to compare her beauty. I asked if I could walk home with her and she said that she was engaged, and while she was as amiable as ever I came to know that night that a kind of wall had risen between us.

I wrote a good hand those days and the leading merchant of the village engaged me to post his books every Saturday at ten cents an hour. Thenceforward until Christmas I gave my free days to that task. I estimated the sum that I should earn and planned to divide it in equal parts and proudly present it to my aunt and uncle on Christmas day.

One Saturday while I was at work on the big ledger of the merchant I ran upon this item:

October 3. S. Wright—To one suit of
clothes for Michael Henry
from measures furnished by
S. Robinson $14.30
Shirts to match 1.70

I knew then the history of the suit of clothes which I had worn since that rainy October night, for I remembered that Sam Robinson, the tailor, had measured me at our house and made up the cloth of Aunt Deel's weaving.

I observed, also, that numerous articles—a load of wood, two sacks of flour, three pairs of boots, one coat, ten pounds of salt pork and four bushels of potatoes—all for "Michael Henry" had been charged to Silas Wright.

So by the merest chance I learned that the invisible "Michael Henry" was the almoner of the modest statesman and really the spirit of Silas Wright feeding the hungry and clothing the naked and warming the cold house, in the absence of its owner. It was the heart of Wright joined to that of the schoolmaster, which sat in the green chair.

I fear that my work suffered a moment's interruption, for just then I began to know the great heart of the Senator. Its warmth was in the clothing that covered my back, its delicacy in the ignorance of those who had shared its benefactions.

I count this one of the great events of my youth. But there was a greater one, although it seemed not so at the time of it. A traveler on the road to Ballybeen had dropped his pocketbook containing a large amount of money—two thousand seven hundred dollars was the sum, if I remember rightly. He was a man who, being justly suspicious of the banks, had withdrawn his money. Posters announced the loss and the offer of a large reward. The village was profoundly stirred by them. Searching parties went up the road stirring its dust and groping in its grass and briers for the great prize which was supposed to be lying there. It was said, however, that the quest had been unsuccessful. So the lost pocketbook became a treasured mystery of the village and of all the hills and valleys toward Ballybeen—a topic of old wives and gabbing husbands at the fireside for unnumbered years.

By and by the fall term of school ended. Uncle Peabody came down to get me the day before Christmas. I had enjoyed my work and my life at the Hackets', on the whole, but I was glad to be going home again. My uncle was in high spirits and there were many packages in the sleigh.

"A merry Christmas to ye both an' may the Lord love ye!" said Mr. Hacket as he bade us good-by. "Every day our thoughts will be going up the hills to your house."

As he was tucking the blankets around my feet old Nick Tubbs came zigzagging up the road from the tavern.

"What stimulation travels with that man!" said the schoolmaster. "He might be worse, God knows. Reeling minds are worse than reeling bodies. Some men are born drunk like our friend Colonel Hand and that kind is beyond reformation."

The bells rang merrily as we hurried through the swamp in the hard snow paths.

"We're goin' to move," said my uncle presently. "We've agreed to get out by the middle o' May."

"How does that happen?" I asked.

"I settled with Grimshaw and agreed to go. If it hadn't 'a' been for Wright and Baldwin we wouldn't 'a' got a cent. They threatened to bid against him at the sale. So he settled. We're goin' to have a new home. We've bought a hundred an' fifty acres from Abe Leonard. Goin' to build a new house in the spring. It will be nearer the village."

He playfully nudged my ribs with his elbow.

"We've had a little good luck, Bart," he went on. "I'll tell ye what it is if you won't say anything about it."

I promised.

"I dunno as it would matter much," he continued, "but I don't want to do any braggin'. It ain't anybody's business but ours, anyway. An old uncle over in Vermont died three weeks ago and left us thirty-eight hundred dollars. It was old Uncle Ezra Baynes o' Hinesburg. Died without a chick or child. Your aunt and me slipped down to Potsdam an' took the stage an' went over an' got the money. It was more money than I ever see before in my life. We put it in the bank in Potsdam to keep it out o' Grimshaw's hands. I wouldn't trust that man as fur as you could throw a bull by the tail."

It was a cold clear night and when we reached home the new stove was snapping with the heat in its fire-box and the pudding puffing in the pot and old Shep dreaming in the chimney corner. Aunt Deel gave me a hug at the door. Shep barked and leaped to my shoulders.

"Why, Bart! You're growin' like a weed—ain't ye?—ayes ye be," my aunt said as she stood and looked at me. "Set right down here an' warm ye—ayes!—I've done all the chores—ayes!"

How warm and comfortable was the dear old room with those beloved faces in it. I wonder if paradise itself can seem more pleasant to me. I have had the best food this world can provide in my time, but never anything that I ate with a keener relish than the pudding and milk and bread and butter and cheese and pumpkin pie which Aunt Deel gave us that night.

Supper over, I wiped the dishes for my aunt while Uncle Peabody went out to feed and water the horses. Then we sat down in the genial warmth while I told the story of my life in "the busy town," as they called it. What pride and attention they gave me then!

Three days before they had heard of my adventure with the flail, as to which Mr. Hacket, the district attorney and myself had maintained the strictest reticence. It seemed that the deacon had blabbed, as they used to say, regarding his own brave part in the subsequent proceedings.

My fine clothes and the story of how I had come by them taxed my ingenuity somewhat, although not improperly. I had to be careful not to let them know that I had been ashamed of the home-made suit. They, somehow, felt the truth about it and a little silence followed the story. Then Aunt Deel drew her chair near me and touched my hair very gently and looked into my face without speaking.

"Ayes! I know," she said presently, in a kind of caressing tone, with a touch of sadness in it. "They ain't used to coarse homespun stuff down there in the village. They made fun o' ye—didn't they, Bart?"

"I don't care about that," I assured them. "'The mind's the measure of the man,'" I quoted, remembering the lines the Senator had repeated to me.

"That's sound!" Uncle Peabody exclaimed with enthusiasm.

Aunt Deel took my hand in hers and surveyed it thoughtfully for a moment without speaking.

"You ain't goin' to have to suffer that way no more," she said in a low tone.

I rose and went to the parlor door.

"Ye mustn't go in there," she warned me.

Delightful suspicions came out of the warning and their smiles.

"We're goin' to be more comf'table—ayes," said Aunt Deel as I resumed my chair. "Yer uncle thought we better go west, but I couldn't bear to go off so fur an' leave mother an' father an' sister Susan an' all the folks we loved layin' here in the ground alone—I want to lay down with 'em by an' by an' wait for the sound o' the trumpet—ayes!—mebbe it'll be for thousands o' years—ayes!"

"You don't suppose their souls are a-sleepin' there—do ye?" my uncle asked.

"That's what the Bible says," Aunt Deel answered.

"Wal the Bible—?" Uncle Peabody stopped. What was in his mind we may only imagine.

To our astonishment the clock struck twelve.

"Hurrah! It's merry Christmas!" said Uncle Peabody as he jumped to his feet and began to sing of the little Lord Jesus.

We joined him while he stood beating time with his right hand after the fashion of a singing master.

"Off with yer boots, friend!" he exclaimed when the stanza was finished. "We don't have to set up and watch like the shepherds."

We drew our boots on the chair round with hands clasped over the knee—how familiar is the process, and yet I haven't seen it in more than half a century! I lighted a candle and scampered up-stairs in my stocking feet, Uncle Peabody following close and slapping my thigh as if my pace were not fast enough for him. In the midst of our skylarking the candle tumbled to the floor and I had to go back to the stove and relight it.

How good it seemed to be back in the old room under the shingles! The heat of the stove-pipe had warmed its hospitality.

"It's been kind o' lonesome here," said Uncle Peabody as he opened the window. "I always let the wind come in to keep me company—it gits so warm."

I lay down between flannel sheets on the old feather bed. What a stage of dreams and slumbers it had been, for it was now serving the third generation of Bayneses! The old popple tree had thrown off its tinkling cymbals and now the winter wind hissed and whistled in its stark branches.

Then the deep, sweet sleep of youth from which it is a joy and a regret to come back to the world again. I wish that I could know it once more.

"Ye can't look at yer stockin' yit," said Aunt Deel when I came down-stairs about eight o'clock, having slept through chore time. I remember it was the delicious aroma of frying ham and buckwheat cakes which awoke me, and who wouldn't rise and shake off the cloak of slumber on a bright, cold winter morning with such provocation?

"This ain't no common Chris'mas—I tell ye," Aunt Deel went on. "Santa Claus won't git here short o' noon I wouldn't wonder—ayes!"

"By thunder!" exclaimed Uncle Peabody as he sat down at the table. "This is goin' to be a day o' pure fun—genuwine an' uncommon. Take some griddlers," he added as three or four of them fell on my plate. "Put on plenty o' ham gravy an' molasses. This ain't no Jackman tavern. I got hold o' somethin' down there that tasted so I had to swaller twice on it."

About eleven o'clock Uncle Hiram and Aunt Eliza and their five children arrived with loud and merry greetings. Then came other aunts and uncles and cousins. With what noisy good cheer the men entered the house after they had put up their horses! I remember how they laid their hard, heavy hands on my head and shook it a little as they spoke of my "stretchin' up" or gave me a playful slap on the shoulder—an ancient token of good will—the first form of the accolade, I fancy. What joyful good humor there was in those simple men and women!—enough to temper the woes of a city if it could have been applied to their relief. They stood thick around the stove warming themselves and taking off its griddles and opening its doors and surveying it inside and out with much curiosity.

Suddenly Uncle Hiram tried to put Uncle Jabez in the wood-box while the others laughed noisily. I remember that my aunts rallied me on my supposed liking for "that Dunkelberg girl."

"Now for the Chris'mas tree," said Uncle Peabody as he led the way into our best room, where a fire was burning in the old Franklin grate. "Come on, boys an' girls."

What a wonderful sight was the Christmas tree—the first we had had in our house—a fine spreading balsam loaded with presents! Uncle Hiram jumped into the air and clapped his feet together and shouted: "Hold me, somebody, or I'll grab the hull tree an' run away with it."

Uncle Jabez held one foot in both hands before him and joyfully hopped around the tree.

These relatives had brought their family gifts, some days before, to be hung on its branches. The thing that caught my eye was a big silver watch hanging by a long golden chain to one of the boughs. Uncle Peabody took it down and held it aloft by the chain, so that none should miss the sight, saying:

"From Santa Claus for Bart!"

A murmur of admiration ran through the company which gathered around me as I held the treasure in my trembling hands.

"This is for Bart, too," Uncle Peabody shouted as he took down a bolt of soft blue cloth and laid it in my arms. "Now there's somethin' that's jest about as slick as a kitten's ear. Feel of it. It's for a suit o' clothes. Come all the way from Burlington."

"Good land o' Goshen! Don't be in such a hurry," said Aunt Deel.

"Sorry, but the stage can't wait for nobody at all—it's due to leave right off," Uncle Peabody remarked as he laid a stuffed stocking on top of the cloth and gave me a playful slap and shouted: "Get-ap, there. You've got yer load."

I moved out of the way in a hurricane of merriment. It was his one great day of pride and vanity. He did not try to conceal them.

The other presents floated for a moment in this irresistible tide of laughing good will and found their owners. I have never forgotten how Uncle Jabez chased Aunt Minerva around the house with a wooden snake cunningly carved and colored. I observed there were many things on the tree which had not been taken down when we younger ones gathered up our wealth and repaired to Aunt Deel's room to feast our eyes upon it and compare our good fortune.

The women and the big girls rolled up their sleeves and went to work with Aunt Deel preparing the dinner. The great turkey and the chicken pie were made ready and put in the oven and the potatoes and the onions and the winter squash were soon boiling in their pots on the stove-top. Meanwhile the children were playing in my aunt's bedroom and Uncle Hiram and Uncle Jabez were pulling sticks in a corner while the other men sat tipped against the wall watching and making playful comments—all save my Uncle Peabody, who was trying to touch his head to the floor and then straighten up with the aid of the broomstick.

By and by I sat on top of the wood with which I had just filled the big wood-box and very conscious of the shining chain on my breast. Suddenly the giant, Rodney Barnes, jumped out of his chair and, embracing the wood-box, lifted it and the wood and me in his great arms and danced lightly around a group of the ladies with his burden and set it down in its place again very gently. What a hero he became in my eyes after that!

"If ye should go off some day an' come back an' find yer house missin' ye may know that Rodney Barnes has been here," said Uncle Hiram. "A man as stout as Rodney is about as dangerous as a fire."

Then what Falstaffian peals of laughter!

In the midst of it Aunt Deel opened the front door and old Kate, the Silent Woman, entered. To my surprise, she wore a decent-looking dress of gray homespun cloth and a white cloud looped over her head and ears and tied around her neck and a good pair of boots.

"Merry Chris'mas!" we all shouted.

She smiled and nodded her head and sat down in the chair which Uncle Peabody had placed for her at the stove side. Aunt Deel took the cloud off her head while Kate drew her mittens—newly knitted of the best yarn. Then my aunt brought some stockings and a shawl from the tree and laid them on the lap of old Kate. What a silence fell upon us as we saw tears coursing down the cheeks of this lonely old woman of the countryside!—tears of joy, doubtless, for God knows how long it had been since the poor, abandoned soul had seen a merry Christmas and shared its kindness. I did not fail to observe how clean her face and hands looked! She was greatly changed.

She took my hand as I went to her side and tenderly caressed it. A gentler smile came to her face than ever I had seen upon it. The old stern look returned for a moment as she held one finger aloft in a gesture which only I and my Aunt Deel understood. We knew it signalized a peril and a mystery. That I should have to meet it, somewhere up the hidden pathway, I had no doubt whatever.

"Dinner's ready!" exclaimed the cheerful voice of Aunt Deel.

Then what a stirring of chairs and feet as we sat down at the table. Old Kate sat by the side of my aunt and we were all surprised at her good manners.

Uncle Jabez—a member of the white church—prayed for a moment as we sat with bowed heads. I have never forgotten his simple eloquence as he prayed for the poor and for him who was sitting in the shadow of death (I knew that he referred to Amos Grimshaw and whispered amen) and for our forgiveness.

We jested and laughed and drank cider and reviewed the year's history and ate as only they may eat who have big bones and muscles and the vitality of oxen. I never taste the flavor of sage and currant jelly or hear a hearty laugh without thinking of those holiday dinners in the old log house on Rattleroad.

Some of the men and two of the women filled their pipes and smoked while the dishes were being picked up and washed. By and by the men and the big boys went with us down to the brook where we chopped holes in the ice to give the sheep and the cattle a chance to drink. Then they looked at the horses.

"Peabody you mus' be gittin' rich," said Hiram Bentley.

"No I ain't. I've had to give up here, but a little windfall come to us t'other day from an old uncle in Vermont. It ain't nothin' to brag of, but it'll give us a start an' we thought that while we had the money we'd do somethin' that we've been wantin' to do for years an' years—give a Chris'mas—an' we've done it. The money'll go some way an' we may never have another chance. Bart is a good boy an' we made up our minds he'd enjoy it better now than he ever would ag'in."

That Christmas brought me nothing better than those words, the memory of which is one of the tallest towers in that long avenue of my past down which I have been looking these many days. About all you can do for a boy, worth while, is to give him something good to remember.

The day had turned dark. The temperature had risen and the air was dank and chilly. The men began to hitch up their horses.

"Kind o' thawin' a little," said Uncle Hiram as he got into his sleigh and drove up to the door. "Come on, there. Stop yer cacklin' an' git into this sleigh," he shouted in great good humor to the women and children who stood on the porch. "It'll be snowin' like sixty 'fore we git home."

So, one by one, the sleighloads left us with cheery good-bys and a grinding of runners and a jingling of bells. When the last had gone Uncle Peabody and I went into the house. Aunt Deel sat by the stove, old Kate by the window looking out at the falling dusk. How still the house seemed!

"There's one thing I forgot," I said as I proudly took out of my wallet the six one-dollar bills which I had earned by working Saturdays and handed three of them to my aunt and three to my uncle, saying:

"That is my Christmas present to you. I earned it myself."

I remember so well their astonishment and the trembling of their hands and the look of their faces.

"It's grand—ayes!" Aunt Deel said in a low tone.

She rose in a moment and beckoned to me and my uncle. We followed her through the open door to the other room.

"I'll tell ye what I'd do," she whispered. "I'd give 'em to ol' Kate—ayes! She's goin' to stay with us till to-morrow."

"Good idee!" said Uncle Peabody.

So I took the money out of their hands and went in and gave it to the Silent Woman.

"That's your present from me," I said.

How can I forget how she held my arm against her with that loving, familiar, rocking motion of a woman who is soothing a baby at her breast and kissed my coat sleeve? She released my arm and, turning to the window, leaned her head upon its sill and shook with sobs. The dusk had thickened. As I returned to my seat by the stove I could dimly see her form against the light of the window. We sat in silence for a little while.

Aunt Deel broke it by singing in a low tone as she rocked:

"My days are passing swiftly by
And I—a pilgrim stranger—
Would not detain them as they fly,
These days of toil and danger."

Uncle Peabody rose and got a candle and lighted it at the hearth.

"Wal, Bart, we'll do the chores, an' then I warn ye that we're goin' to have some fun," he said as he got his lantern. "There's goin' to be some Ol' Sledge played here this evenin' an' I wouldn't wonder if Kate could beat us all."

I held the lantern while Uncle Peabody fed the sheep and the two cows and milked—a slight chore these winter days.

"There's nothing so cold on earth as a fork stale on a winter night," he remarked as he was pitching the hay. "Wish I'd brought my mittens."

"You and I are to go off to bed purty early," he said as we were going back to the house. "Yer Aunt Deel wants to see Kate alone and git her to talk if she can."

Kate played with us, smiling now and then at my uncle's merry ways and words, but never speaking. It was poor fun, for the cards seemed to take her away from us into other scenes so that she had to be reminded of her turn to play.

"I dunno but she'll swing back into this world ag'in," said Uncle Peabody when we had gone up to our little room. "I guess all she needs is to be treated like a human bein'. Yer Aunt Deel an' I couldn't git over thinkin' o' what she done for you that night in the ol' barn. So I took some o' yer aunt's good clothes to her an' a pair o' boots an' asked her to come to Chris'mas. She lives in a little room over the blacksmith shop down to Butterfield's mill. I told her I'd come after her with the cutter but she shook her head. I knew she'd rather walk."

He was yawning as he spoke and soon we were both asleep under the shingles.

CHAPTER XIII

THE THING AND OTHER THINGS

I returned to Mr. Hacket's house late in the afternoon of New Year's day. The schoolmaster was lying on a big lounge in a corner of their front room with the children about him. The dusk was falling.

"Welcome, my laddie buck!" he exclaimed as I entered. "We're telling stories o' the old year an' you're just in time for the last o' them. Sit down, lad, and God give ye patience! It'll soon be over."

Little John led me into the group and the schoolmaster began:—Let us call this bit of a story: *The Guide to Paradise.*

"One day in early June I was lyin' under the big apple tree in the garden—sure I was. It was all white and sweet with the blossoms like a bride in her veil—an' I heard the hum o' the bee's wing an' odors o' the upper world come down to me. I was lookin' at the little bird house that we had hung in the tree-top. Of a sudden I saw a tiny bit o' a 'warf—no longer than the thumb o' Mary—God love her!—on its wee porch an' lookin' down at me.

"'Good luck to ye!' says I. 'Who are you?'

"'Who do ye think I am?' says he.

"'Nobody,' says I.

"'That's just who I am,' says he, 'I'm Nobody from Nowhere—God save you from the like.'

"'Glad to see ye,' says I.

"'Glad to be seen,' says he. 'There's a mighty few people can see me.'

"'Looks to me as if ye were tellin' the truth,' says I.

"'Nobody is the only one that always tells the truth—God help ye,' says he. 'And here's a big chunk o' it. Not one in a thousand ever gets the feet o' his mind in the land o' Nowhere—better luck to them!'

"'Where is it?' says I.

"'Up above the earth where the great God keeps His fiddle,' says he.

"'What fiddle?' says I.

"'The fiddle o' silence,' says he. 'Sure, I'm playin' it now. It has long strings o' gold that reach 'way out across the land o' Nowhere—ye call 'em stars. The winds and the birds play on it. Sure, the birds are my hens.'

"He clapped his little hands and down came a robin and sat beside him. Nobody rumpled up the feathers on her back and she queed like she was goin' to peck me—the hussy!

"'She's my watch hen,' says Nobody. 'Guards the house and lays eggs for me—the darlin'! Sure, I've a wonderful farm up here in the air—millions o' acres, and the flowers and the tops o' the trees and the gold mines o' the sky are in it. The flowers are my cattle and the bees are my hired men. Do ye see 'em milkin' this big herd o' apple-blossoms? My hired men carry their milk away to the hollow trees and churn it into honey. There's towers and towers of it in the land o' Nowhere. If it wasn't for Nowhere your country would be as dark as a pocket and as dry as dust—sure it would. Somewhere must be next to Nowhere—or it wouldn't be anywhere, I'm thinkin'. All the light and rain and beauty o' the world come out o' Nowhere—don't they? We have the widest ocean up here with wonderful ships. I call it God's ferry. Ye see, Nowhere is not to be looked down upon just because ye don't find it in Mary's geography. There's lots o' things ye don't know, man. I'm one o' them. What do ye think o' me?'

"'Sure, I like ye,' says I.

"'Lucky man!' says he. 'Everybody must learn to like me an' play with me as the children do. I can get along with the little folks, but it's hard to teach men how to play with me—God pity them! They forget how to believe. I am the guide to paradise and unless ye become as a little child I can not lead ye.'

"He ran to the edge o' the tree roof and took hold o' the end of a long spider's rope hangin' down in the air. In a jiffy he swung clear o' the tree and climbed, hand over hand, until he had gone awa-a-a-a-y out o' sight in the sky."

"Couldn't anybody do that?" said little John.

"I didn't say they could—did I? ye unbeliever!" said the schoolmaster as he rose and led us in to the supper table. "I said Nobody did it."

We got him to tell this little tale over and over again in the days that followed, and many times since then that impersonal and mysterious guide of the schoolmaster's fancy has led me to paradise.

After supper he got out his boxing-gloves and gave me a lesson in the art of self-defense, in which, I was soon to learn, he was highly accomplished, for we had a few rounds together every day after that. He keenly enjoyed this form of exercise and I soon began to. My capacity for taking punishment without flinching grew apace and before long I got the knack of countering and that pleased him more even than my work in school, I have sometimes thought.

"God bless ye, boy!" he exclaimed one day after I had landed heavily on his cheek, "ye've a nice way o' sneakin' in with yer right. I've a notion ye may find it useful some day."

I wondered a little why he should say that, and while I was wondering he felled me with a stinging blow on my nose.

"Ah, my lad—there's the best thing I have seen ye do—get up an' come back with no mad in ye," he said as he gave me his hand.

One day the schoolmaster called the older boys to the front seats in his room and I among them.

"Now, boys, I'm going to ask ye what ye want to do in the world," he said. "Don't be afraid to tell me what ye may never have told before and I'll do what I can to help ye."

He asked each one to make confession and a most remarkable exhibit of young ambition was the result. I remember that most of us wanted to be statesmen—a fact due probably to the shining example of Silas Wright. Then he said that on a certain evening he would try "to show us the way over the mountains."

For some months I had been studying a book just published, entitled, *Stenographic Sound-Hand* and had learned its alphabet and practised the use of it. That evening I took down the remarks of Mr. Hacket in sound-hand.

The academy chapel was crowded with the older boys and girls and the town folk. The master never clipped his words in school as he was wont to do when talking familiarly with the children.

"Since the leaves fell our little village has occupied the center of the stage before an audience of millions in the great theater of congress. Our leading citizen—the chief actor—has been crowned with immortal fame. We who watched the play were thrilled by the query: Will Uncle Sam yield to temptation or cling to honor? He has chosen the latter course and we may still hear the applause in distant galleries beyond the sea. He has decided that the public revenues must be paid in honest money.

"My friend and classmate, George Bancroft, the historian, has written this letter to me out of a full heart:

"'Your fellow townsman, Silas Wright, is now the largest figure in Washington. We were all worried by the resolution of Henry Clay until it began to crumble under the irresistible attack of Mr. Wright. On the 16th he submitted a report upon it which for lucid and accurate statements presented in the most unpretending manner, won universal admiration and will be remembered alike for its intrinsic excellence and for having achieved one of the most memorable victories ever gained in the United States Senate. After a long debate Clay himself, compelled by the irresistible force of argument in the report of Mr. Wright, was obliged to retire from his position, his resolution having been rejected by a vote of 44 to 1.'"

With what pride and joy I heard of this great thing that my friend had accomplished! The schoolmaster went on:

"It is a very good and proper thing, my boys, that you should be inspired by the example of the great man, whose home is here among us and whose beloved face is as familiar as my own, to try your talents in the service of the state. There are certain things that I would have you remember.

"*First*—Know your subject-inside and outside and round about and from beginning to end.

"*Second*—Know the opinions of wise men and your own regarding it.

"*Third*—Be modest in the use of your own opinions and above all be honest.

"*Fourth*—Remember that it is your subject and not yourself that is of prime importance. You will be tempted to think that you are the great part of the business. My young friends, it will not be true. It can not be true. It is not *you* but *the thing you stand for* that is important.

"*Fifth*—The good of all the people must be the thing you stand for—the United States of America.

"Now I wish you to observe how our great fellow townsman keeps his subject to the fore and himself in the background.

"It was in 1834 that he addressed the Senate regarding the deposits of public money. He rose to voice the wishes of the people of this state. If he had seemed to be expressing his own opinions he would have missed his great point. Now mark how he cast himself aside when he began:

"'I must not be understood as, for one moment, entertaining the vain impression that opinions and views pronounced by me, here or elsewhere, will acquire any importance because they are my opinions and views. I know well, sir, that my name carries not with it authority anywhere, but I know, also, that so far as I may entertain and shall express opinions which are, or which shall be found, in accord with the enlightened public opinion of this country, so far they will be sustained and no further.'

"Then by overwhelming proof he set forth the opinion of our people on the subject in hand. Studiously the Senator has hidden himself in his task and avoided in every possible way attracting attention from his purposes to his personality.

"Invitations to accept public dinners as a compliment to himself have received from him this kind of reply:

"'A proper attention to the duties, on the discharge of which you so kindly desire to compliment me requires that I should decline your invitation.'"

All this was new to me, although much more was said touching his love for simple folk regarding which I needed no instruction. Altogether, it helped me to feel the deep foundations on which my friend, the Senator, had been building in his public life.

Going out with the crowd that evening, I met Sally and Mr. and Mrs. Dunkelberg. The latter did not speak to me and when I asked Sally if I could walk home with her she answered curtly, "No, thank you."

In following the schoolmaster I have got a bit ahead of my history. Soon after the opening of the new year—ten days or so later it may have been—I had begun to feel myself encompassed by a new and subtle force. It was a thing as intangible as heat but as real as fire and more terrible, it seemed to me. I felt it first in the attitude of my play fellows. They denied me the confidence and intimacy which I had enjoyed before. They whispered together in my presence. In all this I had not failed to observe that Henry Wills had taken a leading part. The invisible, inaudible, mysterious thing wrought a great change in me. It followed me through the day and lay down with me at night. I wondered what I had done. I carefully surveyed my clothes. They looked all right to me. My character was certainly no worse than it had been. How it preyed upon my peace and rest and happiness—that mysterious hidden thing!

One day Uncle Peabody came down to see me and I walked through the village with him. We met Mr. Dunkelberg, who merely nodded and hurried along. Mr. Bridges, the merchant, did not greet him warmly and chat with him as he had been wont to do. I saw that The Thing—as I had come to think of it—was following him also. How it darkened his face! Even now I can feel the aching of the deep, bloodless wounds of that day. I could bear it better alone. We were trying to hide our pain from each other when we said good-by. How quickly my uncle turned away and walked toward the sheds! He came rarely to the village of Canton after that.

I was going home at noon one day and while passing a crowd of boys I was shoved rudely into the fence. Turning, I saw Henry Wills and my fist flashed to his face. He fell backward and rising called me a thief and the son of a thief. He had not finished the words when I was upon him. The others formed a ring around us and we began a savage battle. One of Wills' friends tried to trip me. In the midst of it I saw the schoolmaster just outside the ring. He seized a boy by the collar.

"There'll be no more interference," said he. "It's goin' to be a fair fight."

I had felt another unfriendly foot but had not seen its owner. We fought up and down, with lips and noses bleeding. At last the time had come when I was quicker and stronger than he. Soon Henry Wills lay on the ground before me with no disposition to go on with the fight. I helped him up and he turned away from me. Some of the boys began to jeer him.

"He's a gentleman compared with the rest o' you," I said. "He had courage enough to say what he thought. There's not another one o' you would dare do it—not a one o' you."

Then said the schoolmaster:

"If there's any more o' you boys that has any such opinion o' Bart Baynes let him be man enough to step up an' say it now. If he don't he ought to be man enough to change his mind on the spot."

A number of the boys and certain of the townsfolk who had gathered about us clapped their hands. For a long time thereafter I wondered why Henry had called me a thief. I concluded that it was because "thief" was the meanest word he could think of in his anger. However that might be, The Thing forsook me. I felt no more its cold, mysterious shadow between me and my school fellows. It had stepped out of my path into that of Henry Wills. His popularity waned and a lucky circumstance it was for him. From that day he began to take to his books and to improve his standing in the school.

I observed that he did not go about with Sally as he had done. I had had no word with her since the night of Mr. Hacket's lecture save the briefest greeting as we passed each other in the street. Those fine winter days I used to see her riding a chestnut pony with a long silver mane that flowed back to her yellow curls in his lope. I loved the look of her as she went by me in the saddle and a longing came into my heart that she should think well of me. I made an odd resolve. It was this: I would make it impossible for her to think ill of me.

I went home one Saturday, having thought much of my aunt and uncle since The Thing had descended upon us. I found them well and as cheerful as ever. For fear of disturbing their peace I said nothing of my fight with Wills or the cause of it. Uncle Peabody had cut the timber for our new house and hauled it to the mill. I returned to school in a better mind about them.

May had returned—a warm bright May. The roads were dry. The thorn trees had thatched their shapely roofs with vivid green. The maple leaves were bigger than a squirrel's foot, which meant as well, I knew, that the trout were jumping. The robins had returned. I had entered my seventeenth year and the work of the term was finished.

She stopped the pony and leaned toward me.

Having nothing to do one afternoon, I walked out on the road toward Ogdensburg for a look at the woods and fields. Soon I thought that I heard the sound of galloping hoofs behind me. Turning, I saw nothing, but imagined Sally coming and pulling up at my side. I wondered what I should say if she were really to come.

"Sally!" I exclaimed. "I have been looking at the violets and the green fields and back there I saw a thorn tree turning white, but I have seen no fairer thing than you."

They surprised me a little—those fine words that came so easily. What a school of talk was the house I lived in those days!

"I guess I'm getting Mr. Hacket's gift o' gab," I said to myself.

Again I heard the sound of galloping hoofs and as I looked back I saw Sally rounding the turn by the river and coming toward me at full speed, the mane of her pony flying back to her face. She pulled up beside me just as I had imagined she would do.

"Bart, I hate somebody terribly," said she.

"Whom?"

"A man who is coming to our house on the stage to-day. Granny Barnes is trying to get up a match between us. Father says he is rich and hopes he will want to marry me. I got mad about it. He is four years older than I am. Isn't that awful? I am going to be just as mean and hateful to him as I can."

"I guess they're only fooling you," I said.

"No, they mean it. I have heard them talking it over."

"He can not marry you."

"Why?"

It seemed to me that the time had come for me to speak out, and with burning cheeks I said:

"Because I think that God has married you to me already. Do you remember when we kissed each other by the wheat-field one day last summer?"

"Yes." She was looking down at the mane of her pony and her cheeks were red and her voice reminded me of the echoes that fill the cavern of a violin when a string is touched.

"Seems to me we were married that day. Seems so, every time I think of it, God asked me all the questions an' I answered yes to 'em. Do ye remember after we had kissed each other how that little bird sang?"

"Yes."

We had faced about and were walking back toward Canton, I close by the pony's side.

"May I kiss you again?"

She stopped the pony and leaned toward me and our lips met in a kiss the thought of which makes me lay down my pen and bow my head a moment while I think with reverence of that pure, sweet spring of memory in whose waters I love to wash my spirit.

We walked on and a song sparrow followed us perching on the fence-rails and blessing us with his song.

"I guess God has married us again," I declared.

"I knew that you were walking on this road and I had to see you," said she. "People have been saying such terrible things."

"What?"

"They say your uncle found the pocketbook that was lost and kept the money. They say he was the first man that went up the road after it was lost."

Now The Thing stood uncovered before me in all its ugliness—The Thing born not of hate but of the mere love of excitement in people wearied by the dull routine and the reliable, plodding respectability of that countryside. The crime of Amos had been a great help in its way but as a topic it was worn out and would remain so until court convened.

"It's a lie—my uncle never saw the pocketbook. Some money was left to him by a relative in Vermont. That's how it happened that he bought a farm instead of going to the poorhouse when Grimshaw put the screws on him."

"I knew that your uncle didn't do it," she went on. "Father and mother couldn't tell you. So I had to."

"Why couldn't your father and mother tell me?"

"They didn't dare. Mr. Grimshaw made them promise that they would not speak to you or to any of your family. I heard them say that you and your uncle did right. Father told mother that he never knew a man so honest as your Uncle Peabody."

We went on in silence for a moment.

"I guess you know now why I couldn't let you go home with me that night," she remarked.

"Yes, and I think I know why you wouldn't have anything more to do with Henry Wills."

"I hate him. He said such horrid things about you and your uncle."

In a moment she asked: "What time is it?"

I looked at my new watch and answered: "It wants ten minutes of five."

"The stage is in long ago. They will be coming up this road to meet me. Father was going to take him for a walk before supper."

Just then we came upon the Silent Woman sitting among the dandelions by the roadside. She held a cup in her hand with some honey on its bottom and covered with a piece of glass.

"She is hunting bees," I said as we stopped beside her.

She rose and patted my shoulder with a smile and threw a kiss to Sally. Suddenly her face grew stern. She pointed toward the village and then at Sally. Up went her arm high above her head with one finger extended in that ominous gesture so familiar to me.

"She means that there is some danger ahead of you," I said.

The Silent Woman picked a long blade of grass and tipped its end in the honey at the bottom of the cup. She came close to Sally with the blade of grass between her thumb and finger.

"She is fixing a charm," I said.

She smiled and nodded as she put a drop of honey on Sally's upper lip.

She held up her hands while her lips moved as if she were blessing us.

"I suppose it will not save me if I brush it off," said Sally.

We went on and in a moment a bee lighted on the honey. Nervously she struck at it and then cried out with pain.

"The bee has stung you," I said.

She covered her face with her handkerchief and made no answer.

"Wait a minute—I'll get some clay," I said as I ran to the river bank.

I found some clay and moistened it with the water and returned.

"There, look at me!" she groaned. "The bee hit my nose."

She uncovered her face, now deformed almost beyond recognition, her nose having swollen to one of great size and redness.

"You look like Rodney Barnes," I said with a laugh as I applied the clay to her afflicted nose.

"And I feel like the old boy. I think my nose is trying to jump off and run away."

The clay having been well applied she began surveying herself with a little hand mirror which she had carried in the pocket of her riding coat.

"What a fright I am!" she mused.

"But you are the best girl in the world."

"Don't waste your pretty talk on me now. I can't enjoy it—my nose aches so. I'd rather you'd tell me when—when it is easier for you to say it."

"We don't see each other very often."

"If you will come out on this road next Saturday afternoon I will ride until I find you and then we can have another talk."

"All right. I'll be here at four-thirty and I'll be thinking about it every day until then."

"My nose feels better now," she said presently and added: "You might tell me a little more if you want to."

"I love you even when you have ceased to be beautiful," I said with the ardor of the young.

"That is grand! You know old age will sting us by and by, Bart," she answered with a sigh and in a tone of womanly wisdom.

We were nearing the village. She wiped the mud from her prodigious nose and I wet her handkerchief in a pool of water and helped her to wash it. Soon we saw two men approaching us in the road. In a moment I observed that one was Mr. Horace Dunkelberg; the other a stranger and a remarkably handsome young man he was, about twenty-two years of age and dressed in the height of fashion. I remember so well his tall, athletic figure, his gray eyes, his small dark mustache and his admirable manners. Both were appalled at the look of Sally.

"Why, girl, what has happened to you?" her father asked.

Then I saw what a playful soul was Sally's. The girl was a born actress.

"Been riding in the country," said she. "Is this Mr. Latour?"

"This is Mr. Latour, Sally," said her father.

They shook hands.

"I am glad to see you," said the stranger.

"They say I am worth seeing," said Sally. "This is my friend, Mr. Baynes. When you are tired of seeing me, look at him."

I shook the hand he offered me.

"Of course, we can't all be good looking," Sally remarked with a sigh, as if her misfortune were permanent.

Mr. Horace Dunkelberg and I laughed heartily—for I had told him in a whisper what had happened to Sally—while Mr. Latour looked a little embarrassed.

"My face is not beautiful, but they say that I have a good heart," Sally assured the stranger.

They started on. I excused myself and took a trail through the woods to another road. Just there, with Sally waving her hand to me as I stood for a moment in the edge of the woods, the curtain falls on this highly romantic period of my life.

Uncle Peabody came for me that evening. It was about the middle of the next week that I received this letter from Sally:

"DEAR BART—Mr. Latour gave up and drove to Potsdam in the evening. Said he had to meet Mr. Parish. I think that he had seen enough of me. I began to hope he would stay—he was so good looking, but mother is very glad that he went, and so am I, for our minister told us that he is one of the wickedest young men in the state. He is very rich and very bad, they say. I wonder if old Kate knew about him. Her charm worked well anyway—didn't it? My nose was all right in the morning. Sorry that I can't meet you Saturday. Mother and I are packing up to go away for the summer. Don't forget me. I shall be thinking every day of those lovely things you said to me. I don't know what they will try to do with me, and I don't care. I really think as you do, Bart, that God has married us to each other.

"Yours forever,
"SALLY DUNKELBERG."

How often I read those words—so like all the careless words of the young!

CHAPTER XIV

THE BOLT FALLS

Three times that winter I had seen Benjamin Grimshaw followed by the Silent Woman clothed in rags and pointing with her finger. Mr. Hacket said that she probably watched for him out of her little window above the blacksmith shop that overlooked the south road. When he came to town she followed. I always greeted the woman when I passed her, but when she was on the trail of the money-lender she seemed unaware of my presence, so intent was she on the strange task she had set herself. If he were not in sight she smiled when passing me, but neither spoke nor nodded.

Grimshaw had gone about his business as usual when I saw him last, but I had noted a look of the worried rat in his face. He had seemed to be under extreme irritation. He scolded every man who spoke to him. The notion came to me that her finger was getting down to the quick.

The trial of Amos came on. He had had "blood on his feet," as they used to say, all the way from Lickitysplit to Lewis County in his flight, having attacked and slightly wounded two men with a bowie knife who had tried to detain him at Rainy Lake. He had also shot at an officer in the vicinity of Lowville, where his arrest was effected. He had been identified by all these men, and so his character as a desperate man had been established. This in connection with the scar on his face and the tracks, which the boots of Amos fitted, and the broken gun stock convinced the jury of his guilt.

The most interesting bit of testimony which came out at the trial was this passage from a yellow paper-covered tale which had been discovered hidden in the haymow of the Grimshaw barn:

"Lightfoot waited in the bushes with his trusty rifle in hand. When the two unsuspecting travelers reached a point nearly opposite him he raised his rifle and glanced over its shining barrel and saw that the flight of his bullet would cut the throats of both his persecutors. He pulled the trigger and the bullet sped to its mark. Both men plunged to the ground as if they had been smitten by a thunderbolt. Lightfoot leaped from cover and seized the rearing horses, and mounting one of them while he led the other, headed them down the trail, and in no great hurry, for he knew that the lake was between him and Blodgett and that the latter's boat was in no condition to hold water."

It was the swift and deadly execution of Lightfoot which Amos had been imitating, as he presently confessed.

I knew then the power of words—even foolish words—over the minds of the young when they are printed and spread abroad.

I remember well the look of the venerable Judge Cady as he pronounced the sentence of death upon Amos Grimshaw. A ray of sunlight slanting through a window in the late afternoon fell upon his gracious countenance, shining also, with the softer light of his spirit. Slowly, solemnly, kindly, he spoke the words of doom. It was his way of saying them that first made me feel the dignity and majesty of the law. The kind and fatherly tone of his voice put me in mind of that Supremest Court which is above all question and which was swiftly to enter judgment in this matter and in others related to it.

Slowly the crowd moved out of the court room. Benjamin Grimshaw rose and calmly whispered to his lawyer. He had not spoken to his son or seemed to notice him since the trial had begun, nor did he now. Many had shed tears that day, but not he. Mr. Grimshaw never showed but one emotion—that of anger. He was angry now. His face was hard and stern. He muttered as he walked out of the court room, his cane briskly beating the floor. I and others followed him, moved by differing motives. I was sorry for him and if I had dared I should have told him that. I was amazed to see how sturdily he stood under this blow—like a mighty oak in a storm. The look of him thrilled me—it suggested that something was going to happen.

The Silent Woman—as ragged as ever—was waiting on the steps. Out went her bony finger as he came down. He turned and struck at her with his cane and shouted in a shrill voice that rang out like a trumpet in his frenzy:

"*Go 'way from me. Take her away, somebody. I can't stan' it. She's killin' me. Take her away. Take her away. Take her away.*"

His face turned purple and then white. He reeled and fell headlong, like a tree severed from its roots, and lay still on the hard, stone pavement. It seemed as if snow were falling on his face—it grew so white. The Silent Woman stood as still as he, pointing at him with her finger, her look unchanged. People came running toward us. I lifted the head of Mr. Grimshaw and laid it on my knee. It felt like the head of the stranger in Rattleroad. Old Kate bent over and looked at the eyelids of the man, which fluttered faintly and were still.

"Dead!" she muttered.

Then, as if her work were finished, she turned and made her way through the crowd and walked slowly down the street. Men stood aside to let her pass, as if they felt the power of her spirit and feared the touch of her garments.

Two or three men had run to the house of the nearest doctor. The crowd thickened. As I sat looking down at the dead face in my lap, a lawyer who had come out of the court room pressed near me and bent over and looked at the set eyes of Benjamin Grimshaw and said:

"She floored him at last. I knew she would. He tried not to see her, but I tell ye that bony old finger of hers burnt a hole in him. He couldn't stand it. I knew he'd blow up some day under the strain. She got him at last."

"Who got him?" another asked.

"Rovin' Kate. She killed him pointing her finger at him—so."

"She's got an evil eye. Everybody's afraid o' the crazy ol' Trollope!"

"Nonsense! She isn't half as crazy as the most of us," said the lawyer. "In my opinion she had a good reason for pointing her finger at that man. She came from the same town he did over in Vermont. Ye don't know what happened there."

The doctor arrived. The crowds made way for him. He knelt beside the still figure and made the tests. He rose and shook his head, saying:

"It's all over. Let one o' these boys go down and bring the undertaker."

Benjamin Grimshaw, the richest man in the township, was dead, and I have yet to hear of any mourners.

Three days later I saw his body lowered into its grave. The little, broken-spirited wife stood there with the same sad smile on her face that I had noted when I first saw her in the hills. Rovin' Kate was there in the clothes she had worn Christmas day. She was greatly changed. Her hair was neatly combed. The wild look had left her eyes. She was like one whose back is relieved of a heavy burden. Her lips moved as she scattered little red squares of paper into the grave. I suppose they thought it a crazy whim of hers—they who saw her do it. I thought that I understood the curious bit of symbolism and so did the schoolmaster, who stood beside me. Doubtless the pieces of paper numbered her curses.

"The scarlet sins of his youth are lying down with him in the dust," Hacket whispered as we walked away together.

END OF BOOK TWO

BOOK THREE

Which is the Story of the Chosen Ways

CHAPTER XV

UNCLE PEABODY'S WAY AND MINE

I am old and love my ease and sometimes dare to think that I have earned it. Why do I impose upon myself the task of writing down these memories, searching them and many notes and records with great care so that in every voice and deed the time shall speak? My first care has been that neither vanity nor pride should mar a word of all these I have written or shall write. So I keep my name from you, dear reader, for there is nothing you can give me that I want. I have learned my lesson in that distant time and, having learned it, give you the things I stand for and keep myself under a mask. These things urge me to my task. I do it that I may give to you—my countrymen—the best fruitage of the great garden of my youth and save it from the cold storage of unknowing history.

It is a bad thing to be under a heavy obligation to one's self of which, thank God, I am now acquitted. I have known men who were their own worst creditors. Everything they earned went swiftly to satisfy the demands of Vanity or Pride or Appetite. I have seen them literally put out of house and home, thrown neck and crop into the street, as it were, by one or the other of these heartless creditors—each a grasping usurer with unjust claims.

I remember that Rodney Barnes called for my chest and me that fine morning in early June when I was to go back to the hills, my year's work in school being ended. I elected to walk, and the schoolmaster went with me five miles or more across the flats to the slope of the high country. I felt very wise with that year's learning in my head. Doubtless the best of it had come not in school. It had taken me close to the great stage and in a way lifted the curtain. I was most attentive, knowing that presently I should get my part.

"I've been thinking, Bart, o' your work in the last year," said the schoolmaster as we walked. "Ye have studied six books and one—God help ye! An' I think ye have got more out o' the one than ye have out o' the six."

In a moment of silence that followed I counted the books on my fingers: Latin, Arithmetic, Algebra, Grammar, Geography, History. What was this one book he referred to?

"It's God's book o' life, boy, an' I should say ye'd done very well in it."

After a little he asked: "Have ye ever heard of a man who had the Grimshaws?"

I shook my head as I looked at him, not knowing just what he was driving at.

"Sure, it's a serious illness an' it has two phases. First there's the Grimshaw o' greed—swinish, heartless greed—the other is the Grimshaw o' vanity—the strutter, with sword at belt, who would have men bow or flee before him."

That is all he said of that seventh book and it was enough.

"Soon the Senator will be coming," he remarked presently. "I have a long letter from him and he asks about you and your aunt and uncle. I think that he is fond o' you, boy."

"I wish you would let me know when he comes," I said.

"I am sure he will let you know, and, by the way, I have heard from another friend o' yours, my lad. Ye're a lucky one to have so many friends—sure ye are. Here, I'll show ye the letter. There's no reason why I shouldn't. Ye will know its writer, probably. I do not."

So saying he handed me this letter:

"CANTERBURY, VT.,
June 1.

"DEAR SIR—I am interested in the boy Barton Baynes. Good words about him have been flying around like pigeons. When school is out I would like to hear from you, what is the record? What do you think of the soul in him? What kind of work is best for it? If you will let me maybe I can help the plans of God a little. That is my business and yours. Thanking you for reading this, I am, as ever,

"God's humble servant,
KATE FULLERTON."

"Why, this is the writing of the Silent Woman," I said before I had read the letter half through.

"Rovin' Kate?"

"Roving Kate; I never knew her other name, but I saw her handwriting long ago."

"But look—this is a neatly written, well-worded letter an' the sheet is as white and clean as the new snow. Uncanny woman! They say she carries the power o' God in her right hand. So do all the wronged. I tell ye, lad, there's only one thing in the world that's sacred."

I turned to him with a look of inquiry and asked:

"What is it?"

"The one and only miracle we know-the gate o' birth through which comes human life and the lips commanding our love and speaking the wisdom of childhood. Show me how a man treats women an' I'll tell ye what he amounts to. There's the test that shows whether he's a man or a spaniel dog."

There was a little moment of silence then—how well I remember it! The schoolmaster broke the silence by adding:

"Well ye know, lad, I think the greatest thing that Jesus Christ did was showing to a wicked world the sanctity o' motherhood."

That, I think, was the last lesson in the school year. Just beyond us I could see the slant of Bowman's Hill. What an amount of pains they gave those days to the building of character! It will seem curious and perhaps even wearisome now, but it must show here if I am to hold the mirror up to the time.

"I wonder why Kate is asking about me," I said.

"Never mind the reason. She is your friend and let us thank God for it. Think how she came to yer help in the old barn an' say a thousand prayers, my lad. I shall write to her to-day, and what shall I say as to the work?"

"Well, I've been consulting the compass," I answered thoughtfully, as I looked down at the yielding sand under my feet. "I think that I want to be a lawyer."

"Good! I would have guessed it. I suppose your week in the court room with the fine old judge and the lawyers settled that for ye."

"I think that it did."

"Well, the Senator is a lawyer, God prosper him, an' he has shown us that the chief business o' the lawyer is to keep men out o' the law."

Having come to the first flight of the uplands, he left me with many a kind word—how much they mean to a boy who is choosing his way with a growing sense of loneliness!

I reached the warm welcome of our little home just in time for dinner. They were expecting me and it was a regular company dinner—chicken pie and strawberry shortcake.

"I wallered in the grass all the forenoon tryin' to git enough berries for this celebration—ayes!—they ain't many of 'em turned yit," said Aunt Deel. "No, sir—nothin' but pure cream on this cake. I ain't a goin' to count the expense."

Uncle Peabody danced around the table and sang a stanza of the old ballad, which I have forgotten, but which begins:

Come, Philander, let us be a-marchin'.

How well I remember that hour with the doors open and the sun shining brightly on the blossoming fields and the joy of man and bird and beast in the return of summer and the talk about the late visit of Alma Jones and Mr. and Mrs. Lincoln!

While we were eating I told them about the letter of old Kate.

"Fullerton!" Aunt Deel exclaimed. "Are ye sure that was the name, Bart?"

"Yes."

"Goodness gracious sakes alive!"

She and Uncle Peabody gave each other looks of surprised inquiry.

"Do you know anybody by that name?" I asked.

"We used to," said Aunt Deel as she resumed her eating. "Can't be she's one o' the Sam Fullertons, can it?"

"Oh, prob'ly not," said Uncle Peabody. "Back east they's more Fullertons than ye could shake a stick at. Say, I see the biggest bear this mornin' that I ever see in all the born days o' my life.

"It was dark. I'd come out o' the fifty-mile woods an' down along the edge o' the ma'sh an' up into the bushes on the lower side o' the pastur. All to once I heerd somethin'! I stopped an' peeked through the bushes—couldn't see much—so dark. Then the ol' bear riz up on her hind legs clus to me. We didn't like the looks o' one 'nother an' begun to edge off very careful.

"Seems so I kind o' said to the ol' bear: 'Excuse me.'

"Seems so the ol' bear kind o' answered: 'Sart'nly.'

"I got down to a little run, near by, steppin' as soft as a cat. I could just see a white stun on the side o' it. I lifted my foot to step on the stun an' jump acrost. B-r-r-r-r! The stun jumped up an' scampered through the bushes. Then I *was* scairt. Goshtalmighty! I lost confidence in everything. Seemed so all the bushes turned into bears. Jeerusalem, how I run! When I got to the barn I was purty nigh used up."

"How did it happen that the stone jumped?" I asked.

"Oh, I guess 't was a rabbit," said Uncle Peabody.

Thus Uncle Peabody led us off into the trail of the bear and the problem of Kate and the Sam Fullertons concerned us no more at that time.

A week later we had our raising. Uncle Peabody did not want a public raising, but Aunt Deel had had her way. We had hewed and mortised and bored the timbers for our new home. The neighbors came with pikes and helped to raise and stay and cover them. A great amount of human kindness went into the beams and rafters of that home and of others like it. I knew that The Thing was still alive in the neighborhood, but even that could not paralyze the helpful hands of those people. Indeed, what was said of my Uncle Peabody was nothing more or less than a kind of conversational firewood. I can not think that any one really believed it.

We had a cheerful day. A barrel of hard cider had been set up in the dooryard, and I remember that some drank it too freely. The he-o-hee of the men as they lifted on the pikes and the sound of the hammer and beetle rang in the air from morning until night. Mrs. Rodney Barnes and Mrs. Dorothy came to help Aunt Deel with the cooking and a great dinner was served on an improvised table in the dooryard, where the stove was set up. The shingles and sheathes and clapboards were on before the day ended.

When they were about to go the men filled their cups and drank to Aunt Deel.

I knew, or thought I knew, why they had not mentioned my Uncle Peabody, and was very thoughtful about it. Suddenly the giant Rodney Barnes strode up to the barrel. I remember the lion-like dignity of his face as he turned and said:

"Now, boys, come up here an' stand right before me, every one o' you."

He ranged them in a circle around the barrel. He stood at the spigot and filled every cup. Then he raised his own and said:

"I want ye to drink to Peabody Baynes—one o' the squarest men that ever stood in cowhide."

They drank the toast—not one of them would have dared refuse.

"Now three cheers for the new home and every one that lives in it," he demanded.

They cheered lustily and went away.

Uncle Peabody and I put in the floors and stairway and partitions. More than once in the days we were working together I tried to tell him what Sally had told me, but my courage failed.

We moved our furniture. I remember that Uncle Peabody called it "the houseltree." We had greased paper on the windows for a time after we moved until the sash came. Aunt Deel had made rag carpets for the parlor and the bedroom which opened off it. Our windows looked down into the great valley of the St. Lawrence, stretching northward thirty miles or more from our hilltop. A beautiful grove of sugar maples stood within a stone's throw of the back door.

What a rustic charm in the long slant of the green hill below us with its gray, mossy boulders and lovely thorn trees! It was, I think, a brighter, pleasanter home than that we had left. It was built on the cellar of one burned a few years before. The old barn was still there and a little repairing had made it do.

The day came, shortly, when I had to speak out, and I took the straight way of my duty as the needle of the compass pointed. It was the end of a summer day and we had watched the dusk fill the valley and come creeping up the slant, sinking the boulders and thorn tops in its flood, one by one. As we sat looking out of the open door that evening I told them what Sally had told me of the evil report which had traveled through the two towns. Uncle Peabody sat silent and perfectly motionless for a moment, looking out into the dusk.

"W'y, of all things! Ain't that an awful burnin' shame-ayes!" said Aunt Deel as she covered her face with her hand.

"Damn, little souled, narrer contracted—" Uncle Peabody, speaking in a low, sad tone, but with deep feeling, cut off this highly promising opinion before it was half expressed, and rose and went to the water pail and drank.

"As long as we're honest we don't care what they say," he remarked as he returned to his chair.

"If they won't believe us we ought to show 'em the papers—ayes," said Aunt Deel.

"Thunder an' Jehu! I wouldn't go 'round the town tryin' to prove that I ain't a thief," said Uncle Peabody. "It wouldn't make no differ'nce. They've got to have somethin' to play with. If they want to use my name for a bean bag let 'em as long as they do it when I ain't lookin'. I wouldn't wonder if they got sore hands by an' by."

I never heard him speak of it again. Indeed, although I knew the topic was often in our thoughts it was never mentioned in our home but once after that, to my knowledge.

We sat for a long time thinking as the night came on. By and by Uncle Peabody began the hymn in which we joined:

"Oh, keep my heart from sadness, God;
Let not its sorrows stay,
Nor shadows of the night erase
The glories of the day."

"Say—by thunder!—we don't have to set in the shadows. Le's fill the room with the glory of the day," said Uncle Peabody as he lighted the candles. "It ain't a good idee to go slidin' down hill in the summer-time an' in the dark, too. Le's have a game o' cards."

I remember that we had three merry games and went to bed. All outward signs of our trouble had vanished in the glow of the candles.

Next day I rode to the post-office and found there a book addressed to me in the handwriting of old Kate. It was David Hoffman's *Course of Legal Study*. She had written on its fly-leaf:

"To Barton Baynes, from a friend."

"That woman 'pears to like you purty thorough," said Uncle Peabody.

"Well, let her if she wants to—poor thing!" Aunt Deel answered. "A woman has got to have somebody to like—ayes!—or I dunno how she'd live—I declare I don't—ayes!"

"I like her, too," I said. "She's been a good friend to me."

"She has, sart'n," my uncle agreed.

We began reading the book that evening in the candle-light and soon finished it. I was thrilled by the ideal of human service with which the calling of the lawyer was therein lifted up and illuminated. After that I had no doubt of my way.

That week a letter came to me from the Senator, announcing the day of Mrs. Wright's arrival in Canton and asking me to meet and assist her in getting the house to rights. I did so. She was a pleasant-faced, amiable woman and a most enterprising house cleaner. I remember that my first task was mending the wheelbarrow.

"I don't know what Silas would do if he were to get home and find his wheelbarrow broken," said she. "It is almost an inseparable companion of his."

The schoolmaster and his family were fishing and camping upon the river, and so I lived at the Senator's house with Mrs. Wright and her mother until he arrived. What a wonderful house it was, in my view! I was awed by its size and splendor, its soft carpets and shiny brass and mahogany. Yet it was very simple.

I hoed the garden and cleaned its paths and mowed the dooryard and did some painting in the house. I remember that Mrs. Ebenezer Binks—wife of the deacon and the constable—came in while I was at the latter task early one morning to see if there were anything she could do.

She immediately sat down and talked constantly until noon of her family and especially of the heartlessness and general misconduct of her son and daughter-in-law because they had refused to let her apply the name of Divine Submission to the baby. It had been a hard blow to Mrs. Binks, because this was the one and only favor which she had ever asked of them. She reviewed the history of the Binkses from Ebenezer—the First—down to that present day. There had been three Divine Submissions in the family and they had made the name of Binks known wherever people knew anything. When Mrs. Wright left the room Mrs. Binks directed her conversation at me, and when Mrs. Wright returned I only got the spray of it. By dinner time we were drenched in a way of speaking and Mrs. Binks left, assuring us that she would return later and do anything in her power.

"My stars!" Mrs. Wright exclaimed. "If you see her coming lock the door and go and hide in a closet until she goes away. Mrs. Binks always brings her ancestors with her and they fill the house so that there's no room for anybody else."

When the day's work was ended Mrs. Wright exclaimed:

"Thank goodness! the Binkses have not returned."

We always referred to Mrs. Binks as the Binkses after that.

Mrs. Jenison, a friend of the Wrights, came in that afternoon and told us of the visit of young Latour to Canton and of the great relief of the decent people at his speedy departure.

"I wonder what brought him here," said Mrs. Wright.

"It seems that he had heard of the beauty of Sally Dunkelberg. But a bee had stung her nose just before he came and she was a sight to behold."

The ladies laughed.

"It's lucky," said Mrs. Wright. "Doesn't Horace Dunkelberg know about him?"

"I suppose he does, but the man is money crazy."

I couldn't help hearing it, for I was working in the room in which they talked. Well, really, it doesn't matter much now. They are all gone.

"Who is young Latour?" I asked when Mrs. Jenison had left us.

"A rake and dissolute young man whose father is very rich and lives in a great mansion over in Jefferson County," Mrs. Wright answered.

I wondered then if there had been a purpose in that drop of honey from the cup of the Silent Woman.

I remember that the Senator, who returned to Canton that evening on the Watertown stage, laughed heartily when, as we were sitting by the fireside, Mrs. Wright told of the call of the Binkses.

"The good lady enjoys a singular plurality," he remarked.

"She enjoys it better than we do," said Mrs. Wright.

The Senator had greeted me with a fatherly warmth. Again I felt that strong appeal to my eye in his broadcloth and fine linen and beaver hat and in the splendid dignity and courtesy of his manners.

"I've had good reports of you, Bart, and I'm very glad to see you," he said.

"I believe your own marks have been excellent in the last year," I ventured.

"Poorer than I could wish. The teacher has been very kind to me," he laughed. "What have you been studying?"

"Latin (I always mentioned the Latin first), Algebra, Arithmetic, Grammar, Geography and History."

"Including the history of the Binkses," he laughed.

There was never a note of humor in his speeches, but he was playful in his talk at times, especially when trusted friends were with him.

"She is a very excellent woman, after all," he added.

He asked about my aunt and uncle and I told him of all that had befallen us, save the one thing of which I had spoken only with them and Sally.

"I shall go up to see them soon," he said.

The people of the little village had learned that he preferred to be let alone when he had just returned over the long, wearisome way from the scene of his labors. So we had the evening to ourselves.

I remember my keen interest in his account of riding from Albany to Utica on the new railroads. He spoke with enthusiasm of the smoothness and swiftness of the journey.

"With no mishap they now make it in about a half a day," he said, as we listened with wonder. "It is like riding in a house with a good deal of smoke coming out of the chimney and in at the windows. You sit on a comfortable bench with a back and a foot-rest in front and look out of the window and ride. But I tremble sometimes to think of what might happen with all that weight and speed.

"We had a little mishap after leaving Ballston Spa. The locomotive engine broke down and the train stopped. The passengers poured out like bees. We put our hands and shoulders on the train and pushed it backwards about a third of a mile to a passing station. There the engine got out of our way and after an hour's wait a horse was hitched to the train. With the help of the men he started it. At the next town our horse was reinforced by two others. They hauled us to the engine station four miles beyond, where another locomotive engine was attached to the train, and we went on by steam and at a fearful rate of speed."

Mrs. Wright, being weary after the day's work, went to bed early and, at his request, I sat with the Senator by the fire for an hour or so. I have always thought it a lucky circumstance, for he asked me to tell of my plans and gave me advice and encouragement which have had a marked effect upon my career.

I remember telling him that I wished to be a lawyer and my reasons for it. He told me that a lawyer was either a pest or a servant of justice and that his chief aim should be the promotion of peace and good will in his community. He promised to try and arrange for my accommodation in his office in the autumn and meanwhile to lend me some books to read while I was at home.

"Before we go to bed let us have a settlement," said the Senator. "Will you kindly sit down at the table there and make up a statement of all the time you have given me?"

I made out the statement very neatly and carefully and put it in his hands.

"That is well done," said he. "I shall wish you to stay until the day after to-morrow, if you will. So you will please add another day."

I amended the statement and he paid me the handsome sum of seven dollars. I remember that after I went to my room that night I stitched up the opening in my jacket pocket, which contained my wealth, with the needle and thread which Aunt Deel had put in my bundle, and slept with the jacket under my mattress.

The Senator and I were up at five o'clock and at work in the garden. What a contrast to see him spading in his old farm suit! Mrs. Wright cooked our breakfast and called us in at six.

I remember we were fixing the fence around his pasture lot that day when a handsomely dressed gentleman came back in the field. Mr. Wright was chopping at a small spruce.

"Is Senator Wright here?" the stranger inquired of me.

I pointed to the chopper.

"I beg your pardon—I am looking for the distinguished United States Senator," he explained with a smile.

Again I pointed at the man with the ax and said:

"That is the Senator."

Often I have thought of the look of astonishment on the face of the stranger as he said: "Will you have the kindness to tell him that General Macomb would like to speak with him?"

I halted his ax and conveyed the message.

"Is this the hero of Plattsburg?" Mr. Wright asked.

"Well, I have been there," said the General.

They shook hands and went up to the house together.

I walked back to the hills that evening. There I found a letter from Sally. She and her mother, who was in ill health, were spending the summer with relatives at Portsmouth, New Hampshire. She wrote of riding and fishing and sailing, but of all that she wrote I think only of these words now:

"I meet many good-looking boys here, but none of them are like you. I wonder if you remember what you said to me that day. If you want to unsay it, you can do it by letter, you know. I think that would be the best way to do it. So don't be afraid of hurting my feelings. Perhaps I would be glad. You don't know. What a long day that was! It seems as if it wasn't over yet. How lucky for me that it was such a beautiful day! You know I have forgotten all about the pain, but I laugh when I think how I looked and how Mr. Latour looked. He laughed a good deal going home, as if thinking of some wonderful joke. In September I am going away to a young ladies' school in Albany. I hate it. Can you imagine why? I am to learn fine manners and French and Spanish and dancing and be good enough for any man's wife. Think of that. Father says that I must marry a big man. Jiminy Crimps! As if a big man wouldn't know better. I am often afraid that you will know too much. I know what will happen when your intellect sees how foolish I am. My grandmother says that I am frivolous and far from God. I am afraid it's true, but sometimes I want to be good—only sometimes. I remember you said, once, that you were going to be like Silas Wright. Honestly I believe that you could. So does mother. I want you to keep trying, but it makes me afraid. Oh, dear! How sad and homesick I feel to-day! Tell me the truth now, when you write."

That evening I wrote my first love-letter—a fairly warm and moving fragment of history. My family have urged me to let it go in the record, but I have firmly refused. There are some things which I can not do even in this little masquerade. It is enough to say that when the day ended I had deliberately chosen two of the many ways that lay before me.

CHAPTER XVI

I USE MY OWN COMPASS AT A FORK IN THE ROAD

Swiftly now I move across the border into manhood—a serious, eager, restless manhood. It was the fashion of the young those days.

I spent a summer of hard work in the fields. Evenings I read the books which Mr. Wright had loaned to me, Blackstone's *Commentaries* and *Greenleaf on Evidence* and a translation by Doctor Bowditch of LaPlace's *Mécanique Celeste*. The latter I read aloud. I mention it because in a way it served as an antidote for that growing sense of expansion in my intellect. In the vastness of infinite space I found the littleness of man and his best accomplishments.

Mr. Wright came up for a day's fishing in July. My uncle and I took him up the river. I remember that after he had landed a big trout he sat down and held the fish up before him and looked proudly at the graceful, glowing, arrowy shape.

"I never did anything in the Senate that seemed half so important as this," he remarked thoughtfully.

While we ate our luncheon he described Jackson and spoke of the famous cheese which he had kept on a table in the vestibule of the White House for his callers. He described his fellow senators—Webster, Clay, Rives, Calhoun and Benton. I remember that Webster was, in his view, the least of them, although at his best the greatest orator. We had a delightful day, and when I drove back to the village with him that night he told me that I could go into the office of Wright and Baldwin after harvesting.

"It will do for a start," he said. "A little later I shall try to find a better place for you."

I began my work taking only the studies at school which would qualify me for surveying. I had not been in Canton a week when I received a rude shock which was my first lesson in the ungentle art of politics. Rodney Barnes and Uncle Peabody were standing with me in front of a store. A man came out with Colonel Hand and said in a loud voice that Sile Wright was a spoilsman and a drunkard—in politics for what he could get out of it.

My uncle turned toward the stranger with a look of amazement. Rodney Barnes dropped the knife with which he had been whittling. I felt my face turning red.

"What's that, mister?" asked Rodney Barnes.

The stranger repeated his statement and added that he could prove it.

"Le's see ye," said Barnes as he approached him.

There was a half moment of silence.

"Go on with yer proof," Rodney insisted, his great right hand trembling as he whittled.

"There are plenty of men in Albany that know the facts," said the stranger.

"Any other proof to offer?"

"That's enough."

"Oh, I see, ye can't prove it to-day, but ye don't mind sayin' it to-day. Say, mister, where do you live?"

"None o' your dam' business."

Swift as a cat's paw the big, right hand of Rodney caught the man by his shoulder and threw him down. Seizing him by the collar and the seat of his trousers our giant friend lifted the slanderer and flung him to the roof of a wooden awning in front of the grocer's shop near which we stood.

"Now you stay there 'til I git cooled off or you'll be hurt," said Rodney. "You better be out o' my reach for a few minutes."

A crowd had begun to gather.

"I want you all to take a look at that man," Rodney shouted. "He says Sile Wright is a drunkard an' a thief."

Loud jeers followed the statement, then a volley of oaths and a moment of danger, for somebody shouted:

"Le's tar an' feather him."

"No, we'll just look at him a few minutes," Rodney Barnes shouted. "He's one o' the greatest curiosities that ever came to this town."

The slanderer, thoroughly frightened, stood silent a few moments like a prisoner in the stocks. Soon the grocer let him in at an upper window.

Then the loud voice of Rodney Barnes rang like a trumpet in the words:

"Any man who says a mean thing of another when he can't prove it ought to be treated in the same way."

"That's so," a number of voices answered.

The slanderer stayed in retirement the rest of the day and the incident passed into history, not without leaving its impression on the people of the two towns.

My life went on with little in it worth recording until the letter came. I speak of it as "the letter," because of its effect upon my career. It was from Sally, and it said:

"DEAR BART—It's all over for a long time, perhaps forever—that will depend on you. I shall be true to you, if you really love me, even if I have to wait many, many years. Mother and father saw and read your letter. They say we are too young to be thinking about love and that we have got to stop it. How can I stop it? I guess I would have to stop living. But we shall have to depend upon our memories now. I hope that yours is as good as mine. Father says no more letters without his permission, and he stamped his foot so hard that I think he must have made a dent in the floor. Talk about slavery—what do you think of that? Mother says that we must wait—that it would make father a great deal of trouble if it were known that I allowed you to write. I guess the soul of old Grimshaw is still following you. Well, we must stretch out that lovely day as far as we can. Its words and its sunshine are always in my heart. I am risking the salvation of my soul in writing this. But I'd rather burn forever than not tell you how happy your letter made me, dear Bart. It is that Grimshaw trouble that is keeping us apart. On the third of June, 1844, we shall both be twenty-one—and I suppose that we can do as we please then. The day is a long way off, but I will agree to meet you that day at eleven in the morning under the old pine on the river where I met you that day and you told me that you loved me. If either or both should die our souls will know where to find each other. If you will solemnly promise, write these words and only these to my mother—Amour omnia vincit, but do not sign your name.

"SALLY."

What a serious matter it seemed to me then! I remember that it gave Time a rather slow foot. I wrote the words very neatly and plainly on a sheet of paper and mailed it to Mrs. Dunkelberg. I wondered if Sally would stand firm and longed to know the secrets of the future. More than ever I was resolved to be the principal witness in some great matter, as my friend in Ashery Lane had put it.

I was eight months with Wright and Baldwin when I was offered a clerkship in the office of Judge Westbrook, at Cobleskill, in Schoharie

County, at two hundred a year and my board. I knew not then just how the offer had come, but knew that the Senator must have recommended me. I know now that he wanted a reliable witness of the rent troubles which were growing acute in Schoharie, Delaware and Columbia Counties.

It was a trial to go so far from home, as Aunt Deel put it, but both my aunt and uncle agreed that it was "for the best."

"Mr. Purvis" had come to work for my uncle. In the midst of my preparations the man of gristle decided that he would like to go with me and see the world and try his fortune in another part of the country.

How it wrung my heart, when Mr. Purvis and I got into the stage at Canton, to see my aunt and uncle standing by the front wheel looking up at me. How old and lonely and forlorn they looked! Aunt Deel had her purse in her hand. I remember how she took a dollar bill out of it—I suppose it was the only dollar she had—and looked at it a moment and then handed it up to me.

"You better take it," she said. "I'm 'fraid you won't have enough."

How her hand and lips trembled! I have always kept that dollar.

I couldn't see them as we drove away.

I enjoyed the ride and the taverns and the talk of the passengers and the steamboat journey through the two lakes and down the river, but behind it all was a dark background. The shadows of my beloved friends fell every day upon my joys. However, I would be nearer Sally. It was a comfort when we were in Albany to reflect that she was somewhere in that noisy, bewildering spread of streets and buildings. I walked a few blocks from the landing, taking careful note of my way—mentally blazing a trail for fear of getting lost—and looked wistfully up a long street. There were many people, but no Sally.

The judge received me kindly and gave Purvis a job in his garden. I was able to take his dictation in sound-hand and spent most of my time in taking down contracts and correspondence and drafting them into proper form, which I had the knack of doing rather neatly. I was impressed by the immensity of certain towns in the neighborhood, and there were some temptations in my way. Many people, and especially the prominent men, indulged in ardent spirits.

One of my young friends induced me to go to dinner with him at Van Brocklin's, the fashionable restaurant of a near city. We had a bottle of wine and some adventures and I was sick for a week after it. Every day of that week I attended a convention of my ancestors and received much good advice. Toward the end of it my friend came to see me.

"There's no use of my trying to be a gentleman," I said. "I fear that another effort would hang my pelt on the door. It's a disgrace, probably, but I've got to be good. I'm driven to it."

"The way I look at it is this," said he. "We're young fellows and making a good deal of money and we can't tell when we'll die and leave a lot that we'll never get any good of."

It was a down-country, aristocratic view of the responsibilities of youth and quite new to me. Caligula was worried in a like manner, I believe. We had near us there a little section of the old world which was trying, in a half-hearted fashion, to maintain itself in the midst of a democracy. It was the manorial life of the patroons—a relic of ancient feudalism which had its beginning in 1629, when The West Indies Company issued its charter of Privileges and Exemptions. That charter offered to any member of the company who should, within four years, bring fifty adults to the New Netherlands and establish them along the Hudson, a liberal grant of land, to be called a manor, of which the owner or patroon should be full proprietor and chief magistrate. The settlers were to be exempt from taxation for ten years, but under bond to stay in one place and develop it. In the beginning the patroon built houses and barns and furnished cattle, seed and tools. The tenants for themselves and their heirs agreed to pay him a fixed rent forever in stock and produce and, further, to grind at the owner's mill and neither to hunt nor fish.

Judge Westbrook, in whose office I worked, was counsel and collector for the patroons, notably for the manors of Livingston and Van Renssalaer—two little kingdoms in the heart of the great republic.

I spent two years at my work and studied in the office of the learned judge with an ever-present but diminishing sense of homesickness. I belonged to the bowling and athletic club and had many friends.

Mr. Louis Latour, of Jefferson County, whom I had met in the company of Mr. Dunkelberg, came during my last year there to study law in the office of the judge, a privilege for which he was indebted to the influence of Senator Wright, I understood. He was a gay Lothario, always boasting of his love affairs, and I had little to do with him.

One day in May near the end of my two years in Cobleskill Judge Westbrook gave me two writs to serve on settlers in the neighborhood of Baldwin Heights for non-payment of rent. He told me what I knew, that there was bitter feeling against the patroons in that vicinity and that I might encounter opposition to the service of the writs. If so I was not to press the matter, but bring them back and he would give them to the sheriff.

"I do not insist on your taking this task upon you," he added. "I want a man of tact to go and talk with these people and get their point of view. If you don't care to undertake it I'll send another man."

"I think that I would enjoy the task," I said in ignorance of that hornet's nest back in the hills.

"Take Purvis with you," he said. "He can take care of the horses, and as those back-country folk are a little lawless it will be just as well to have a witness with you. They tell me that Purvis is a man of nerve and vigor."

Thus very deftly and without alarming me he had given me a notion of the delicate nature of my task. He had great faith in me those days. Well, I had had remarkably good luck with every matter he had put into my hands. He used to say that I would make a diplomat and playfully called me "Lord Chesterfield"—perhaps because I had unconsciously acquired a dignity and courtesy of manner beyond my years a little.

"Mr. Purvis" had been busy building up a conversational reputation for frightfulness in the gardens. He was held in awe by a number of the simple-minded men with whom he worked. For him life had grown very pleasant again—a sweet, uninterrupted dream of physical power and fleeing enemies. I tremble to think what might have happened if his strength and courage had equaled his ambition. I smiled when the judge spoke of his nerve and vigor. Still I was glad of his company, for I enjoyed Purvis.

I had drafted my letters for the day and was about to close my desk and start on my journey when Louis Latour came in and announced that he had brought the writs from the judge and was going with me.

"You will need a sheriff's deputy anyhow, and I have been appointed for just this kind of work," he assured me.

"I don't object to your going but you must remember that I am in command," I said, a little taken back, for I had no good opinion either of his prudence or his company.

He was four years older than I but I had better judgment, poor as it was, and our chief knew it.

"The judge told me that I could go but that I should be under your orders," he answered. "I'm not going to be a fool. I'm trying to establish a reputation for good sense myself."

We got our dinners and set out soon after one o'clock. Louis wore a green velvet riding coat and handsome top boots and snug-fitting, gray trousers. He was a gallant figure on the high-headed chestnut mare which his father had sent to him. Purvis and I, in our working suits, were like a pair of orderlies following a general. We rode two of the best saddle horses in the judge's stable and there were no better in that region.

I had read the deeds of the men we were to visit. They were brothers and lived on adjoining farms with leases which covered three hundred and fifty acres of land. Their great-grandfather had agreed to pay a yearly rent forever of sixty-two bushels of good, sweet, merchantable, winter wheat, eight yearling cattle and four sheep in good flesh and sixteen fat hens, all to be delivered in the city of Albany on the first day of January of each year. So, feeling that I was engaged in a just cause, I bravely determined to serve the writs if possible.

It was a delightful ride up into the highlands through woods just turning green. Full flowing noisy brooks cut the road here and there on their way to the great river. Latour rode along beside me for a few miles and began to tell of his sentimental adventures and conquests. His talk showed that he had the heart of a stone. It made me hate him and the more because he had told of meeting Sally on the street in Albany and that he was in love with her. It was while he was telling me how he had once fooled a country girl that I balked. He thought it a fine joke, for his father had cut his allowance two hundred a year so that the sum they had had to pay in damages had kept his nose "on the grindstone" for two years. Then I stopped my horse with an exclamation which would have astonished Lord Chesterfield, I am sure.

The young man drew rein and asked:

"What's the matter?"

"Only this. I shall have to try to lick you before we go any further."

"How's that?"

I dismounted and tightened the girth of my saddle. My spirit was taking swift counsel with itself at the brink of the precipice. It was then that I seemed to see the angry face of old Kate—the Silent Woman—at my elbow, and it counseled me to speak out. Again her spirit was leading me. Calmly and slowly these words came from my lips:

"Because I think you are a low-lived, dirty-souled dog of a man and if you can stand that without fighting you are a coward to boot."

This was not the language of diplomacy but at the time it seemed to me rather kind and flattering.

Latour flashed red and jumped off his horse and struck at me with his crop. I caught it in my hand and said:

"Hold on. Let's proceed decently and in order. Purvis, you hold these horses while we fight it out."

Purvis caught Latour's horse and brought the others close to mine and gathered the reins in his hand. I shall never forget how pale he looked and how fast he was breathing and how his hands trembled.

I jumped off and ran for my man. He faced me bravely. I landed a stunning blow squarely on his nose and he fell to the ground. Long before, Hacket had told me that a swift attack was half the battle and I have found it so more than once, for I have never been slow to fight for a woman's honor or a friend's or my own—never, thank God! Latour lay so quietly for a moment that I was frightened. His face was covered with blood. He came to and I helped him up and he rushed at me like a tiger. I remember that we had a long round then with our fists. I knew how to take care of my face and stomach and that I did while he wore himself out in wild blows and desperate lunges.

We had dismounted near the end of a bridge. He fought me to the middle of it and when his speed slackened I took the offensive and with such energy that he clinched. I threw him on the planks and we went down together, he under me, in a fall so violent that it shook the bridge and knocked the breath out of him. This seemed to convince Latour that I was his master. His distress passed quickly and he got up and began brushing the dust from his pretty riding coat and trousers. I saw that he was winded and in no condition to resume the contest.

I felt as fresh as if I had mowed only once around the field, to quote a saying of my uncle.

"We'll have to fight it out some other day," he said. "I'm weak from the loss of blood. My nose feels as if it was turned wrong side out."

"It ought to be used to the grindstone after two years of practise," I remarked. "Come down to the brook and let me wash the blood off you."

Without a word he followed me and I washed his face as gently as I could and did my best to clean his shirt and waistcoat with my handkerchief. His nose was badly swollen.

"Latour, women have been good to me," I said. "I've been taught to think that a man who treats them badly is the basest of all men. I can't help it. The feeling has gone into my bones. I'll fight you as often as I hear you talk as you did."

He reeled with weakness as he started toward his horse. I helped him into the saddle.

"I guess I'm not as bad as I talk," he remarked.

If it were so he must have revised his view of that distinction which he had been lying to achieve. It was a curious type of vanity quite new to me then.

Young Mr. Latour fell behind me as we rode on. The silence was broken presently by "Mr. Purvis," who said:

"You can hit like the hind leg of a horse. I never sees more speed an' gristle in a feller o' your age."

"Nobody could swing the scythe and the ax as much as I have without getting some gristle, and the schoolmaster taught me how to use it," I answered. "But there's one thing that no man ought to be conceited about."

"What's that?"

"His own gristle. I remember Mr. Hacket told me once that the worst kind of a fool was the man who was conceited over his fighting power and liked to talk about it. If I ever get that way I hope that I shall have it licked out of me."

"I never git conceited—not that I ain't some reason to be," said Mr. Purvis with a highly serious countenance. He seemed to have been blind to that disparity between his acts and sayings which had distinguished him in Lickitysplit.

I turned my head away to hide my smiles and we rode on in silence.

"I guess I've got somethin' here that is cocollated to please ye," he said.

He took a letter from his pocket and gave it to me. My heart beat faster when I observed that the superscription on the envelope was in Sally's handwriting. The letter, which bore neither signature nor date line, contained these words:

"Will you please show this to Mr. Barton Baynes? I hope it will convince him that there is one who still thinks of the days of the past and of the days that are coming—especially one day."

Tears dimmed my eyes as I read and re-read the message. More than two of those four years had passed and, as the weeks had dragged along I had thought more and more of Sally and the day that was coming. I had bought a suit of evening clothes and learned to dance and gone out to parties and met many beautiful young ladies but none of them had the charm of Sally. The memory of youth—true-hearted, romantic, wonder-working youth—had enthroned her in its golden castle and was defending her against the present commonplace herd of mere human beings. No one of them had played with me in the old garden or stood by the wheat-field with flying hair, as yellow as the grain, and delighted me with the sweetest words ever spoken. No one of them had been glorified with the light and color of a thousand dreams.

I rode in silence, thinking of her and of those beautiful days now receding into the past and of my aunt and uncle. I had written a letter to them every week and one or the other had answered it. Between the lines I had detected the note of loneliness. They had told me the small news of the countryside. How narrow and monotonous it all seemed to me then! Rodney Barnes had bought a new farm; John Axtell had been hurt in a runaway; my white mare had got a spavin!

"Hello, mister!"

I started out of my reverie with a little jump of surprise. A big, rough-dressed, bearded man stood in the middle of the road with a gun on his shoulder.

"Where ye goin'?"

"Up to the Van Heusen place."

"Where do ye hail from?"

"Cobleskill."

"On business for Judge Westbrook?"

"Yes."

"Writs to serve?"

"Yes," I answered with no thought of my imprudence.

"Say, young man, by hokey nettie! I advise you to turn right around and go back."

"Why?"

"'Cause if ye try to serve any writs ye'll git into trouble."

"That's interesting," I answered. "I am not seeking a quarrel, but I do want to see how the people feel about the payment of their rents."

"Say mister, look down into that valley there," the stranger began. "See all them houses—they're the little houses o' the poor. See how smooth the land is? Who built them houses? Who cleaned that land? Was it Mr. Livingston? By hokey nettie! I guess not. The men who live there built the houses an' cleaned the land. We ain't got nothin' else—not a dollar! It's all gone to the landlord. I am for the men who made every rod o' that land an' who own not a single rod of it. Years an' years ago a king gave it to a man who never cut one tree or laid one stone on another. The deeds say that we must pay a rent o' so many bushels o' wheat a year but the land is no good for wheat, an' ain't been for a hundred years. Why, ye see, mister, a good many things have happened in three hundred years. The land was willin' to give wheat then an' a good many folks was willin' to be slaves. By hokey nettie! they had got used to it. Kings an' magistrates an' slavery didn't look so bad to 'em as they do now. Our brains have changed—that's what's the matter—same as the soil has changed. We want to be free like other folks in this country. America has growed up around us but here we are livin' back in old Holland three hundred years ago. It don't set good. We see lots o' people that don't have to be slaves. They own their land an' they ain't worked any harder than we have or been any more savin'. That's why I say we can't pay the rents no more an' ye mustn't try to make us. By hokey nettie! You'll have trouble if ye do."

The truth had flashed upon me out of the words of this simple man. Until then I had heard only one side of the case. If I were to be the servant of justice, as Mr. Wright had advised, what was I to do? These tenants had been Grimshawed and were being Grimshawed out of the just fruits of their toil by the feudal chief whose remote ancestor had been a king's favorite. For half a moment I watched the wavering needle of my compass and then:

"If what you say is true I think you are right," I said.

"I don't agree with you," said young Latour. "The patroons have a clear title to this land. If the tenants don't want to pay the rents they ought to get out and make way for others."

"Look here, young man, my name is Josiah Curtis," said the stranger. "I live in the first house on the right-hand side o' the road. You may tell the judge that I won't pay rent no more—not as long as I live—and I won't git out, either."

"Mr. Latour, you and Purvis may go on slowly—I'll overtake you soon," I said.

They went on and left me alone with Curtis. He was getting excited and I wished to allay his fears.

"Don't let him try to serve no writs or there'll be hell to pay in this valley," said Curtis.

"In that case I shall not try to serve the writs. I don't want to stir up the neighborhood, but I want to know the facts. I shall try to see other tenants and report what they say. It may lead to a settlement."

We went on together to the top of the hill near which we had been standing. Far ahead I saw a cloud of dust but no other sign of Latour and Purvis. They must have spurred their horses into a run. The fear came to me that Latour would try to serve the writs in spite of me. They were in his pocket. What a fool I had been not to call for them. My companion saw the look of concern in my face.

"I don't like that young feller," said Curtis. "He's in fer trouble."

He ran toward his house, which was only a few rods beyond us, while I started on in pursuit of the two men at top speed. Before my horse had taken a dozen jumps I heard a horn blowing behind me and its echo in the hills. Within a half a moment a dozen horns were sounding in the valleys around me. What a contrast to the quiet in which we had been riding was this pandemonium which had broken loose in the countryside. A little ahead I could see men running out of the fields. My horse had begun to lather, for the sun was hot. My companions were far ahead. I could not see the dust of their heels now. I gave up trying to catch them and checked the speed of my horse and went on at a walk. The horns were still sounding. Some of them seemed to be miles away. About twenty rods ahead I saw three riders in strange costumes come out of a dooryard and take the road at a wild gallop in pursuit of Latour and Purvis. They had not discovered me. I kept as calm as I could in the midst of this excitement. I remember laughing when I thought of the mess in which "Mr. Purvis" would shortly find himself.

I passed the house from which the three riders had just turned into the road. A number of women and an old man and three or four children stood on the porch. They looked at me in silence as I was passing and then began to hiss and jeer. It gave me a feeling I have never known since that day. I jogged along over the brow of a hill when, at a white, frame house, I saw the center toward which all the men of the countryside were coming.

Suddenly I heard the hoof-beats of a horse behind me. I stopped, and looking over my shoulder saw a rider approaching me in the costume of an Indian chief. A red mask covered his face. A crest of eagle feathers circled the edge of his cap. Without a word he rode on at my side. I knew not then that he was the man Josiah Curtis—nor could I at any time have sworn that it was he.

A crowd had assembled around the house ahead. I could see a string of horsemen coming toward it from the other side. I wondered what was going to happen to me. What a shouting and jeering in the crowded dooryard! I could see the smoke of a fire. We reached the gate. Men in Indian masks and costumes gathered around us.

"Order! Sh-sh-sh," was the loud command of the man beside me in whom I recognized—or thought that I did—the voice of Josiah Curtis.

"What has happened?"

"One o' them tried to serve a writ an' we have tarred an' feathered him."

Just then I heard the voice of Purvis shouting back in the crowd this impassioned plea:

"Bart, for God's sake, come here."

I turned to Curtis and said:

"If the gentleman tried to serve the writ he acted without orders and deserves what he has got. The other fellow is simply a hired man who came along to take care of the horses. He couldn't tell the difference between a writ and a hole in the ground."

"Men, you have gone fur enough," said Curtis. "This man is all right. Bring the other men here and put 'em on their horses an' I'll escort 'em out o' the town."

They brought Latour on a rail amidst roars of laughter. What a bear-like, poultrified, be-poodled object he was!—burred and sheathed in rumpled gray feathers from his hair to his heels. The sight and smell of him scared the horses. There were tufts of feathers over his ears and on his chin. They had found great joy in spoiling that aristocratic livery in which he had arrived.

Then came poor Purvis. They had just begun to apply the tar and feathers to him when Curtis had stopped the process. He had only a shaking ruff of long feathers around his neck. They lifted the runaways into their saddles. Purvis started off at a gallop, shouting "Come on, Bart," but they stopped him.

"Don't be in a hurry, young feller," said one of the Indians, and then there was another roar of laughter.

"Go back to yer work now," Curtis shouted, and turning to me added: "You ride along with me and let our feathered friends follow us."

So we started up the road on our way back to Cobleskill. Soon Latour began to complain that he was hot and the feathers pricked him.

"You come alongside me here an' raise up a little an' I'll pick the inside o' yer legs an' pull out yer tail feathers," said Curtis. "If you got 'em stuck into yer skin you'd be a reg'lar chicken an' no mistake."

I helped in the process and got my fingers badly tarred.

"This is a dangerous man to touch—his soul is tarred," said Curtis. "Keep away from him."

"What a lookin' skunk you be!" he laughed as he went on with the picking.

We resumed our journey. Our guide left us at the town line some three miles beyond.

"Thank God the danger is over," said Purvis. "The tar on my neck has melted an' run down an' my shirt sticks like the bark on a tree. I'm sick o' the smell o' myself. If I could find a skunk I'd enjoy holdin' him in my lap a while. I'm goin' back to St. Lawrence County about as straight as I can go. I never did like this country anyway."

He had picked the feathers out of his neck and Latour was now busy picking his arms and shoulders. Presently he took off his feathered coat and threw it away, saying:

"They'll have to pay for this. Every one o' those jackrabbits will have to settle with me."

"You brought it on yourself," I said. "You ran away from me and got us all into trouble by being too smart. You tried to be a fool and succeeded beyond your expectation. My testimony wouldn't help you any."

"You're always against the capitalist," he answered.

It was dark when I left my companions in Cobleskill. I changed my clothes and had my supper and found Judge Westbrook in his home and reported the talk of Curtis and our adventure and my view of the situation back in the hills. I observed that he gave the latter a cold welcome.

"I shall send the sheriff and a posse," he said with a troubled look.

"Pardon me, but I think it will make a bad matter worse," I answered.

"We must not forget that the patroons are our clients," he remarked.

I yielded and went on with my work. In the next week or so I satisfied myself of the rectitude of my opinions. Then came the most critical point in my history—a conflict with Thrift and Fear on one side and Conscience on the other.

The judge raised my salary. I wanted the money, but every day I would have to lend my help, directly or indirectly, to the prosecution of claims which I could not believe to be just. My heart went out of my work. I began to fear myself. For weeks I had not the courage to take issue with the learned judge.

One evening I went to his home determined to put an end to my unhappiness. After a little talk I told him frankly that I thought the patroons should seek a friendly settlement with their tenants.

"Why?" he asked.

"Because their position is unjust, un-American and untenable," was my answer.

He rose and gave me his hand and a smile of forbearance in consideration of my youth, as I took it.

I left much irritated and spent a sleepless night in the course of which I decided to cling to the ideals of David Hoffman and Silas Wright.

In the morning I resigned my place and asked to be relieved as soon as the convenience of the judge would allow it. He tried to keep me with gentle persuasion and higher pay, but I was firm. Then I wrote a long letter to my friend the Senator.

Again I had chosen my way and with due regard to the compass.

CHAPTER XVII

THE MAN WITH THE SCYTHE

It was late in June before I was able to disengage myself from the work of the judge's office. Meanwhile there had been blood shed back in the hills. One of the sheriff's posse had been severely wounded by a bullet and had failed to serve the writs. The judge had appealed to the governor. People were talking of "the rent war."

Purvis had returned to St. Lawrence County and hired to my uncle for the haying. He had sent me a letter which contained the welcome information that the day he left the stage at Canton, he had seen Miss Dunkelberg on the street.

"She was lookin' top-notch—stop't and spoke to me," he went on. "You cood a nocked me down with a fether I was that scairt. She ast me how you was an' I lookt her plum in the eye an' I says: all grissul from his head to his heels, mam, an' able to lick Lew Latour, which I seen him do in quick time an' tolable severe. He can fight like a bob-tailed cat when he gits a-goin', I says."

What a recommendation to the sweet, unsullied spirit of Sally! Without knowledge of my provocation what would she think of me? He had endowed me with all the frightfulness of his own cherished ideal, and what was I to do about it? Well, I was going home and would try to see her.

What a joy entered my heart when I was aboard the steamboat, at last, and on my way to all most dear to me! As I entered Lake Champlain I consulted the map and decided to leave the boat at Chimney Point to find Kate Fullerton, who had written to the schoolmaster from Canterbury. My aunt had said in a letter that old Kate was living there and that a great change had come over her. So I went ashore and hired a horse of the ferryman—one of those "Green Mountain ponies" of which my uncle had told me: "They'll take any gait that suits ye, except a slow one, an' keep it to the end o' the road."

I think that I never had a horse so bent on reaching that traditional "end of the road." He was what they called a "racker" those days, and a rocking-chair was not easier to ride. He took me swiftly across the wide flat and over the hills and seemed to resent my effort to slow him.

I passed through Middlebury and rode into the grounds of the college, where the Senator had been educated, and on out to Weybridge to see where he had lived as a boy. I found the Wright homestead—a comfortable white house at the head of a beautiful valley with wooded hills behind it—and rode up to the door. A white-haired old lady in a black lace cap was sitting on its porch looking out at the sunlit fields.

"Is this where Senator Wright lived when he was a boy?" I asked.

"Yes, sir," the old lady answered.

"I am from Canton."

She rose from her chair.

"You from Canton!" she exclaimed. "Why, of all things! That's where my boy's home is. I'm glad to see you. Go an' put your horse in the barn."

I dismounted and she came near me.

"Silas Wright is my boy," she said. "What is your name?"

"Barton Baynes," I answered as I hitched my horse.

"Barton Baynes! Why, Silas has told me all about you in his letters. He writes to me every week. Come and sit down."

We sat down together on the porch.

"Silas wrote in his last letter that you were going to leave your place in Cobleskill," she continued to my surprise. "He said that he was glad you had decided not to stay."

It was joyful news to me, for the Senator's silence had worried me and I had begun to think with alarm of my future.

"I wish that he would take you to Washington to help him. The poor man has too much to do."

"I should think it a great privilege to go," I answered.

"My boy likes you," she went on. "You have been brought up just as he was. I used to read to him every evening when the candles were lit. How hard he worked to make a man of himself! I have known the mother's joy. I can truly say, 'Now let thy servant depart in peace.'"

"'For mine eyes have seen thy salvation,'" I quoted.

"You see I know much about you and much about your aunt and uncle," said Mrs. Wright.

She left me for a moment and soon the whole household was gathered about me on the porch, the men having come up from the fields. The Senator had told them on his last visit of my proficiency as a sound-hand writer and I amused them by explaining the art of it. They put my horse in the barn and pressed me to stay for dinner, which I did. It was a plain boiled dinner at which the Senator's cousin and his hired man sat down in their shirt-sleeves and during which I heard many stories of the boyhood of the great man. As I was going the gentle old lady gave me a pair of mittens which her distinguished son had worn during his last winter in college. I remember well how tenderly she handled them!

"I hope that Silas will get you to help him"—those were the last words she said to me when I bade her good-by.

The visit had set me up a good deal. The knowledge that I had been so much in the Senator's thoughts, and that he approved my decision to leave the learned judge, gave me new heart. I had never cherished the thought that he would take me to Washington although, now and then, a faint star of hope had shone above the capitol in my dreams. As I rode along I imagined myself in that great arena and sitting where I could see the flash of its swords and hear the thunder of Homeric voices. That is the way I thought of it. Well, those were no weak, piping times of peace, my brothers. They were times of battle and as I rode through that peaceful summer afternoon I mapped my way to the fighting line. I knew that I should enjoy the practise of the law but I had begun to feel that eventually my client would be the people whose rights were subject to constant aggression as open as that of the patroons or as insidious as that of the canal ring.

The shadows were long when I got to Canterbury. At the head of its main street I looked down upon a village green and some fine old elms. It was a singularly quiet place. I stopped in front of a big white meeting house. An old man was mowing in its graveyard near the highway. Slowly he swung his scythe.

"It's a fine day," I said.

"No, it ain't, nuther-too much hard work in it," said he.

"Do you know where Kate Fullerton lives?" I asked.

"Well, it's purty likely that I do," he answered as he stood resting on his snath. "I've lived seventy-two years on this hill come the fourteenth day o' June, an' if I didn't know where she lived I'd be 'shamed of it."

He looked at me thoughtfully for a moment and added:

"I know everybody that lives here an' everybody that dies here, an' some that orto be livin' but ain't an' some that orto be dead which ye couldn't kill `em with an ax—don't seem so—I declare it don't. Do ye see that big house down there in the trees?"

I could see the place at which he pointed far back from the village street in the valley below us, the house nearly hidden by tall evergreens.

"Yes," I answered.

"No ye can't, nuther—leastways if ye can ye've got better eyes'n mos' people, ye can't see only a patch o' the roof an' one chimney—them pine trees bein' thicker'n the hair on a dog. It's the gloomiest ol' house in all creation, I guess. Wal, that's the Squire Fullerton place—he's Kate's father."

"Does the squire live there?"

"No, sir—not eggzac'ly. He's dyin' there—been dyin' there fer two year er more. By gosh! It's wonderful how hard 'tis fer some folks to quit breathin'. Say, be you any o' his fam'ly?"

"No."

"Nor no friend o' his?"

"No!"

"Course not. He never had a friend in his life—too mean! He's too mean to die, mister—too mean fer hell an' I wouldn't wonder—honest, I wouldn't—mebbe that's why God is keepin' him here—jest to meller him up a little. Say, mister, be you in a hurry?"

"No."

"Yis ye be. Everybody's in a hurry—seems to me—since we got steam power in the country. Say, hitch yer hoss an' come in here. I want to show ye suthin'."

He seemed to enjoy contradicting me.

"Nobody seems in a hurry in this town," I said.

"Don't, hey? Wal, ye ought to 'a' seen Deacon Norton run when some punkins on his side hill bu'st their vines an' come rollin' down an' chased him half a mile into the valley."

I dismounted and hitched my horse to the fence and followed him into the old churchyard, between weather-stained mossy headstones and graves overgrown with wild roses. Near the far end of these thick-sown acres he stopped.

"Here's where the buryin' begun," said my guide. "The first hole in the hill was dug for a Fullerton."

There were many small monuments and slabs of marble—some spotted with lichens and all in commemoration of departed Fullertons.

"Say, look a' that," said my guide as he pulled aside the stem of a leafy brier red with roses. "Jest read that, mister."

My keen eyes slowly spelled out the time-worn words on a slab of stained marble:

Sacred to the memory of
Katherine Fullerton
1787-1806
"Proclaim his Word in every place
That they are dead who fall from grace."

A dark shadow fell upon the house of my soul and I heard a loud rapping at its door which confused me until, looking out, I saw the strange truth of the matter. Rose leaves and blossoms seemed to be trying to hide it with their beauty, but in vain.

"I understand," I said.

"No ye don't. Leastways I don't believe ye do—not correct. Squire Fullerton dug a grave here an' had an empty coffin put into it away back in 1806. It means that he wanted everybody to understan' that his girl was jest the same as dead to him an' to God. Say, he knew all about God's wishes—that man. Gosh! He has sent more folks to hell than there are in it, I guess. Say, mister, do ye know why he sent her there?"

I shook my head.

"Yis ye do, too. It's the same ol' thing that's been sendin' women to hell ever since the world begun. Ye know hell must 'a' been the invention of a man—that's sartin—an' it was mostly fer women an' children—that's sartiner—an' fer all the men that didn't agree with him. Set down here an' I'll tell ye the hull story. My day's work is done."

We sat down together and he went on as follows:

"Did ye ever see Kate Fullerton?"

"Yes."

"No ye didn't, nuther. Yer too young. Mebbe ye seen her when she was old an' broke down but that wa'n't Kate—no more'n I'm Bill Tweedy, which I ain't. Kate was as handsome as a golden robin. Hair yeller as his breast an' feet as spry as his wings an' a voice as sweet as his song, an' eyes as bright as his'n—yis, sir—ye couldn't beat her fer looks. That was years and years ago. Her mother died when Kate was ten year old—there's her grave in there with the sickle an' the sheaf an' the portry on it. That was unfort'nit an' no mistake. Course the squire married ag'in but the new wife wa'n't no kind of a mother to the girl an' you know, mister, there was a young scoundrel here by the name o' Grimshaw. His father was a rich man—owned the cooper shop an' the saw-mill an' the tannery an' a lot o' cleared land down in the valley. He kep' comp'ny with her fer two or three year. Then all of a sudden folks began to talk—the women in partic'lar. Ye know men invented hell an' women keep up the fire. Kate didn't look right to 'em. Fust we knew, young Grimshaw had dropped her an' was keepin' comp'ny with another gal—yis, sir. Do ye know why?"

Before I could answer he went on:

"No ye don't—leastways I don't believe ye do. It was 'cause her father was richer'n the squire an' had promised his gal ten thousan' dollars the day she was married. All of a sudden Kate disappeared. We didn't know what had happened fer a long time."

"One day the ol' squire got me to dig this grave an' put up the headstun an' then he tol' me the story. He'd turned the poor gal out o' doors. God o' Israel! It was in the night—yis, sir—it was in the night that he sent her away. Goldarn him! He didn't have no more heart than a grasshopper—no sir—not a bit. I could 'a' brained him with my shovel, but I didn't.

"I found out where the gal had gone an' I follered her—yis I did—found her in the poorhouse way over on Pussley Hill—uh huh! She jes' put her arms 'round my neck an' cried an' cried. I guess 'twas 'cause I looked kind o' friendly—uh huh! I tol' her she should come right over to our house an' stay jest as long as she wanted to as soon as she got well—yis, sir, I did.

"She was sick all summer long—kind o' out o' her head, ye know, an' I used to go over hossback an' take things fer her to eat. An' one day when I was over there they was wonderin' what they was goin' to do with her little baby. I took it in my arms an' I'll be gol dummed if it didn't grab hold o' my nose an' hang on like a puppy to a root. When they tried to take it away it grabbed its fingers into my whiskers an' hollered like a panther—yis, sir. Wal, ye know I jes' fetched that little baby boy home in my arms, ay uh! My wife scolded me like Sam Hill—yis, sir—she had five of her own. I tol' her I was goin' to take it back in a day er two but after it had been in the house three days ye couldn't 'a' pulled it away from her with a windlass.

"We brought him up an' he was alwuss a good boy. We called him Enoch—Enoch Rone—did ye ever hear the name?"

"'No.'

"I didn't think 'twas likely but I'm alwuss hopin'.

"Early that fall Kate got better an' left the poorhouse afoot. Went away somewheres—nobody knew where. Some said she'd crossed the lake an' gone away over into York State, some said she'd drowned herself. By'm by we heard that she'd gone way over into St. Lawrence County where Silas Wright lives an' where young Grimshaw had settled down after he got married.

"Wal, 'bout five year ago the squire buried his second wife—there 'tis over in there back o' Kate's with the little speckled angel on it. Nobody had seen the squire outside o' his house for years until the funeral—he was crippled so with rheumatiz. After that he lived all 'lone in the big house with ol' Tom Linney an' his wife, who've worked there fer 'bout forty year, I guess.

"Wal, sir, fust we knew Kate was there in the house livin' with her father. We wouldn't 'a' knowed it, then, if it hadn't been that Tom Linney come over one day an' said he guessed the ol' squire wanted to see me—no, sir, we wouldn't—fer the squire ain't sociable an' the neighbors never darken his door. She must 'a' come in the night, jest as she went—nobody see her go an' nobody see her come, an' that's a fact. Wal, one day las' fall after the leaves was off an' they could see a corner o' my house through the bushes, Tom was walkin' the ol' man 'round the room. All to once he stopped an' p'inted at my house through the winder an' kep' p'intin'. Tom come over an' said he ca'llated the squire wanted to see me. So I went there. Kate met me at the door. Gosh! How old an' kind o' broke down she looked! But I knew her the minute I set my eyes on her—uh huh—an' she knew me—yis, sir—she smiled an' tears come to her eyes an' she patted my hand like she wanted to tell me that she hadn't forgot, but she never said a word—not a word. The ol' squire had the palsy, so 't he couldn't use his hands an' his throat was paralyzed—couldn't speak ner nothin'. Where do ye suppose he was when I found him?"

"In bed?" I asked.

"No, sir—no, siree! He was in hell—that's where he was—reg'lar ol' fashioned, down-east hell, burnin' with fire an' brimstun, that he'd had the agency for an' had recommended to every sinner in the neighborhood. He was settin' in his room. God o' Isr'el! You orto 'a' seen the motions he made with his hands an' the way he tried to speak when I went in there, but all I could hear was jest a long yell an' a kind of a rattle in his throat. Heavens an' airth! how desperit he tried to spit out the thing that was gnawin' his vitals. Ag'in an' ag'in he'd try to tell me. Lord God! how he did work!

"All to once it come acrost me what he wanted—quick as ye could say scat. He wanted to have Kate's headstun took down an' put away—that's what he wanted. That stun was kind o' layin' on his stummick an' painin' of him day an' night. He couldn't stan' it. He knew that he was goin' to die purty soon an' that Kate would come here an' see it an' that everybody would see her standin' here by her own grave, an' it worried him. It was kind o' like a fire in his belly.

"I guess, too, he couldn't bear the idee o' layin' down fer his las' sleep beside that hell hole he'd dug fer Kate—no, sir!

"Wal, ye know, mister, I jes' shook my head an' never let on that I knew what he meant an' let him wiggle an' twist like a worm on a hot griddle, an' beller like a cut bull 'til he fell back in a swoon.

"Damn him! it don't give him no rest. He tries to tell everybody he sees—that's what they say. He bellers day an' night an' if you go down there he'll beller to you an' you'll know what it's about, but the others don't.

"You an' me are the only ones that knows the secret, I guess. Some day, 'fore he dies, I'm goin' to take up that headstun an' hide it, but he'll never know it's done—no, sir—not 'til he gits to the judgment seat, anyway."

The old man stopped and rubbed his hands together as if he were washing them of the whole matter. The dusk of evening had fallen and crocked the white marble and blurred the lettered legends around us. The mossy stones now reminded me only of the innumerable host of the dead. Softly the notes of a song sparrow scattered down into the silence that followed the strange story.

The old man rose and straightened himself and blew out his breath and brushed his hands upon his trousers by way of stepping down into this world again out of the close and dusty loft of his memory. But I called him back.

"What has become of Enoch?" I asked.

"Wal, sir, Enoch started off west 'bout three year ago an' we ain't heard a word from him since that day—nary a word, mister. I suppose we will some time. He grew into a good man, but there was a kind of a queer streak in the blood, as ye might say, on both sides kind o'. We've wrote letters out to Wisconsin, where he was p'intin' for, an' to places on the way, but we can't git no news 'bout him. Mebbe he was killed by the Injuns."

We walked out of the graveyard together in silence. Dimly above a distant ridge I could see stark, dead timber looming on a scarlet cloud in the twilight. It is curious how carefully one notes the setting of the scene in which his spirit has been deeply stirred.

I could see a glimmer of a light in the thicket of pines down the valley. I unhitched and mounted my horse.

"Take the first turn to the right," said the old man as he picked up his scythe.

"I'm very much obliged to you," I said.

"No ye ain't, nuther," he answered. "Leastways there ain't no reason why ye should be."

My horse, impatient as ever to find the end of the road, hurried me along and in a moment or two we were down under the pine grove that surrounded the house of old Squire Fullerton—a big, stone house with a graveled road around it. A great black dog came barking and growling at me from the front porch. I rode around the house and he followed. Beyond the windows I could see the gleam of candle-light and moving figures. A man came out of the back door as I neared it.

"Who's there?" he demanded.

"My name is Barton Baynes from St. Lawrence County. Kate Fullerton is my friend and I wish to see her."

"Come up to the steps, sor. Don't git off yer horse—'til I've chained the dog. Kate'll be out in a minute."

He chained the dog to the hitching post and as he did so a loud, long, wailing cry broke the silence of the house. It put me in mind of the complaint of the damned which I remembered hearing the minister describe years before at the little schoolhouse in Lickitysplit. How it harrowed me!

The man went into the house. Soon he came out of the door with a lighted candle in his hand, a woman following. How vividly I remember the little murmur of delight that came from her lips when he held the candle so that its light fell upon my face! I jumped off my horse and gave the reins to the man and put my arms around the poor woman, whom I loved for her sorrows and for my debt to her, and rained kisses upon her withered cheek. Oh God! what a moment it was for both of us!

The way she held me to her breast and patted my shoulder and said "my boy!"—in a low, faint, treble voice so like that of a child—it is one of the best memories that I take with me into the new life now so near, from which there is no returning.

"My boy!'" Did it mean that she had appointed me to be a kind of proxy for the one she had lost and that she had given to me the affection which God had stored in her heart for him? Of that, I know only what may be conveyed by strong but unspoken assurance.

She led me into the house. She looked very neat now—in a black gown over which was a spotless white apron and collar of lace—and much more slender than when I had seen her last. She took me into a large room in the front of the house with a carpet and furniture, handsome once but now worn and decrepit. Old, time-stained engravings of scenes from the Bible, framed in wood, hung on the walls.

She gave me a chair by the candle-stand and sat near me and looked into my face with a smile of satisfaction. In a moment she pointed toward the west with that forefinger, which in my presence had cut down her enemy, and whispered the one word:

"News?"

I told all that I had heard from home and of my life in Cobleskill but observed, presently, a faraway look in her eyes and judged that she was not hearing me. Again she whispered:

"Sally?"

"She has been at school in Albany for a year," I said. "She is at home now and I am going to see her."

"You love Sally?" she whispered.

"Better than I love my life."

Again she whispered: "Get married!"

"We hope to in 1844. I have agreed to meet her by the big pine tree on the river bank at eleven o'clock the third of June, 1844. We are looking forward to that day."

A kind of shadow seemed to come out of her spirit and rest upon her face and for a moment she looked very solemn. I suppose that she divined the meaning of all that. She shook her head and whispered:

"Money thirst!"

A tall, slim woman entered the room then and said that supper was ready. Kate rose with a smile and I followed her into the dining-room where two tables were spread. One had certain dishes on it and a white cover, frayed and worn. She led me to the other table which was neatly covered with snowy linen. The tall woman served a supper on deep, blue china, cooked as only they could cook in old New England. Meanwhile I could hear the voice of the aged squire—a weird, empty, inhuman voice it was, utterly cut off from his intelligence. It came out of the troubled depths of his misery.

So that house—the scene of his great sin which would presently lie down with him in the dust—was flooded, a hundred times a day, by the unhappy spirit of its master. In the dead of the night I heard its despair echoing through the silent chambers.

Kate said little as we ate, or as we sat together in the shabby, great room after supper, but she seemed to enjoy my talk and I went into the details of my personal history. How those years of suffering and silence had warped her soul and body in a way of speaking! They were a poor fit in any company now. Her tongue had lost its taste for speech I doubt not; her voice was gone, although I had heard a low plaintive murmur in the words "my boy."

The look of her face, even while I was speaking, indicated that her thoughts wandered restlessly, in the gloomy desert of her past. I thought of that gay bird—like youth of hers of which the old man with the scythe had told me and wondered. As I was thinking of this there came a cry from the aged squire so loud and doleful that it startled me and I turned and looked toward the open door.

Kate rose and came to my side and leaning toward my ear whispered:

"It is my father. He is always thinking of when I was a girl. He wants me."

She bade me good night and left the room. Doubtless it was the outraged, departed spirit of that golden time which was haunting the old squire. A Bible lay on the table near me and I sat reading it for an hour or so. A tall clock in a corner solemnly tolled the hour of nine. In came the tall woman and asked in the brogue of the Irish:

"Would ye like to go to bed?"

"Yes, I am tired."

She took a candle and led me up a broad oaken stairway and into a room of the most generous proportions. A big four-post bedstead, draped in white, stood against a wall. The bed, sheeted in old linen, had quilted covers. The room was noticeably clean; its furniture of old mahogany and its carpet comparatively unworn.

When I was undressed I dreaded to put out the candle. For the first time in years I had a kind of child-fear of the night. But I went to bed at last and slept rather fitfully, waking often when the cries of the old squire came flooding through the walls. How I longed for the light of morning! It came at last and I rose and dressed and seeing the hired man in the yard, went out-of-doors. He was a good-natured Irishman.

"I'm glad o' the sight o' ye this fine mornin'," said he. "It's a pleasure to see any one that has all their senses—sure it is."

I went with him to the stable yard where he did his milking and talked of his long service with the squire.

"We was glad when he wrote for Kate to come," he said. "But, sure, I don't think it's done him any good. He's gone wild since she got here. He was always fond o' his family spite o' all they say. Did ye see the second table in the dinin'-room? Sure, that's stood there ever since his first wife et her last meal on it, just as it was then, sor—the same cloth, the same dishes, the same sugar in the bowl, the same pickles in the jar. He was like one o' them big rocks in the field there—ye couldn't move him when he put his foot down."

Kate met me at the door when I went back into the house and kissed my cheek and again I heard those half-spoken words, "My boy." I ate my breakfast with her and when I was about to get into my saddle at the door I gave her a hug and, as she tenderly patted my cheek, a smile lighted her countenance so that it seemed to shine upon me. I have never forgotten its serenity and sweetness.

CHAPTER XVIII

I START IN A LONG WAY

I journeyed to Canton in the midst of the haying season. After the long stretches of forest road we hurried along between fragrant fields of drying hay. At each tavern we first entered the barroom where the landlord—always a well-dressed man of much dignity and filled with the news of the time, that being a part of his entertainment—received us with cheerful words. His housekeeper was there and assigned our quarters for the night. Our evenings were spent playing cards or backgammon or listening to the chatter of our host by the fireside. At our last stop on the road I opened my trunk and put on my best suit of clothes.

We reached Canton at six o'clock in the evening of a beautiful summer day. I went at once to call upon the Dunkelbergs and learned from a man at work in the dooryard that they had gone away for the summer. How keen was my disappointment! I went to the tavern and got my supper and then over to Ashery Lane to see Michael Hacket and his family. I found the schoolmaster playing his violin.

"Now God be praised—here is Bart!" he exclaimed as he put down his instrument and took my hands in his. "I've heard, my boy, how bravely ye've weathered the capes an' I'm proud o' ye—that I am!"

I wondered what he meant for a second and then asked:

"How go these days with you?"

"Swift as the weaver's shuttle," he answered. "Sit you down, while I call the family. They're out in the kitchen putting the dishes away. Many hands make light labor."

They came quickly and gathered about me—a noisy, happy group. The younger children kissed me and sat on my knees and gave me the small news of the neighborhood.

How good were the look of those friendly faces and the full-hearted pleasure of the whole family at my coming!

"What a joy for the spare room!" exclaimed the schoolmaster. "Sure I wouldn't wonder if the old bed was dancin' on its four legs this very minute."

"I intend to walk up to the hills to-night," I said.

"Up to the hills!" he exclaimed merrily. "An' the Hackets lyin' awake thinkin' o' ye on the dark road! Try it, boy, an' ye'll get a crack with the ruler and an hour after school. Yer aunt and uncle will be stronger to stand yer comin' with the night's rest upon them. Ye wouldn't be routin' them out o' bed an' they after a hard day with the hayin'! Then, my kind-hearted lad, ye must give a thought to Michael Henry. He's still alive an' stronger than ever—thank God!"

So, although I longed for those most dear to me up in the hills, I spent the night with the Hackets and the schoolmaster and I sat an hour together after the family had gone to bed.

"How are the Dunkelbergs?" I asked.

"Sunk in the soft embrace o' luxury," he answered. "Grimshaw made him; Grimshaw liked him. He was always ready to lick the boots o' Grimshaw. It turned out that Grimshaw left him an annuity of three thousand dollars, which he can enjoy as long as he observes one condition."

"What is that?"

"He must not let his daughter marry one Barton Baynes, late o' the town o' Ballybeen. How is that for spite, my boy? They say it's written down in the will."

I think that he must have seen the flame of color playing on my face, for he quickly added:

"Don't worry, lad. The will o' God is greater than the will o' Grimshaw. He made you two for each other and she will be true to ye, as true as the needle to the north star."

"Do you think so?"

"Sure I do. Didn't she as much as tell me that here in this room—not a week ago? She loves ye, boy, as true as God loves ye, an' she's a girl of a thousand.

"Her father is a bit too fond o' money. I've never been hard struck with him. It has always seemed to me that he was afflicted with perfection—a camellia man!—so invariably neat and proper and conventional! Such precise and wearisome rectitude! What a relief it would be to see him in his shirt-sleeves or with soiled boots or linen or to hear him say something—well-unexpected! Six shillings a week to the church and four to charity, as if that were the contract—no more, no less! But did ye ever hear o' his going out o' his way to do a good thing—say to help a poor woman left with a lot o' babies or a poor lad that wants to go to school? 'No, I'm very sorry, but I give four shillings a week to charity and that's all I can afford.'"

"Why did they go away? Was it because I was coming?"

"I think it likely, my fine lad. The man heard o' it some way—perhaps through yer uncle. He's crazy for the money, but he'll get over that. Leave him to me. I've a fine course o' instruction ready for my Lord o' Dunkelberg."

"I think I shall go and try to find her," I said.

"I am to counsel ye about that," said the schoolmaster. "She's as keen as a brier—the fox! She says, 'Keep away. Don't alarm him, or he'll bundle us off to Europe for two or three years.'

"So there's the trail ye travel, my boy. It's the one that keeps away. Don't let him think ye've anything up the sleeve o' yer mind. Ye know, lad, I believe Sally's mother has hold o' the same rope with her and when two clever women get their wits together the divvle scratches his head. It's an old sayin', lad, an' don't ye go out an' cut the rope. Keep yer head cool an' yer heart warm and go right on with yer business. I like the whole plan o' this remarkable courtship o' yours."

"I guess you like it better than I do," was my answer.

"Ah, my lad, I know the heart o' youth! Ye'd like to be puttin' yer arms around her—wouldn't ye, now? Sure, there's time enough! You two young colts are bein' broke' an' bitted. Ye've a chance now to show yer quality—yer faith, yer loyalty, yer cleverness. If either one o' ye fails that one isn't worthy o' the other. Ye're in the old treadmill o' God—the both o' ye! Ye're bein' weighed an' tried for the great prize. It's not pleasant, but it's better so. Go on, now, an' do yer best an' whatever comes take it like a man."

A little silence followed. He broke it with these words:

"Ye're done with that business in Cobleskill, an' I'm glad. Ye didn't know ye were bein' tried there—did ye? Ye've stood it like a man. What will ye be doin' now?"

"I'd like to go to Washington with the Senator."

He laughed heartily.

"I was hopin' ye'd say that," he went on. "Well, boy, I think it can be arranged. I'll see the Senator as soon as ever he comes an' I believe he'll be glad to know o' yer wishes. I think he's been hopin', like, that ye would propose it. Go up to the farm and spend a happy month or two with yer aunt an' uncle. It'll do ye good. Ye've been growin' plump down there. Go an' melt it off in the fields."

"How is Deacon Binks?" I asked presently.

"Soul buried in fat! The sparkler on his bosom suggests a tombstone stickin' out of a soiled snowbank."

A little more talk and we were off to bed with our candles.

Next morning I went down into the main street of the village before leaving for home. I wanted to see how it looked and, to be quite frank, I wanted some of the people of Canton to see how I looked, for my clothes were of the best cloth and cut in the latest fashion. Many stopped me and shook my hand—men and women who had never noticed me before, but there was a quality in their smiles that I didn't quite enjoy. I know now that they thought me a little too grand on the outside. What a stern-souled lot those Yankees were! "All ain't gold that glitters." How often I had heard that version of the old motto!

"Why, you look like the Senator when he is just gittin' home from the capital," said Mr. Jenison.

They were not yet willing to take me at the par of my appearance.

I met Betsy Price—one of my schoolmates—on the street. She was very cordial and told me that the Dunkelbergs had gone to Saratoga.

"I got a letter from Sally this morning," Betsy went on. "She said that young Mr. Latour was at the same hotel and that he and her father were good friends."

I wonder if she really enjoyed sticking this thorn into my flesh—a thorn which made it difficult for me to follow the advice of the schoolmaster and robbed me of the little peace I might have enjoyed. My faith in Sally wavered up and down until it settled at its wonted level and reassured me.

It was a perfect summer morning and I enjoyed my walk over the familiar road and up into the hill country. The birds seemed to sing a welcome to me. Men and boys I had known waved their hats in the hay-fields and looked at me. There are few pleasures in this world like that of a boy getting home after a long absence. My heart beat fast when I saw the house and my uncle and Purvis coming in from the twenty-acre lot with a load of hay. Aunt Deel stood on the front steps looking down the road. Now and then her waving handkerchief went to her eyes. Uncle Peabody came down the standard off his load and walked toward me.

"Say, stranger, have you seen anything of a feller by the name o' Bart Baynes?" he demanded.

"Have you?" I asked.

"No, sir, I ain't. Gosh a'mighty! Say! what have ye done with that boy of our'n?"

"What have you done to our house?" I asked again.

"Built on an addition."

"That's what I've done to your boy," I answered.

"Thunder an' lightnin'! How you've raised the roof!" he exclaimed as he grabbed my satchel. "Dressed like a statesman an' bigger'n a bullmoose. I can't 'rastle with you no more. But, say, I'll run ye a race. I can beat ye an' carry the satchel, too."

We ran pell-mell up the lane to the steps like a pair of children.

Aunt Deel did not speak. She just put her arms around me and laid her dear old head upon my breast. Uncle Peabody turned away. Then what a silence! Off in the edge of the woodland I heard the fairy flute of a wood-thrush.

"Purvis, you drive that load on the floor an' put up the hosses," Uncle Peabody shouted in a moment. "If you don't like it you can hire 'nother man. I won't do no more till after dinner. This slave business is played out."

"All right," Purvis answered.

"You bet it's all right. I'm fer abolition an' I've stood your domineerin', nigger-driver ways long enough fer one mornin'. If you don't like it you can look for another man."

Aunt Deel and I began to laugh at this good-natured, make-believe scolding of Uncle Peabody and the emotional strain was over. They led me into the house where a delightful surprise awaited me, for the rooms had been decorated with balsam boughs and sweet ferns. A glowing mass of violets, framed in moss, occupied the center of the table. The house was filled with the odors of the forest, which, as they knew, were dear to me. I had written that they might expect me some time before noon, but I had begged them not to meet me in Canton, as I wished to walk home after my long ride. So they were ready for me.

I remember how they felt the cloth on my back and how proudly they surveyed it.

"Couldn't buy them goods 'round these parts," said Uncle Peabody. "Nor nothin' like 'em—no, sir."

"Feels a leetle bit like the butternut trousers," said Aunt Deel as she felt my coat.

"Ayes, but them butternut trousers ain't what they used to be when they was young an' limber," Uncle Peabody remarked. "Seems so they was gettin' kind o' wrinkled an' baldheaded-like, 'specially where I set down."

"Ayes! Wal I guess a man can't grow old without his pants growin' old, too—ayes!" said Aunt Deel.

"If yer legs are in 'em ev'ry Sunday they ketch it of ye," my uncle answered. "Long sermons are hard on pants, seems to me."

"An' the longer the legs the harder the sermons—in them little seats over 't the schoolhouse—ayes!" Aunt Deel added by way of justifying his complaint. "There wouldn't be so much wear in a ten-mile walk—no!"

The chicken pie was baking and the strawberries were ready for the shortcake.

"I've been wallerin' since the dew was off gittin' them berries an' vi'lets—ayes!" said Aunt Deel, now busy with her work at the stove.

"Aunt, you look as young as ever," I remarked.

She slapped my arm and said with mock severity:

"Stop that! W'y! You know better—ayes!"

How vigorously she stirred the fire then.

"I can't return the compliment—my soul! how you've changed!—ayes!" she remarked. "I hope you ain't fit no more, Bart. I can't bear to think o' you flyin' at folks an' poundin' of 'em. Don't seem right—no, it don't!"

"Why, Aunt Deel, what in the world do you mean?" I asked.

"It's Purvis's brain that does the poundin', I guess," said my uncle. "It's kind o' got the habit. It's a reg'lar beetle brain. To hear him talk, ye'd think he an' you could clean out the hull Mexican nation—barrin' accidents. Why, anybody would suppose that yer enemies go to climbin' trees as soon as they see ye comin' an' that you pull the trees up by the roots to git at 'em."

"A certain amount of such deviltry is necessary to the comfort of Mr. Purvis," I remarked. "If there is nobody else to take the responsibility for it he assumes it himself. His imagination has an intense craving for blood and violence. It's that type of American who, egged on by the slave power, is hurrying us into trouble with Mexico."

Purvis came in presently with a look in his face which betrayed his knowledge of the fact that all the cobwebs spun by his fancy were now to be brushed away. Still he enjoyed them while they lasted and there was a kind of tacit claim in his manner that there were subjects regarding which no honest man could be expected to tell the truth.

As we ate our dinner they told me that an escaped slave had come into a neighboring county and excited the people with stories of the auction block and of negroes driven like yoked oxen on plantations in South Carolina, whence he had escaped on a steamboat.

"I b'lieve I'm goin' to vote for abolition," said Uncle Peabody. "I wonder what Sile Wright will say to that."

"He'll probably advise against it, the time isn't ripe for so great a change," was my answer. "He thinks that the whole matter should be left to the glacial action of time's forces."

Indeed I had spoken the view of the sounder men of the North. The subject filled them with dread alarm. But the attitude of Uncle Peabody was significant. The sentiment in favor of a change was growing. It was now to be reckoned with, for the abolition party was said to hold the balance of power in New York and New England and was behaving itself like a bull in a china shop.

After dinner I tried to put on some of my old clothes, but found that my nakedness had so expanded that they would not cover it, so I hitched my white mare on the spring wagon and drove to the village for my trunk.

Every week day after that I worked in the fields until the Senator arrived in Canton about the middle of August. On one of those happy days I received a letter from old Kate, dated, to my surprise, in Saratoga. It said:

"DEAR BARTON BAYNES—I thought I would let you know that my father is dead. I have come here to rest and have found some work to do. I am better now. Have seen Sally. She is very beautiful and kind. She does not know that I am the old witch, I have changed so. The others do not know—it is better that way. I think it was the Lord that brought me here. He has a way of taking care of some people, my boy. Do you remember when I began to call you my boy—you were very little. It is long, long ago since I first saw you in your father's dooryard—you said you were going to mill on a butterfly's back. You looked just as I thought my boy would look. You gave me a kiss. What a wonderful gift it was to me then! I began to love you. I have no one else to think of now. I hope you won't mind my thinking so much of you.

"God bless you,
KATE FULLERTON."

I understood now why the strong will and singular insight of this woman had so often exercised themselves in my behalf. I could not remember the far day and the happy circumstance of which she spoke, but I wrote her a letter which must have warmed her heart I am sure.

Silas Wright arrived in Canton and drove up to our home. He reached our door at eight in the morning with his hound and rifle. He had aged rapidly since I had seen him last. His hair was almost white. There were many new lines in his face. He seemed more grave and dignified. He did not lapse into the dialect of his fathers when he spoke of the ancient pastimes of hunting and fishing as he had been wont to do.

"Bart," he said when the greetings were over, "let's you and me go and spend a day in the woods. I'll leave my man here to help your uncle while you're gone."

We went by driving south a few miles and tramping in to the foot of the stillwater on our river—a trail long familiar to me. The dog left us soon after we took it and began to range over thick wooded hills. We sat down among small, spire-like spruces at the river's edge with a long stretch of water in sight while the music of the hound's voice came faintly to our ears from the distant forest.

"Oh, I've been dreaming of this for a long time," said the Senator as he leaned back against a tree and filled his lungs and looked out upon the water, green with lily-pads along the edge and flecked with the last of the white blossoms. "I believe you want to leave this lovely country."

"I am waiting for the call to go," I said.

"Well, I'm inclined to think you are the kind of man who ought to go," he answered almost sadly. "You are needed. I have been waiting until we should meet to congratulate you on your behavior at Cobleskill. I think you have the right spirit—that is the all-important matter. You will encounter strange company in the game of politics. Let me tell you a story."

He told me many stories of his life in Washington, interrupted by a sound like that of approaching footsteps. We ceased talking and presently a flock of partridges came near us, pacing along over the mat of leaves in a leisurely fashion. We sat perfectly still. A young cock bird with his beautiful ruff standing out, like the hair on the back of a frightened dog, strode toward us with a comic threat in his manner. It seemed as if he were of half a mind to knock us into the river. But we sat as still as stumps and he spared us and went on with the others.

The baying of the hound was nearer now. Suddenly we saw a big buck come down to the shore of the cove near us and on our side of the stream. He looked to right and left. Then he made a long leap into the water and waded slowly until it covered him. He raised his nose and laid his antlers back over his shoulders and swam quietly down-stream, his nose just showing above the water. His antlers were like a bit of driftwood. If we had not seen him take the water his antlers might easily have passed for a bunch of dead sticks. Soon the buck slowly lifted his head and turned his neck and looked at both shores. Then very deliberately he resumed his place under water and went on. We watched him as he took the farther shore below us and made off in the woods again.

"I couldn't shoot at him, it was such a beautiful bit of politics," said the Senator.

Soon the hound reached the cove's edge and swam the river and ranged up and down the bank for half an hour before he found the buck's trail again.

"I've seen many a rascal, driven to water by the hounds, go swimming away as slyly as that buck, with their horns in the air, looking as innocent as a bit of driftwood. They come in from both shores—the Whig and the Democratic—and they are always shot at from one bank or the other."

I remember it surprised me a little to hear him say that they came in from both shores.

"Just what do you want to do?" he asked presently.

"I should like to go down to Washington with you and help you in any way that I can."

"All right, partner—we'll try it," he answered gravely. "I hope that I don't forget and work you as hard as I work myself. It wouldn't be decent. I have a great many letters to write. I'll try thinking out loud while you take them down in sound-hand. Then you can draft them neatly and I'll sign them. You have tact and good manners and can do many of my errands for me and save me from those who have no good reason for taking up my time. You will meet the best people and the worst. There's just a chance that it may come to something worth while—who knows? You are young yet. It will be good training and you will witness the making of some history now and then."

What elation I felt!

Again the voice of the hound which had been ringing in the distant hills was coming nearer.

"We must keep watch—another deer is coming," said the Senator.

We had only a moment's watch before a fine yearling buck came down to the opposite shore and stood looking across the river. The Senator raised his rifle and fired. The buck fell in the edge of the water.

"How shall we get him?" my friend asked.

"It will not be difficult," I answered as I began to undress. Nothing was difficult those days. I swam the river and towed the buck across with a beech withe in his gambrel joints. The hound joined me before I was half across with my burden and nosed the carcass and swam on ahead yelping with delight.

We dressed the deer and then I had the great joy of carrying him on my back two miles across the country to the wagon. The Senator wished to send a guide for the deer, but I insisted that the carrying was my privilege.

"Well, I guess your big thighs and broad shoulders can stand it," said he.

"My uncle has always said that no man could be called a hunter until he can go into the woods without a guide and kill a deer and bring it out on his back. I want to be able to testify that I am at least partly qualified."

"Your uncle didn't say anything about fetching the deer across a deep river without a boat, did he?" Mr. Wright asked me with a smile.

Leaves of the beeches, maples and basswoods—yellowed by frost—hung like tiny lanterns, glowing with noonday light, above the dim forest-aisle which we traveled.

The sun was down when we got to the clearing.

"What a day it has been!" said Mr. Wright when we were seated in the wagon at last with the hound and the deer's head between his feet and mine.

"One of the best in my life," I answered with a joy in my heart the like of which I have rarely known in these many years that have come to me.

We rode on in silence with the calls of the swamp robin and the hermit thrush ringing in our ears as the night fell.

"It's a good time to think, and there we take different roads," said my friend. "You will turn into the future and I into the past."

"I've been thinking about your uncle," he said by and by. "He is one of the greatest men I have ever known. You knew of that foolish gossip about him—didn't you?"

"Yes," I answered.

"Well, now, he's gone about his business the same as ever and showed by his life that it couldn't be true. Not a word out of him! But Dave Ramsey fell sick—down on the flat last winter. By and by his children were crying for bread and the poor-master was going to take charge of them. Well, who should turn up there, just in the nick of time, but Delia and Peabody Baynes. They fed those children all winter and kept them in clothes so that they could go to school. The strange thing about it is this: it was Dave Ramsey who really started that story. He got up in church the other night and confessed his crime. His conscience wouldn't let him keep it. He said that he had not seen Peabody Baynes on that road the day the money was lost but had only heard that he was there. He knew now that he couldn't have been there. Gosh t'almighty! as your uncle used to say when there was nothing else to be said."

It touched me to the soul—this long-delayed vindication of my beloved Uncle Peabody.

The Senator ate supper with us and sent his hired man out for his horse and buggy. When he had put on his overcoat and was about to go he turned to my uncle and said:

"Peabody Baynes, if I have had any success in the world it is because I have had the exalted honor and consciousness that I represented men like you."

He left us and we sat down by the glowing candles. Soon I told them what Ramsey had done. There was a moment of silence. Uncle Peabody rose and went to the water-pail for a drink.

"Bart, I believe I'll plant corn on that ten-acre lot next spring—darned if I don't," he said as he returned to his chair.

None of us ever spoke of the matter again to my knowledge.

CHAPTER XIX

ON THE SUMMIT

My mental assets would give me a poor rating I presume in the commerce of modern scholarship when I went to Washington that autumn with Senator and Mrs. Wright. Still it was no smattering that I had, but rather a few broad areas of knowledge which were firmly in my possession. I had acquired, quite by myself since leaving the academy, a fairly serviceable reading knowledge of French; I had finished the *Æneid*; I had read the tragedies of Shakespeare and could repeat from them many striking passages; I had read the histories of Abbott and the works of Washington Irving and certain of the essays of Carlyle and Macaulay. My best asset was not mental but spiritual, if I may be allowed to say it, in all modesty, for, therein I claim no special advantage, saving, possibly, an unusual strength of character in my aunt and uncle. Those days the candles were lighting the best trails of knowledge all over the land. Never has the general spirit of this republic been so high and admirable as then and a little later. It was to speak, presently, in the immortal voices of Whittier, Emerson, Whitman, Greeley and Lincoln. The dim glow of the candles had entered their souls and out of them came a light that filled the land and was seen of all men. What became of this mighty spirit of democracy? My friend, it broke down and came near its death in a long, demoralizing war which gave to our young men a thorough four-year course in the ancient school of infamy.

The railroads on which we traveled from Utica, the great cities through which we passed, were a wonder and an inspiration to me. I was awed by the grandeur of Washington itself. I took lodgings with the Senator and his wife.

"Now, Bart," said he, when we had arrived, "I'm going to turn you loose here for a little while before I put harness on you. Go about for a week or so and get the lay of the land and the feel of it. Mrs. Wright will be your guide until the general situation has worked its way into your consciousness."

It seemed to me that there was not room enough in my consciousness for the great public buildings and the pictures and the statues and the vast machinery of the government. Beauty and magnitude have a wonderful effect when they spring fresh upon the vision of a youth out of the back country. I sang of the look of them in my letters and soon I began to think about them and imperfectly to understand them. They had their epic, lyric and dramatic stages in my consciousness.

One afternoon we went to hear Senator Wright speak. He was to answer Calhoun on a detail of the banking laws. The floor and galleries were filled. With what emotion I saw him rise and begin his argument as all ears bent to hear him! He aimed not at popular sentiments in highly finished rhetoric, as did Webster, to be quoted in the school-books and repeated on every platform. But no words of mine—and I have used many in the effort—are able to convey a notion of the masterful ease and charm of his manner on the floor of the Senate or of the singular modesty, courtesy, aptness and simplicity of his words as they fell from his lips. There were the thunderous Webster, the grandeur of whose sentences no American has equaled; the agile-minded Clay, whose voice was like a silver clarion; the farseeing, fiery Calhoun, of "the swift sword"—most formidable in debate—but I was soon to learn that neither nor all of these men—gifted of heaven so highly—could cope with the suave, incisive, conversational sentences of Wright, going straight to the heart of the subject and laying it bare to his hearers. That was what people were saying as we left the Senate chamber, late in the evening; that, indeed, was what they were always saying after they had heard him answer an adversary.

He had a priceless and unusual talent for avoiding school-reader English and the arts of declamation and for preparing a difficult subject to enter the average brain. The underlying secret of his power was soon apparent to me. He stood always for that great thing in America which, since then, Whitman has called "the divine aggregate," and seeing clearly how every measure would be likely to affect its welfare, he followed the compass. It had led him to a height of power above all others and was to lead him unto the loneliest summit of accomplishment in American history.

Not much in my term of service there is important to this little task of mine. I did my work well, if I may believe the Senator, and grew familiar with the gentle and ungentle arts of the politician.

One great fact grew in magnitude and sullen portent as the months passed: the gigantic slave-holding interests of the South viewed with growing alarm the spread of abolition sentiment. Subtly, quietly and naturally they were feeling for the means to defend and increase their power. Straws were coming to the surface in that session which betrayed this deep undercurrent of purpose. We felt it and the Senator was worried I knew, but held his peace. He knew how to keep his opinions until the hour had struck that summoned them to service. The Senator never played with his lance. By and by Spencer openly sounded the note of conflict.

The most welcome year of my life dawned on the first of January, 1844. I remember that I arose before daylight that morning and dressed and went out on the street to welcome it.

I had less than six months to wait for that day appointed by Sally. I had no doubt that she would be true to me. I had had my days of fear and depression, but always my sublime faith in her came back in good time.

Oh, yes, indeed, Washington was a fair of beauty and gallantry those days. I saw it all. I have spent many years in the capital and I tell you the girls of that time had manners and knew how to wear their clothes, but again the magic of old memories kept my lady on her throne. There was one of them—just one of those others who, I sometimes thought, was almost as graceful and charming and noble-hearted as Sally, and she liked me I know, but the ideal of my youth glowed in the light of the early morning, so to speak, and was brighter than all others. Above all, I had given my word to Sally and—well, you know, the old-time Yankee of good stock was fairly steadfast, whatever else may be said of him—often a little too steadfast, as were Ben Grimshaw and Squire Fullerton.

The Senator and I went calling that New Year's day. We saw all the great people and some of them were more cheerful than they had a right to be. It was a weakness of the time. I shall not go into details for fear of wandering too far from my main road. Let me step aside a moment to say, however, that there were two clouds in the sky of the Washington society of those days. One was strong drink and the other was the crude, rough-coated, aggressive democrat from the frontiers of the West. These latter were often seen in the holiday regalia of farm or village at fashionable functions. Some of them changed slowly and, by and by, reached the stage of white linen and diamond breast-pins and waistcoats of figured silk. It must be said, however, that their motives were always above their taste.

The winter wore away slowly in hard work. Mr. Van Buren came down to see the Senator one day from his country seat on the Hudson. The Ex-president had been solicited to accept the nomination again. I know that Senator Wright strongly favored the plan but feared that the South would defeat him in convention, it being well known that Van Buren was opposed to the annexation of Texas—a pet project of the slave-holders. However, he advised his friend to make a fight for the nomination and this the latter resolved to do. Thenceforward until middle May I gave my time largely to the inditing of letters for the Senator in Van Buren's behalf.

The time appointed for the convention in Baltimore drew near. One day the Senator received an intimation that he would be put in nomination if Van Buren failed. Immediately he wrote to Judge Fine, of Ogdensburg, chairman of the delegation from the northern district of New York, forbidding such use of his name on the ground that his acquiescence would involve disloyalty to his friend the Ex-president.

He gave me leave to go to the convention on my way home to meet Sally. I had confided to Mrs. Wright the details of my little love affair—I had to—and she had shown a tender, sympathetic interest in the story.

The Senator had said to me one day, with a gentle smile:

"Bart, you have business in Canton, I believe, with which trifling matters like the choice of a president and the Mexican question can not be permitted to interfere. You must take time to spend a day or two at the convention in Baltimore on your way.... Report to our friend Fine, who will look after your comfort there. The experience ought to be useful to a young man who, I hope, will have work to do in future conventions."

I took the stage to Baltimore next day—the twenty-sixth of May. The convention thrilled me—the flags, the great crowd, the bands, the songs, the speeches, the cheering—I see and hear it all in my talk. The uproar lasted for twenty minutes when Van Buren's name was put in nomination.

Then the undercurrent! The slave interest of the South was against him as Wright had foreseen. The deep current of its power had undermined certain of the northern and western delegations. Ostensibly for Van Buren and stubbornly casting their ballots for him, they had voted for the two-thirds rule, which had accomplished his defeat before the balloting began. It continued for two days without a choice. The enemy stood firm. After adjournment that evening many of the Van Buren delegates were summoned to a conference. I attended it with Judge Fine.

The Ex-president had withdrawn and requested his friends in the convention to vote for Silas Wright. My emotions can be more readily imagined than described when I heard the shouts of enthusiasm which greeted my friend's name. Tears began to roll down my cheeks. Judge Fine lifted his hand. When order was at last restored he began:

"Gentlemen, as a friend of the learned Senator and as a resident of the county which is the proud possessor of his home, your enthusiasm has a welcome sound to me; but I happen to know that Senator Wright will not allow his name to go before the convention."

He read the letter of which I knew.

Mr. Benjamin F. Butler then said:

"When that letter was written Senator Wright was not aware that Mr. Van Buren's nomination could not be accomplished, nor was he aware that his own nomination would be the almost unanimous wish of this convention. I have talked with the leading delegates from Missouri and Virginia to-day. They say that he can be nominated by acclamation. Is it possible that he—a strong party man—can resist this unanimous call of the party with whose help he has won immortal fame? No, it is not so. It can not be so. We must dispatch a messenger to him by horse at once who shall take to him from his friend Judge Fine a frank statement of the imperious demand of this convention and a request that he telegraph a withdrawal of his letter in the morning."

The suggestion was unanimously approved and within an hour, mounted on one of the best horses in Maryland—so his groom informed me—I was on my way to Washington with the message of Judge Fine in my pocket. Yes, I had two days to spare on my schedule of travel and reckoned that, by returning to Baltimore next day I should reach Canton in good time.

It was the kind of thing that only a lithe, supple, strong-hearted lad such as I was in the days of my youth, could relish—speeding over a dark road by the light of the stars and a half-moon, with a horse that loved to kick up a wind. My brain was in a fever, for the notion had come to me that I was making history.

The lure of fame and high place hurried me on. With the Senator in the presidential chair I should be well started in the highway of great success. Then Mr. H. Dunkelberg might think me better than the legacy of Benjamin Grimshaw. A relay awaited me twenty-three miles down the road.

Well, I reached Washington very sore, but otherwise in good form, soon after daybreak. I was trembling with excitement when I put my horse in the stable and rang the bell at our door. It seemed to me that I was crossing the divide between big and little things. A few steps more and I should be looking down into the great valley of the future. Yet, now that I was there, I began to lose confidence.

The butler opened the door.

Yes, the Senator was up and had just returned from a walk and was in his study. I found him there.

"Well, Bart, how does this happen?" he asked.

"It's important business," I said, as I presented the letter.

Something in his look and manner as he calmly adjusted his glasses and read the letter of Judge Fine brought the blood to my face. It seemed to puncture my balloon, so to speak, and I was falling toward the earth and so swiftly my head swam. He laid the letter on his desk and, without looking up and as coolly as if he were asking for the change of a dollar, queried:

"Well, Bart, what do you think we had better do about it?"

"I—I was hoping—you—you would take it," I stammered.

"That's because the excitement of the convention is on you," he answered. "Let us look at the compass. They have refused to nominate Mr. Van Buren because he is opposed to the annexation of Texas. On that subject the will of the convention is now clear. It is possible that they would nominate me. We don't know about that, we never shall know. If they did, and I accepted, what would be expected of me is also clear. They would expect me to abandon my principles and that course of conduct which I conceive to be best for the country. Therefore I should have to accept it under false pretenses and take their yoke upon me. Would you think the needle pointed that way?"

"No," I answered.

Immediately he turned to his desk and wrote the telegram which fixed his place in history. It said no.

Into the lives of few men has such a moment fallen. I am sure the Lord God must have thought it worth a thousand years of the world's toil. It was that moment in the life of a great leader when Satan shows him the kingdoms of the earth and their glory. I looked at him with a feeling of awe. What sublime calmness and serenity was in his face! As if it were a mere detail in the work of the day, and without a moment's faltering, he had declined a crown, for he would surely have been nominated and elected. He rose and stood looking out of the open window. Always I think of him standing there with the morning sunlight falling upon his face and shoulders. He had observed my emotion and I think it had touched him a little. There was a moment of silence. A curious illusion came to me then, for it seemed as if I heard the sound of distant music. Looking thoughtfully out of the window he asked:

"Bart, do you know when our first fathers turned out of the trail of the beast and found the long road of humanity? I think it was when they discovered the compass in their hearts."

So now at last we have come to that high and lonely place, where we may look back upon the toilsome, adventurous way we have traveled with the aid of the candle and the compass. Now let us stop a moment to rest and to think. How sweet the air is here! The night is falling. I see the stars in the sky. Just below me is the valley of Eternal Silence. You will understand my haste now. I have sought only to do justice to my friend and to give my country a name, long neglected, but equal in glory to those of Washington and Lincoln.

Come, let us take one last look together down the road we have traveled, now dim in the evening shadows. Scattered along it are the little houses of the poor of which I have written. See the lights in the windows—the lights that are shining into the souls of the young—the eager, open, expectant, welcoming souls of the young!—and the light carries many things, but best of all a respect for the old, unchanging way of the compass. After all that is the end and aim of the whole matter—believe me.

My life has lengthened into these days when most of our tasks are accomplished by machinery. We try to make men by the thousand, in vast educational machines, and no longer by the one as of old. It was the loving, forgiving, forbearing, patient, ceaseless toil of mother and father on the tender soul of childhood, which quickened that inextinguishable sense of responsibility to God and man in these people whom I now leave to the judgment of my countrymen.

I have lived to see the ancient plan of kingcraft, for self-protection, coming back into the world. It demands that the will and conscience of every individual shall be regulated and controlled by some conceited prince, backed by an army. It can not fail, I foresee, to accomplish such devastation in the human spirit as shall imperil the dearest possession of man.

If one is to follow the compass he can have but one king—his God.

I am near the end. I rode back to Baltimore that forenoon. They had nominated Mr. Polk, of Tennessee, for president and Silas Wright for vice-president, the latter by acclamation. I knew that Wright would decline the honor, as he did.

I hurried northward to keep my appointment with Sally. The boats were slowed by fog. At Albany I was a day behind my schedule. I should have only an hour's leeway if the boats on the upper lakes and the stage from Plattsburg were on time. I feared to trust them. So I caught the west-bound train and reached Utica three hours late. There I bought a good horse and his saddle and bridle and hurried up the north road. When he was near spent I traded him for a well-knit Morgan mare up in the little village of Sandy Creek. Oh, I knew a good horse as well as the next man and a better one than she I never owned—never. I was back in my saddle at six in the afternoon and stopped for feed and an hour's rest at nine and rode on through the night. I reached the hamlet of Richville soon after daybreak and put out for a rest of two hours. I could take it easy then. At seven o'clock the mare and I started again, well fed and eager to go on.

It was a summer morning that shortens the road—even that of the young lover. Its air was sweet with the breath of the meadows. The daisies and the clover and the cornflowers and the wild roses seemed to be waving a welcome to me and the thorn trees—shapely ornament of my native hills—were in blossom. A cloud of pigeons swept across the blue deep above my head. The great choir of the fields sang to me—bobolinks, song sparrows, meadowlarks, bluebirds, warblers, wrens, and far away in the edge of a spruce thicket I heard the flute of the white-throated sparrow in this refrain:

When, years later, I heard the wedding march in Lohengrin I knew where Wagner had got his theme.

I bathed at a brook in the woods and put on a clean silk shirt and tie out of my saddlebags. I rode slowly then to the edge of the village of Canton and turned at the bridge and took the river road, although I had time to spare. How my heart was beating as I neared the familiar scene! The river slowed its pace there, like a discerning traveler, to enjoy the beauty of its shores. Smooth and silent was the water and in it were the blue of the sky and the feathery shadow-spires of cedar and tamarack and the reflected blossoms of iris and meadow rue. It was a lovely scene.

There was the pine, but where was my lady? I dismounted and tied my mare and looked at my watch. It lacked twenty minutes of eleven. She would come—I had no doubt of it. I washed my hands and face and neck in the cool water. Suddenly I heard a voice I knew singing: *Barney Leave the Girls Alone.* I turned and saw—your mother, my son[1]. She was in the stern of a birch canoe, all dressed in white with roses in her hair. I raised my hat and she threw a kiss at me. Old Kate sat in the bow waving her handkerchief. They stopped and Sally asked in a tone of playful seriousness:

[1] These last lines were dictated to his son.

"Young man, why have you come here?"

"To get you," I answered.

"What do you want of me?" She was looking at her face in the water.

"I want to marry you," I answered bravely.

"Then you may help me ashore if you please. I am in my best, white slippers and you are to be very careful."

Beautiful! She was the spirit of the fields of June then and always.

I helped her ashore and held her in my arms and, you know, the lips have a way of speaking then in the old, convincing, final argument of love. They left no doubt in our hearts, my son.

"When do you wish to marry me?" she whispered.

"As soon as possible, but my pay is only sixty dollars a month now."

"We shall make it do," she answered. "My mother and father and your aunt and uncle and the Hackets and the minister and a number of our friends are coming in a fleet of boats."

"We are prepared either for a picnic or a wedding," was the whisper of Kate.

"Let's make it both," I proposed to Sally.

"Surely there couldn't be a better place than here under the big pine—it's so smooth and soft and shady," said she.

"Nor could there be a better day or better company," I urged, for I was not sure that she would agree.

The boats came along. Sally and I waved a welcome from the bank and she merrily proclaimed:

"It's to be a wedding."

Then a cheer from the boats, in which I joined.

I shall never forget how, when the company had landed and the greetings were over, Uncle Peabody approached your mother and said:

"Say, Sally, I'm goin' to plant a kiss on both o' them red cheeks o' yours, an' do it deliberate, too." He did it and so did Aunt Deel and old Kate, and I think that, next to your mother and me, they were the happiest people at the wedding.

There is a lonely grave up in the hills—that of the stranger who died long ago on Rattleroad. One day I found old Kate sitting beside it and on a stone lately erected there was the name, Enoch Rone.

"It is very sorrowful," she whispered. "He was trying to find me when he died."

We walked on in silence while I recalled the circumstances. How strange that those tales of blood and lawless daring which Kate had given to Amos Grimshaw had led to the slaying of her own son! Yet, so it happened, and the old wives will tell you the story up there in the hills.

The play ends just as the night is falling with Kate and me entering the little home, so familiar now, where she lives and is ever welcome with Aunt Deel and Uncle Peabody. The latter meets us at the door and is saying in a cheerful voice:

"Come in to supper, you rovers. How solemn ye look! Say, if you expect Sally and me to do all the laughin' here you're mistaken. There's a lot of it to be done right now, an' it's time you j'ined in. We ain't done nothin' but laugh since we got up, an' we're in need o' help. What's the matter, Kate? Look up at the light in God's winder. How bright it shines to-night! When I feel bad I always look at the stars."

THE END

EPILOGUE

Wanted by all the people—
A servant
Born of those who serve and aspire
Who has known want and trouble
And all that passes in The Little House of the Poor:
Lonely thought, counsels of love and prudence,
The happiness born of a penny,
The need of the strange and mighty dollar
And the love of things above all its power of measurement.
The dreams that come of weariness and the hard bed,
The thirst for learning as a Great Deliverer.
Who has felt in his heart the weakness and the strength of his brothers
And, above all, the divinity that dwells in them.
Who, therefore, shall have faith in men and women
And knowledge of their wrongs and needs and of their proneness to error.
Humbly must he listen to their voice, as one who knows that God will often speak in it,
And have charity even for his own judgments.
Thus removed, far removed from the conceit and vanity of Princes
Shall he know how great is the master he has chosen to serve.

CPSIA information can be obtained
at www.ICGtesting.com
Printed in the USA
LVHW101711010323
740520LV00002B/627

9 789356 892187